# CHRISTIANITY, DEVELOPMENT AND MODERNITY IN AFRICA

PAUL GIFFORD

# Christianity, Development and Modernity in Africa

OXFORD
UNIVERSITY PRESS

# OXFORD

UNIVERSITY PRESS

Oxford University Press is a department of the
University of Oxford. It furthers the University's objective
of excellence in research, scholarship, and education
by publishing worldwide.

Oxford   New York
Auckland   Cape Town   Dar es Salaam   Hong Kong   Karachi
Kuala Lumpur   Madrid   Melbourne   Mexico City   Nairobi
New Delhi   Shanghai   Taipei   Toronto

With offices in
Argentina   Austria   Brazil   Chile   Czech Republic   France   Greece
Guatemala   Hungary   Italy   Japan   Poland   Portugal   Singapore
South Korea   Switzerland   Thailand   Turkey   Ukraine   Vietnam

Oxford is a registered trade mark of Oxford University Press
in the UK and certain other countries.

Published in the United States of America by
Oxford University Press
198 Madison Avenue, New York, NY 10016

Library of Congress Cataloging-in-Publication Data is available
Paul Gifford.
Christianity, Development and Modernity in Africa.
ISBN: 9780190495732

Printed in India on acid-free paper

# CONTENTS

# ABBREVIATIONS

| | |
|---|---|
| AFER | *African Ecclesial Review* |
| AIC | African Independent Church |
| ANC | African National Congress |
| CAFOD | Catholic Fund for Overseas Development |
| CAN | Christian Association of Nigeria |
| CAR | Central African Republic |
| CBCN | Catholic Bishops' Conference of Nigeria |
| CEJ | Catholic Economic Justice (group) |
| CISA | Catholic Information Service Africa |
| CMMB | Catholic Medical Mission Board |
| CRS | Catholic Relief Services |
| DRC | The Democratic Republic of the Congo |
| CUEA | Catholic University of Eastern Africa |
| EU | European Union |
| GDP | Gross Domestic Product |
| IMF | International Monetary Fund |
| JDPC | Justice, Development and Peace Committee |
| KANU | Kenya African National Union |
| MFHM | Marian Faith Healing Ministry |
| MFM | Mountain of Fire and Miracles Ministries |
| NGO | Non-governmental Organisation |
| SACBC | Southern African Catholic Bishops Conference |
| SACC | South African Council of Churches |
| SCIAF | Scottish Catholic International Aid Fund |
| SDA | Seventh Day Adventist |
| SECAM | Symposium of Episcopal Conferences of Africa and Madagascar |

# ABBREVIATIONS

| | |
|------|------|
| TLS | *Times Literary Supplement* |
| UMG | Uganda Martyrs Guild |
| UN | United Nations |
| UNDP | United Nations Development Programme |
| USAID | United States Agency for International Development |
| WCC | World Council of Churches |
| WEF | World Economic Forum |
| WHO | World Health Organization |
| WVS | World Values Survey |
| ZACH | Zimbabwe Association of Church-Related Hospitals |

# INTRODUCTION

E.P. Thompson remarked of early British Methodism: 'Too much writing on Methodism commences with the assumption that we all know what Methodism was, and gets on with discussing its growth-rates or its organizational structures'.[1] Sometimes I think the same is true of contemporary African Christianity. Not enough effort goes into establishing exactly what it is. In the case of Africa's contemporary Christianity, the problem is compounded because I suspect some issues are studiously avoided, most notably what I here call the enchanted religious imagination. This has meant that the picture presented is sometimes misleading. I have been hesitant to give this enchanted imagination the salience I have long thought it deserved, because it is a difficult topic to treat appropriately. I have been encouraged to attempt it by Isak Niehaus' very sympathetic account of the harrowing death from AIDS of his research assistant, who was convinced all his troubles came from witchcraft. Niehaus' motivation well expresses my own in this book:

In the face of severe crises—failed development, domestic violence, way too many early deaths, and inappropriate coping strategies—silence is a far more serious abuse of intellectual freedom than the revelation of unpalatable truths. The alternatives—selectively reporting on the achievements of [Africa's post-Independence governments], constructing contrived realities about humane sociality (*ubuntu*), and ethnographic romanticism—are infinitely worse options.[2]

---

[1] E.P. Thompson, *The Making of the English Working Class*, London: Gollancz, 1963, 91.
[2] Isak Niehaus, *Witchcraft and a Life in the New South Africa*, Cambridge

I am attempting to open, not close, a debate. I have long been inspired by the words with which I once heard the polymath James Barr begin a lecture. I make them my own here. 'As an academic, it is not my job to be right. It is my job to say what I think as clearly and as carefully as I can. Where I am wrong, I rely on you [listeners in Barr's case, readers in mine] to correct me.'

Many points raised in this book I have broached in previous articles, although not precisely in this form. It would be tedious continually to refer to these previous publications, so such references will be deliberately kept to a minimum.

---

University Press for International African Institute, 2013, 26. Within my brackets Niehaus wrote 'South Africa's post-apartheid government'.

# 1

# THE ISSUES

In December 1998 I attended the Eighth General Assembly of the World Council of Churches, in Harare, as an observer. All the major problems of the world were addressed: Third World debt; the rights of women; the rights of minorities, including sexual minorities; intellectual property rights; the plight of child soldiers; the status of Jerusalem; the evils of unrestricted capital flows; global warming. I was struck by how recognizable and identifiable WCC Christianity is. This is a North Atlantic Christianity, greatly shaped by the Western Enlightenment. Evil was conceived structurally. Invariably the theological reflections at this gathering were politically, sociologically and economically informed. However, at other times during the assembly I had the opportunity to visit some churches manifesting a very different Christianity, most notably the Universal Church of the Kingdom of God, a Pentecostal church of Brazilian origin which has in the last two decades spread widely around the world. It had not existed in Zimbabwe five years previously, but in 1998 it already flourished in six cities, and in Harare drew about 450 people to each of its five Sunday services. The issues addressed were very different from those addressed by the WCC. These were not structural but personal: joblessness, homelessness, sickness, childlessness, business failure, failure to find a spouse. But even more striking was the underlying religious imagination, so different from that on display at the World Council Assembly; this was the worldview that sees spirits, demons, spiritual

3

powers at play in all areas of life, and responsible for every ill. Spirits and witchcraft were said to be responsible for illness, misery, poverty, hunger and misfortune. One particular spirit was said to cause AIDS, and 'to have put HIV blood in the veins' of one sufferer called up to be cured. Here the remedy for the problem of evil was not structural analysis and political-economic reform; it was diagnosis of the spirit responsible and deliverance or exorcism by the ministers.

Everyone is aware of diversity within Christianity, like the historical divisions between East and West, or Catholics and Protestants, or Anglicans and Methodists. But the far more profound difference revealed in Harare is largely ignored. This difference has nothing to do with historical denominations. The WCC is made up of most of the mainline denominations. But denominational differences did not arise at the Universal Church of the Kingdom of God. Those present were from Catholic, Anglican, Methodist and other churches, and in many cases still considered themselves members of their original denominations, and would still attend their services. These dynamics are not captured in conventional discussions of world Christianity.

Much writing on global Christianity, or the southward shift of Christianity, is built on an assumed essentialism. Most studies assume that a Christian is a Christian is a Christian (or a Catholic is a Catholic is a Catholic). Consider Barrett's *World Christian Encyclopedia*, remarkable for its countless columns of statistics.[1] He claims that in the year 2000 there were 1,999,564,000 Christians in the world, presuming that we all know what a Christian is and that if we add up all the national totals we have 1,999,564,000 instances of that certain something we all recognize so easily. His statistics presume that there is something that makes a Baptist, and that's what you have wherever Baptists are found, and that is different from what makes a Presbyterian. In Chile in 1995, for example, we had 40,000 Baptists and 15,000 Presbyterians. By contrast Denmark had 10,000 Baptists and 534 Presbyterians. The presumption is that the Baptists in Chile and the Baptists in Denmark are one and the same; we can add them together with Baptists from all other countries and get a grand total of 46.7 million worldwide in 2000. Likewise Benin had 90,000 Methodists

[1] David Barrett, George Kurian and Todd Johnson, *World Christian Encyclopedia: 2nd Edition*, New York: Oxford University Press, 2001. Also David Barrett and Todd Johnson, *World Christian Trends AD 30—AD 2200: Interpreting the Annual Christian Megacensus*, Pasadena, CA: William Carey Library, 2001.

and Britain had 1.2 million; added to those in other countries, there were 22.3 million Methodists in the world. This picture is built on questionable assumptions. While Christians in, say, Ghana may readily divide themselves into such groupings, it may be that the significant religious characteristics of Presbyterians in Ghana are shared in the main with Ghanaian Catholics. In other words, it is something else (something local and cultural, something Ghanaian or African) that constitutes the really significant characteristic of all Ghana's Christians—which may also characterize other Ghanaians, even Muslims.

The problems are even greater in discussing looser categories of Christians, like 'Evangelicals' or 'Pentecostals'. It seems widely accepted that the defining marks of Evangelicalism are four: personal conversion, biblicism, the cross and mission. The presumption in many studies that African churches labelling themselves evangelical necessarily manifest all four qualities is quite unwarranted. Noll is one who sets out to study global Evangelicalism. He charts the origins of this sector of Christianity from the late seventeenth-century renewal movements within state-church European Protestant regimes. He proceeds to include all Pentecostals under the label 'Evangelical', on the grounds that both represent 'conversionist' Christianity.[2] As we shall see, it is far from self-evident that 'conversionist' is a quality of much African Pentecostalism; in many cases, I will argue, quite the opposite is true.

When talking about Christianity in Africa, it is necessary to be very clear what level one is working on. Consider these words of Peel:

The only *workable* definition of conversion is the process by which people come to regard themselves, and be regarded by others, as Christians. This social identification is what being a Christian most immediately and unarguably *is*, rather than holding certain beliefs or behaving in certain ways specified a priori... By taking social identification as the real thing to be explained we avoid the analytical problems which arise if—as often occurs in practice—Christians maintain or later adopt 'non-Christian' beliefs and practices but still insist on regarding themselves as Christians and are so regarded by others.[3]

Peel is quite clear what level he is working on; he is discussing all those calling themselves or called Christians, whatever their beliefs or

---

[2] Mark Noll, *The New Shape of World Christianity*, Downers Grove: InterVarsity Press, 2009. For the problems involved in identifying Evangelicals, see especially *New Shape*, 22, 42–6, 53, 84–5, 90, 96.

[3] J.D.Y. Peel, *Religious Encounter and the Making of the Yoruba*, Bloomington and Indianapolis: Indiana University Press, 2000, 216, emphasis in original.

behaviour. They constitute a perfectly valid group to study, and many issues can fruitfully be addressed on the basis of such labelling. However, many other observers, though in fact working with the group externally identified as Christians, insinuate exactly what Peel warns against: that the group so identified is characterized by certain specific beliefs and behaviour. They presume that some qualitative change necessarily accompanies the label.

My argument in this book concerns diversity within the group labelled Christian, and the different public effects that in all likelihood flow from this diversity. I will make my case through a comparison between two different forms of Christianity particularly salient in sub-Saharan Africa (henceforth simply Africa). One form I will call Pentecostalism. I am well aware of the diversity within Pentecostalism, but it would be tiresome to allow for that by using a term like 'Pentecostal-like' at every turn. I will outline Pentecostalism through particular detailed examples. I will not presume that these examples are 'representative' in a hard sense, but nevertheless will argue that they are representative enough to allow me to make my case. The form of Christianity I will compare with Pentecostalism is Roman Catholicism (henceforth simply Catholicism). Catholicism, though supposedly monolithic, has its own internal tensions, as we shall see. Despite these tensions, I will claim that there is an overarching trajectory within African Catholicism which, again, is sufficient to support my case. My case is that Pentecostalism on the one hand, and Catholicism on the other, illustrate forms of Christianity whose diversity is unacknowledged in the usual studies of African Christianity, and that these differences have significant bearing on questions of development and modernity. (I do not argue it here, but I suspect that much of what I say about Catholicism applies, *mutatis mutandis*, to other mainline mission-founded churches, too.)

My method calls for explanation. I will not make much use of official pronouncements, even in the case of Catholicism, which is rich in them. I will leave aside much writing on African Christianity, which often deliberately avoids the very difference I want to address. While freely using quantitative data when they suit me, I am not constructing my argument from surveys and statistics. In matters like religion, surveys may reveal only the bluntest reality. Respondents largely know what is expected of them, and often respond accordingly. For example, nearly every African Christian, when asked, would assert the existence and importance of heaven and hell. Yet, as I shall argue, for many Africans it is the this-worldly nature of their Christianity that is characteristic, something that could entirely be missed by someone operating only from responses to surveys.

My approach is built on personal experience. I have been researching various branches of African Christianity for thirty years. Although for most of that time also teaching in London, I have been fortunate to average at least six months of each of the last thirty years in Africa. In Africa, I spend my time attending churches, Bible studies, conventions and crusades—every sort of Christian gathering—and when in London, I do the same with African immigrant churches. My interest has been wide ranging. I spent two years researching Africa's mainline Protestant churches for the All Africa Conference of Churches, in a job that took me across the entire continent. At other times, my primary focus has been African Pentecostalism.

The early-modern historian Keith Thomas has spent a lifetime steeping himself in the world he describes, drawing on everything he considers relevant. He cites approvingly an anonymous assessor of his work. Thomas's argument (said the assessor) is both contained and artfully concealed in examples:

According to strict and even censorious critical criteria, these materials cannot stand as proof of any argument, since the reader is in the hands of the author and of what he has chosen to serve up as, strictly speaking, illustrations of his own contentions—it being, in principle, always possible to build up a different picture with the aid of different examples. The last thing that one will find... is the allegedly knock-down evidence of statistics, but the wholly justified implication is that these matters are best understood with the aid of what German social scientists and theorists call the faculty of *Verstehen*.

That, says Thomas, captures exactly what he tries to do: so to draw on his findings that he can present for consideration a reasoned, coherent, defensible—even convincing—picture.[4] His defence of that method has application here. I am fully aware that my examples (sometimes from several years apart) are not 'conclusive' in any hard sense, but I've selected them because I think they are revealing of the reality I am describing, and my reason for thinking so is my 30 years of exposure and experience. Naturally my experience is not exhaustive nor my insight unerring. In my research I have collected all I could, from pas-

---

[4] Keith Thomas, 'Diary', *London Review of Books*, 10 June 2010, 37.

toral letters to obscure ephemera, and taken copious notes of every-thing I considered relevant, from services to interviews to events. (Keith Thomas in the article just referred to laments that the private archive that it has taken him a lifetime to build up by painful accumu-lation can now be achieved by a moderately diligent student surfing the web in the course of a morning; I am aware of that too.) There is noth-ing illegitimate in building a general case from exposure, experience and reflection, bearing in mind the provisos just made. It is an invita-tion to those with more representative examples and deeper *Verstehen* to step forward.

Other words in the title deserve explanation; first of all 'Africa'. Collier, in his *Bottom Billion*, argued that past attempts to think in terms of the developing world as opposed to the developed world founder on the fact that most of the developing world has recently done rather well.[5] The recent advances of countries like Brazil, China and India has been staggering. That doesn't mean they have solved all their problems—far from it—but it forces us to discriminate within the developing block. In Collier's view, we have a developed world of about a billion. Of the former 'developing world', about five billion are doing quite well. There is a residual category, though, that is being left behind, and he named this the bottom billion. In this bottom billion he places all sub-Saharan Africa, the '-stans' of the former Soviet block, and only Bolivia in Latin America. Collier's division not only saves us from including Brazil and Chad in the one analytical category of 'developing world', but shows that there is some basis for talking of sub-Saharan Africa as one unit of study. I am fully aware that this does not solve all our problems in considering sub-Saharan Africa as a unit; after all, within Africa, Botswana and Niger exhibit all sorts of differ-ences. I will try to be sensitive to this throughout, but since we must generalize, generalizing about sub-Saharan Africa alone is more defen-sible than generalizing about a bloc containing countries as diverse as Uruguay, China and Malawi.

My particular understanding of the African context will be impor-tant for the argument of this book, and I will briefly outline it here. European powers had been impacting on Africa since the fifteenth cen-tury—most crucially in the slave trade from the mid-fifteenth till well

[5] Paul Collier, *The Bottom Billion: Why the Poorest Countries are Failing and What can be Done about it*, Oxford University Press, 2007.

into the nineteenth century. It was not until the 'Scramble for Africa' that European powers set about carving the continent up into their own colonies. The scramble lasted about three decades, being complete by about 1912. Colonialism had considerable effects, creating capital cities, railway networks, administrative structures, introducing European schooling and languages, and above all fixing national boundaries. Its effects on African peoples varied, not least because colonialism in Africa had a very short life—in some places it lasted only a single generation—and the end, when it came, was remarkably swift. The scramble out of Africa (1957–68) was pursued at the same headlong pace as the scramble into it. Most African countries became independent in the 1960s, the local elite taking over the instruments of rule from the colonial powers. Independence coincided with a period of unparalleled world-wide economic growth (1945–75). Thus Africa came to independence on a surge of optimism, even euphoria. The new governments set about modernizing their societies, for which there was no effective model other than Western economic and techno-scientific development, in either its capitalist or its socialist variant, promoted during the Cold War by the American and Soviet blocs respectively.

Before long, however, the euphoria of the early 1960s turned sour. What became Africa's characteristic political order is best described as 'neo-patrimonialism'. It is almost defined in contrast to Western 'rational-legal' administrations in which power is exercised through legally defined structures for publicly acknowledged aims. This rational-legal ideal (admittedly nowhere achieved in its fulness) has proved the most efficient and legitimate way of managing a complex modern state. In Africa's neo-patrimonial states, by contrast, support is ensured by clientelism, a relationship of exchange in which a superior provides security for an inferior, who as a client then provides political support for his patron. Those lower in a hierarchy are not subordinate officials with defined powers and functions of their own, but retainers whose position depends on a 'Big Man' to whom they owe allegiance. Control of the state carries with it access to wealth, the ability to provide (and of course to withhold) security and to allocate benefits in the form of jobs, development projects and so on. The system is held together by loyalty or kinship ties rather than by a hierarchy of administrative grades and functions.

Of course colonialism has affected today's Africa. Colonial states had to secure the obedience of an alien people, so control was always a defining characteristic. Moreover, as the colonial states had to pay for themselves, provision of services was limited. There was thus little merging of state and society as common expressions of shared values, and little in the way of legitimacy, or popular commitment to public institutions. So too the Cold War, the debt burden and unfair terms of trade have had their effect. Nevertheless, it is its dysfunctional neo-patrimonial political culture that is primarily responsible for Africa's present plight. So in the 1980s, with African states effectively bankrupt, and internal and external pressure for reform increasing, the demand arose for 'structural adjustment', to bring about 'good governance' (understood to include elements like transparency and accountability, pluralism, participation, predictability, openness, competence and efficiency, respect for human rights and property rights, a flourishing civil society and the rule of law). This attempt involved enormous contradictions; in Africa it was almost bound to fail, for structural adjustment 'struck directly at the basis for economic and hence political control maintained by African governing elites over their own societies. That was indeed precisely the point.'[6] Governing elites, even if in theory forced by their debt crisis to implement structural adjustment, were able to thwart its implementation; indeed, 'winning', in the view of many African rulers, 'consisted in gaining as much external finance as possible, while delivering as little economic reform as possible in exchange'.[7]

The power of Western donors to change Africa's political culture was further undermined in the late 1990s by the increasing demand (led by the Chinese) for Africa's raw materials. Investment, mainly but not exclusively in extractive industries, has flowed in. This investment has given rise to the impressive economic growth statistics of the first decade of the twenty-first century, leading some to claim that Africa is joining the modern world and will even be the Asia of the future. I am less convinced, at least on evidence adduced so far. For example, Angola is sometimes held up as the fastest growing economy in the world, with growth rates of 10 per cent for a decade. Yet this has not changed the elite running Angola. Angola's long-running civil war was prolonged by politicians, several of whom 'pocketed huge "commissions" on arms to blast the rebels'. It was only when they realized they

---

[6] Christopher Clapham, 'Governmentality and Economic Policy in Sub-Saharan Africa', *Third World Quarterly*, 17 (1996), 812; my indebtedness throughout this book to Clapham's wide-ranging output is gratefully acknowledged.

[7] Ibid., 813.

could do well out of the disarmament process that the war could be ended: 'The same men who used to grow fat on weapons contracts have now taken charge of ordering tents, medical kits and rations for demobilized rebels'.[8] In 2013, Forbes named Africa's first woman dollar billionaire. How did she make her money? In manufacturing or trade, or pioneering some new form of software? No. She happens to be daughter of Africa's longest-serving president, José Eduardo dos Santos of Angola.[9]

Development and modernity are concepts that will feature largely in what follows. Both are fiercely contested concepts, too. We will return to them often below, but already my general perspective is clear. My view is that Africa's only hope of joining the modern world is to transcend neo-patrimonialism, enforce the rule of law, build institutions, and adopt rational bureaucratic structures, systems, and procedures in education, health, agriculture, transport and so on. It is the contribution of different forms of Christianity to that agenda that I want to address here.

The key word in the title is Christianity, and that requires some brief context too. Christianity's profile in Africa has changed over the last century. Mission churches have always dominated, with African Independent Churches (AICs) a significant presence in some countries. Mainline Protestantism was the dominant influence until about the time of the Second World War; after that, Catholicism. Christian missionaries were closely associated with the colonial project (the nature of the link is variously understood, as we shall see). At independence it was widely thought that Christianity in Africa would become increasingly less significant, because it was so closely associated with colonialism, and because it depended so strongly on mission school systems, which would be taken over by the new African governments. This prediction has proved completely false. The increasing importance of Christianity is not just in its numbers. When Africa's one-party states

---

[8] *Economist*, 23 May 2002.

[9] *Guardian*, 25 Jan. 2013. It is not my intention to give extensive analysis of Africa's persisting neo-patrimonial abuses, enriching the elite but impoverishing the general population, but for recent examples, see Greenpeace's *The Plunder of a Nation's Birthright; a Drama in Five Acts*, launched 10 Oct. 2012, on the abuse of Senegal's fishing resources; and the Africa Progress Report *Equity in Extractives*, launched 10 May 2013 at WEF on Africa, Cape Town, on the abuse of the Congo's (DRC) mineral resources.

imploded in the 1980s, it was the mainline churches (in Francophone countries, specifically the Catholic Church) that led civil society's demands for reform. Their public profile was enormously enhanced. With the proliferation of Pentecostal churches from about the same time, Christianity is now perhaps the most salient social force in sub-Saharan Africa.

It is the public significance of Christianity that will be our concern here. I will not be debating the essence of Christianity, or identifying true, pure or pristine Christianity. This book is not concerned with assessing the orthodoxy of Christianity, but with identifying two very different forms of it, and speculating on their effects.

2

# ENCHANTED CHRISTIANITY

In traditional African religion there is (most often) a supreme being, and lesser deities, ancestors, and spirits dwelling in rocks, rivers, trees, animals and various objects. All spirits have powers which can affect humans. The physical realm and the realm of the spirit are not separate from each other. Nothing is purely matter. This world is one of action and counteraction of potent forces, spirit acting upon spirit. A stronger or higher being can easily destroy or impair the weaker or lower, and since humans are relatively low beings, they can be controlled by the former. A stronger or higher spirit acting negatively upon the spirit of any human may affect the whole family, clan or state. It therefore becomes a central concern to avoid this or, where it is suspected to be imminent, ward it off quickly. The absence of such negative forces forms the idea of the good life. Religion is very largely the means of manipulating these forces. Deities are consulted to ward off negative influence in important matters, but consultations are also used for lesser evils like failure to find a husband, infertility, giving birth to unhealthy offspring, and failure in business and education. Of course, these spirits may be manipulated by others, particularly to inflict evil. Consulting at shrines serves normally to discover why individual persons or communities are suffering particular afflictions. Causality is to be discerned primarily in the spirit realm, although natural causality is not entirely disregarded.

This enchanted religious imagination has not, as many missionaries predicted, died out. It is widely encountered in Africa today, particularly in what we can call 'witchcraft'. Admittedly, the word is unsatisfactory, but since it is the word most often used, let it stand. Let me illustrate the persistence of this enchanted religious imagination in Africa.

## Persistence

A form of enchanted religion was brought to the attention of the West during the Liberian (and Sierra Leonean) wars in the 1990s, when media exposed the phenomenon of 'heartmen'. This flows from religious conceptions. In the Liberian hinterland, society was ruled by secret societies, *Poro* for men and *Sande* for women. To reach high office in those, a human sacrifice was necessary, usually of one's own child. Since this demand was particularly heavy, the practice effectively regulated itself. However, when in the 1920s the Americo-Liberians on the coast extended their reach into the hinterland, one way to extend their political control was to become influential in these societies. Americo-Liberian politicians were less keen on sacrificing one of their own, so the practice was modified somewhat and body parts could be provided for them—hence the origin of the office of heartman. After that, of course, restraint was lessened, and at the time of the civil war after the overthrow of President Samuel Doe (1990), when all social institutions virtually collapsed, any restraint vanished. Now any illiterate teenager, high on drugs, could find body parts for himself to increase his power.[1]

Equally recent are the albino killings in East Africa. Albinism is a melanin deficiency that leaves sufferers vulnerable to cancer. The incidence in Europe and North America is one in 20,000 persons, but in East Africa it is reckoned to be 500 per cent higher, about one in

---

[1] See Stephen Ellis, *Mask of Anarchy: the Destruction of Liberia and the Religious Dimension of an African Civil War*, London: Hurst, 2001. There was almost an epidemic of such ritual murders in Liberia around election time; see Paul Gifford, *Christianity and Politics in Doe's Liberia*, Cambridge University Press, 1993, 30f. This phenomenon is attested elsewhere. Around elections in Gabon, an increase in ritual killings is regular, and one finds the same trade from suppliers to middlemen to politicians (East African *Standard*, 18 April 2008, 29). In March 2013 in Gabon, the Association for the Prevention of Ritual Crimes denounced twenty ritual murders recorded since the beginning of the year (*Walfadjri*, 27 March 2013, 4).

4,000. Tanzania is estimated to have about 200,000 albinos. In late 2008 reports emerged that about thirty-five albinos had been killed in Tanzania that year (unreported cases were probably much higher). The reason was the belief that albino body parts could help politicians win elections and businessmen become fantastically rich overnight, and could cure infertility and ward off evil spirits. The demand was particularly strong among the fishing people around the south of Lake Victoria, and the alluvial miners in the gold and diamond fields south of the lake. The Tanzanian government appointed an albino woman to parliament to protect albinos' rights. In early 2009 the police chief in Dar es Salaam distributed mobile phones to several hundred albinos, with a direct line to the police, to be used if they thought they were being tracked by body-harvesters. The problem continues. Early in 2013, the UN High Commissioner for Human Rights deplored a recent outbreak of albino killing—four in the first two weeks of February.[2] So too on the opposite side of the continent, in Senegal, in the run up to general elections in 2012, mysterious deaths were widely seen as ritual human sacrifice for success in the elections; children were warned not to go home from school unaccompanied, and albinos were considered to be in particular danger.[3] After the elections, in the Legislative Assembly a deputy shouted across to the benches of the previous government: 'Since you have lost power, albinos have found peace and we no longer find human remains in the streets.'[4] Nobody asked: What was he saying? What did that mean? Everyone knows full well.

Most spectacular of all are cases of penis snatching in West Africa. People are accused of causing the genitals to disappear or shrink, or in the case of women, breasts to disappear and vaginas to seal up, by touching their victims, brushing against them, or shaking their hand. Witchdoctors or medicine men are said to use the genitals in certain rituals. Nigeria had a month-long outbreak in the early 1990s,[5] Cameroon

[2] *Walfadjri*, 7 March 2013, 6.

[3] *Quotidien*, 13 Feb. 2012, 9; *Populaire*, 10 Feb. 2012, 11; *Populaire*, 11/12 Feb. 2012, 10; *Populaire*, 13 Feb. 2012, 2; *Walfadjri*, 16 Feb. 2012, 6 & 12; *Observateur*, 17 Feb. 2012, 4; *Quotidien*, 18/19 Feb. 2012, 7–9; *Quotidien*, 23 Feb. 2012, 7; *Walfadjri*, 25/26 Feb. 2012, 7; *Gazette*, 23 Feb.–1 March 2012, 31–3.

[4] *Observateur*, 18 Dec. 2012, 8.

[5] 'Although the police and some enlightened members of society had denied that supernatural means could cause people's genitals to vanish, the predominant fear in Nigeria is to the contrary' (*African Concord*, 26 Nov. 1990, 39).

in the mid-1990s, and in the week ending 18 January 1997 there was a serious scare in Ghana. It began in Accra, but before long had spread to Kumasi and the north. Mobs formed to lynch suspected witches (ten were killed in a week), in one case battling the police for several hours, forcing the police to fire over a crowd. Ghana's Inspector General of Police was ready to call out the army if needed to restore order.[6] Cases are reported regularly in various places—even as I write this, in Senegal in 2013.[7]

This enchanted religious imagination pervades African football. In a semi-final of the 2002 Africa Cup of Nations, Cameroon's coach and his assistant were arrested by the Malian police, ostensibly for trying to place a magic charm on the pitch. The coach was standing on the sidelines when he was wrestled to the ground and handcuffed in full view of spectators, carried off by at least eight policeman, leading to Cameroon's threatened refusal to play the game. The incident was played down, as the African Football Federation was desperate to throw off the image that they considered a major reason for the decision not to award South Africa the 2006 World Cup, and indeed fear of the repetition of such incidents persisted right up to the successful staging of the cup in South Africa in 2010. In 2001 *African Soccer* did a ten page supplement on the role of witchdoctors in African football, showing how widespread the phenomenon is, and giving copious examples: animals sacrificed and their parts buried, midnight rituals, powders and lotions. For example, the then national captain of Côte d'Ivoire recalled: 'During the African Nations Cup in 1984, we had more than 150 witch doctors with us at the Golfe Hotel. Our rooms were loaded with pots of various sizes and filled with all kinds of concoctions. Every player was made to take a bath with the odious liquids... after which he would be invited to say his wishes privately into the ear of a living pigeon.' In 1994 Roy Barreto, a white, resigned as coach of the Zimbabwean team Highlanders, complaining bitterly about the club spending thousands of dollars consulting *n'angas* while players' wages were left unpaid. But the then chairman of the club,

<hr>

[6] Covered on the front page of the Catholic *Weekly Standard*, 26 Jan.–1 Feb. 1997 under the headline 'The Case of the Missing Genitals'. The *Spectator* reported that other witchdoctors were going around the city claiming to have the cure for those whose organs had vanished, charging between one and five million cedis (up to US $700); *Weekly Spectator*, 18 Jan. 1997, 1.

[7] *Populaire*, 20 Dec. 2013, 11.

Roger Muhiwa, who was vice-chairman of the Zimbabwe Football Association, reacted swiftly, insisting that the practice was not only in order, but in line with tradition which 'must be preserved'. In December 1997, during Africa's Club Championship final between Accra's Hearts of Oak and Hafia of Guinea, Hearts' 'native doctor' predicted that the scorer of the first goal would die. Ghanaians were very reluctant to score, and when given an easy penalty, the Ghanaian deliberately shot wide. The Guineans eventually won 1–0. One of the Hearts' players that day later commented: 'You can't condemn Anas for throwing away that penalty. I would have done the same thing. The juju man had said the man to score the first goal would die. It was a time when witchdoctors words were believed to be gospel and no one wanted to take a risk.'[8] (For my argument below, an important observation in that *African Soccer* supplement is the comment that 'native doctors' are being replaced by Pentecostal pastors in directing these spiritual forces.)

In Ghana, camps exist where witches are banished, often for life—Gambaga (dating back to 1870), Duabone, Tendang, Kukuo, Ngani and Kpatinga. There is no need to continue. I will just add that, according to a recent UN report (although written before the subsequent implosion of that country), in the Central African Republic 25 per cent of all cases brought to court in the capital Bangui, and 80–90 per cent in the CAR's rural courts, concern witchcraft. As a result 70 per cent of prisoners in Bangui's central prison are there on the basis of witchcraft accusations.[9] Let this suffice to establish the pervasiveness of this enchanted religious imagination.

---

[8] *African Soccer*, Aug.–Sept. 2001, 14–21. More recently, in February 2012, Senegal went to the Africa Cup of Nations in Gabon/Equatorial Guinea among the favourites, but were immediately eliminated, losing all three preliminary games, and by the same score 1–2. It was widely believed that witchcraft caused the team's downfall (see *Observateur*, 1 Feb. 2012, 15; *Observateur*, 2 Feb. 2012, 16; *Les Stades*, 30 Jan. 2012, 9; *Populaire*, 2 Feb. 2012, 7; *Populaire*, 9 Feb. 2012, 6). Senegal's national sport, *lutte avec frappe*, is as much a 'mystical' contest between the wrestlers' *marabouts* as a physical contest between the wrestlers themselves. The father of the winner of a championship bout in June 2013 admitted he had paid 50 million CFA francs (US$100,000) to *marabouts* to ensure his son's success (*Observateur*, 5 June 2013, 16). For an excellent and exhaustive study of enchanted popular beliefs in Senegal, see Ibrahima Sow, *Le maraboutage au Sénégal*, Dakar: IFAN Cheikh Anta Diop, 2013.

[9] UNICEF, *Children Accused of Witchcraft: an Anthropological Study of Contemporary Practices in Africa*, Dakar: UNICEF/WCARO, 2010, 39f.

## Enchanted Christianity

In a seminal article, Robin Horton argued that religion in Africa was concerned with explanation, prediction, and control of events in this world. Western religion, including mission Christianity by the nineteenth century, had ceased to be so concerned, having surrendered most of these functions to science, and instead was concerned with communion with the deity, in both this world and the next. Nigerians became Christians, argued Horton, but before long realized that this new religion did not meet the first requirements of a functioning African religion, so they broke away in the early twentieth century to form their own kind of Christianity—the Christianity of the independent churches—which did precisely that.[10]

A form of Christianity meeting these needs has recently become more widely known. Beginning around 2001, the issue of Congo's alleged child witches became international news. Reports claimed that there were about 40,000 street children in Kinshasa, of whom about 80 per cent were expelled from their extended families because they were considered witches, many as young as five or six years old. As the Democratic Republic of the Congo (DRC) descended into economic freefall, the extended family system, which had always been a communal support system to adopt orphans and take in war refugees, came under great strain. Although one's own children were relatively safe, if children were not one's own they became vulnerable. To handle these evil spirits an entire range of Pentecostal pastors has arisen. The phenomenon soon appeared in Britain, after children of immigrants from the DRC and Angola came to be diagnosed as witches and subjected to all sorts of physical abuse under the guise of exorcism. Kristi Bamu, a fifteen-year-old Congolese youth, was brutally killed by his sister and 'uncle' on Christmas Day 2010 for being a witch. The police admitted they knew very little about the beliefs of these communities on witchcraft and spirit possession, and had to invent an entirely new category of 'faith crimes'. In Britain, where the number of Pentecostal churches increased by 670 between 2005 and 2010, taking the total to 3,900, there have been eighty-three cases of abuse stemming from witchcraft exorcisms up to 2012, but this represents only the tip of the iceberg, because it reflects only those cases resulting in police investigations. Such cases represent a growing problem within the immigrant community.[11]

[10] R. Horton, 'African Conversion', *Africa*, 41, 2 (1971), 85–108.
[11] *Guardian*, 1 March 2012.

Since 2007 a similar phenomenon in Nigeria has received considerable attention, with wide publicity given to Helen Ukpabio, a Pentecostal prophetess of the 150-branch Liberty Gospel Church, and especially her famous video called 'End of the Wicked' which many credit with fuelling a witch frenzy. In the video, children are shown becoming possessed and being inducted into covens, eating human flesh and causing general misfortune. Helen Ukpabio tells parents how to identify a witch, through symptoms like crying and screaming in the night to general sickliness. Nigeria's Delta Region manifests many of the same signs of cultural, social and economic breakdown as Kinshasa.[12]

I visited Zimbabwe in April 2013. There was much publicity about two schoolchildren being turned into baboons after being given rings and bracelets by their Pentecostal teacher.[13] The Pentecostal pastor of the teacher's church had not long before trumpeted his mystical abilities. His followers were reported to 'receive miracle money in their pockets, instantly lose weight, have hair covering bald heads and their missing teeth replaced, while gold dust and other precious minerals fall during church services'. When the Reserve Bank of Zimbabwe was asked to investigate whether the miracle money could be a violation of the country's currency laws, the Governor of the Reserve Bank, Dr Gideon Gono, and the pastor held a joint press conference to confirm that no laws had been violated, and to dismiss the belief that such miracle money 'would negatively impact the (nation's) money supply'.[14]

This enchanted Christianity is widespread. Rather than amass examples from different countries, let me give an extended example of an African Pentecostal church illustrating this enchanted religious imagination, the Mountain of Fire and Miracles Ministries (MFM), founded by Daniel Olukoya in Lagos in 1989. The church claims that its regular Sunday attendance at headquarters makes it the largest single Christian congregation in Africa (the figure has usually been given as 120,000, but a 2012 church magazine increased this to 200,000). It has spread widely, even outside Africa. Its founder has promoted his Christianity in over 200 books (in 2012, 217 publications were listed,

---

[12] In Britain, the publicity arose around the Channel 4 documentary, 'Saving Africa's Witch Children', screened 12 November 2008, which featured an organization 'Stepping Stones Nigeria' set up to protect Nigeria's alleged child witches.

[13] *Herald*, 8 Mar. 2013, 1.

[14] *Herald*, 6 Feb. 2013, 1.

of which thirty-six were translated into French). I make no claim to have read all Olukoya's literature (many books are out of print), nor to have attended the church regularly, but over the last twenty years it is one of the churches in which I have taken a special interest. The following treatment of his particular Christianity is based on his literature, his website, and attendance at MFM church services in Nigeria, Ghana, and London. For the moment, I am not presenting Olukoya's church as representative of African Pentecostalism; rather as an example of this form of Christianity pushed to its limits. I present it as an example that enables me to make my main point as clearly, simply and strongly as I can.

Olukoya teaches that all Christians have a glorious God-given destiny here in this world. 'Every born again Christian is destined for an all-round success. Success is your kingdom right. It is your covenant and redemptive right.'[15] But we are all prey to spiritual forces determined 'to pollute, trap and destroy people's destiny'.[16] Most frequently mentioned is witchcraft, the exercise of supernatural powers by people who are in league with the devil, through manipulation, even with the use of satanic weapons. One becomes a witch either by inheritance (often through one's witch-mother), or through a personal decision (perhaps to obtain great wealth), or by force (some are simply not strong enough to resist initiation), but many are unaware they are witches ('blind witches'), either because they think their nocturnal activities are simply dreams, or because they have been unconsciously ensnared through sex with witchcraft agents.

The signs of being bewitched are any denial of your divine destiny: being 'almost there' but never arriving; the discovery on moving to a new place that you no longer progress; financial embarrassment; financial or spiritual stagnation; the need to work unnecessarily hard before achieving anything; investing in your business but nevertheless eventually losing all; inexplicably high debts; mysterious sicknesses; perpetually losing money ('leaking pockets'); feeling rejected by everyone. And so on—Olukoya admits that 'the list is almost endless'.[17]

[15] D.K. Olukoya, *Praying against the Spirit of the Valley*, Lagos: Battle Cry, 2005, 15; 'Success is your birthright as a born again child of God' (D.K. Olukoya, *Power to Achieve Success*, Lagos: Battle Cry, 2012, 22).

[16] D.K. Olukoya, *The Star Hunters*, Lagos: MFM, 2002, 24.

[17] D.K. Olukoya, *Overpowering Witchcraft*, Lagos: Battle Cry, 1999, 35.

Another category of destructive spirits is marine spirits, which are particularly destructive satanic agents, found widely in Africa. They control riverine areas, and thus are particularly to be found among riverine peoples, whose propensity to sexual laxity and general backwardness owe much to them.[18] Marine spirits are more powerful than witchcraft spirits, and nothing is outside their sphere of influence. 'Survey the entire complete range of calamities (that affect humans) and you discover that most of them are planned and executed by marine spirits.'[19] Many people have been initiated into the marine kingdom unbeknown to themselves. Marine spirits can deposit strange items (like beads, mirrors, necklaces, snakes, fish and plates) into people's bodies.

Marine spirits are closely associated with sex. They inspire sexual dreams. Marine spirits are particularly associated with female beauty; a woman attractive to men is almost certainly one, and 'most of the attractive ladies which litter our streets are from the marine kingdom'.[20] Their sway is extensive. Among other things, they control commerce, trade and the economy; they control alcohol production and the world of cosmetics, hair styling and fashion: 'Most of the styles which are in vogue today are introduced by water spirits... The seductive dresses which most ladies put on today are fashioned from the marine kingdom.'[21]

Marine bondage has many sources, including the following: polygamy (of many wives, you can be sure that at least one is a member of the marine kingdom); ancestors; parents who are marine agents 'unbeknown to you'; friends who belong to water societies; fetish priests; 'white garment churches' (AICs); dedication of babies near rivers; parties and discos (especially with women in seductive dresses and dancing suggestively); marine hair styles; Satan-inspired music; clothes borrowed from people who are marine agents; gifts of rings, bangles, necklaces; sex with marine agents; visiting rivers or streams for cultural reasons. Again, the list is almost endless.

Signs of bondage include: difficulty in praying, fasting and living the Christian life; unprovoked anger; dreaming of water; difficulty in find-

---

[18] D.K. Olukoya, *Disgracing Water Spirits: Deliverance Manual for Indigenes of Riverine Areas*, Lagos: MFM, 2012.
[19] D.K. Olukoya, *Power against Marine Spirits*, Lagos: Battle Cry, 1999, 4.
[20] Ibid., 17.
[21] Ibid., 60.

ing a partner; an unstable marriage and uncontrollable sexual urges; strange sicknesses and a general failure to progress. The only solution to the problem of marine spirits is repentance, a holy life, and deliverance, often extensive deliverance—one man who fell into a river, and was detained in the marine kingdom for six months, on release needed twenty-five deliverance sessions before he was set free.

Yet another category of spiritual forces is a spirit spouse. There are different forms of spiritual marriage. Some know they are involved in such a marriage, but over 90 per cent who are spiritually married are unconscious of the fact. Some are forced into spiritual marriages (by, for example, being raped in dreams). 'The problem is so pronounced that 90 per cent of African women are trapped spiritually.'[22]

One becomes married spiritually in many different ways: through immorality; through receiving gifts from an evil agent whose demonic identity is usually unknown to the recipient; through involvement in African cultural entertainment and dances; through inheriting a family priesthood (which normally involves marriage to some deity); through wearing seductive dresses which attract spirit husbands (such spirits 'introduce the majority of the styles that are prevalent today',[23] and for a woman to persist in wearing trousers is to offer herself in marriage to demonic husbands); through hairstyles and artificial hair attachments; through the sexual covenant established with your first sexual partner; through masturbation; through religious baths; through alcohol and drugs; through manipulation of articles of underwear so they become points of contact with spiritual spouses; through sexual perversion. Sex with a prostitute automatically gives entrance to the demons of the last seven men who had sex with the prostitute, and to all the spirit husbands of the prostitute. Children of a prostitute or concubine are automatically affected.

The indications of spiritual marriage are many, but essentially the absence of the victory that should be a Christian's. All these are signs of spiritual marriage: marital, social, financial and spiritual emptiness; misfortune; 'profitless hard work'; disharmony in marriage; irregular or painful menstruating. The indications are so many that 'the activities of a spirit husband or wife can hardly be completely enumerated'.[24]

---

[22] D.K. Olukoya, *Deliverance from Spirit Husband and Spirit Wife; Incubi and Succubi*, Lagos: Battle Cry, 1999, 108.

[23] Ibid., 23.

[24] Olukoya, *Deliverance from Spirit Husbands*, 33.

The solution to manipulation by spiritual spouses includes repentance, atonement, a holy life, returning gifts which created the relationship, and especially the binding and casting out of spouses by oneself or more probably by a deliverance minister.

Another source of spiritual bondage is a curse made against a person or group of people. Curses are of various kinds. They include curses of divorce, poverty, stagnancy, backwardness, defeat, oppression, and general failure. Ancestral curses are ubiquitous, especially in Africa where 95 per cent of problems stem from ancestors,[25] which is 'why nine out of ten Africans would need to go through deliverance to enjoy their lives'.[26] Ancestral bondage can last up to 500 years. Places also can be cursed. There are forty different problems (ranging from poverty to wastage and to 'lack of maintenance') that Olukoya lists as stemming from one's place of origin.[27]

Once again, you can recognize you are under a curse from signs like the following: struggling without fulfilment or 'profitless hard work'; failure to gain promotion; the recurrence of misfortune; failure where others succeed; promising beginnings which nevertheless always turn to failure; recurring sickness; being robbed of the blessings you are entitled to; encountering a ceiling curtailing your achievements. If your mother has been divorced several times and you are undergoing marital troubles yourself, the cause is probably a curse. If you come from a village where no one has ever built his own house, the whole village is probably under a curse.

A very frequent way of discovering you are under a curse or attacked by some spirit is through dreams. Dreams reveal what is going on in the spirit realm. More than that, they effect what they reveal.[28] Dreams about accidents, carrying loads, closed doors, hair, begging, wearing rags, leaking pockets, thieves, rats, growing old, chains, having property confiscated, coffins, being lost in the forest, black shadows, screaming, eating assorted foods, snakes, water, dead relatives or masquerades all indicate that the devil is attacking you. Olukoya interprets the content of dreams, thereby identifying the particular area under attack and the satanic agent responsible. A dream about carrying a

---

[25] D.K. Olukoya, *Your Foundation and Your Destiny*, Lagos: Battle Cry, 2001, 71.
[26] Olukoya, *Deliverance from Spirit Husbands*, 99.
[27] Olukoya, *Your Foundation*, 255.
[28] The origins of MFM lie in a dream; see D.K. Olukoya, *Criminals in the House of God*, Lagos: MFM, 2nd ed, 2002, 35.

basket indicates a satanic plan to make you suffer loss. Consuming alcohol indicates the spirit of confusion. Corpses indicate the spirit of death. Cobwebs indicate the spirit of rejection: 'The devil is trying to render your life useless'.[29] Earrings indicate the enemy's attempt to turn you into a slave. Padlocks indicate that your blessings have been locked up. A broken-down car indicates an attack 'on the wheel of your progress'.[30] And so on. Olukoya says of the indications of satanic attack: 'The list is almost endless'.[31]

In this enchanted world, boundaries are not hard and fast; the spiritual and the physical world interpenetrate one another. 'The enemy has the power to take an animal, dematerialize it and programme it into the human body. They can make it to come out, alive, through the mouth.'[32] People vomit snails, snakes, calabashes, pins, pots, cowries, rings, lizards, hair, live birds and small coffins; such things had been satanically programmed into the stomach. Women menstruate maggots. Cockroaches come out of a man's head. Cats talk. Domestic pets are often spies for the devil ('If you want to carry out a test, pour anointing oil on your animals at home and see what happens').[33] Demons manifest in the form of human beings. Women act as perfectly normal wives until somehow they are identified as coming from the marine kingdom; upon discovery, they return to their watery origins, never to be seen again. Women preparing for illicit sex can find a proposed partner transformed into a python. A new husband (married against the advice of the pastor) discovers that his wife has horns. A husband (married likewise against the advice of the pastor) turns into a gorilla every time he is alone with his wife. A woman can trap a man by getting him to drink soup prepared by boiling her underwear.

It is *Africa* that has the problem with spiritual forces. 'As a black, you have to be aware of your background, or participation in masquerades, tribal rituals, collection of your name from an oracle, being born by a father who has charms, armlets and idols at home, parents who accept services from demons, parents who were harsh to slaves

[29] D.K. Olukoya, *Victory over Satanic Dreams*, Lagos: MFM, 1996, 26.
[30] Ibid., 29.
[31] Ibid., 14.
[32] D.K. Olukoya, *Dining Table of Darkness*, Lagos: Battle Cry, 2005, 9.
[33] D.K. Olukoya, *When the Wicked is on the Rampage*, Lagos: Battle Cry, 2012, 43. 'Witches use black cats, but the deception of the devil is to conceal the fact that they actually prefer white ones' (ibid., 43); also D.K. Olukoya, *Deliverance from Evil Load*, Lagos: MFM, 2009, 42.

and being born in a polygamous set-up. You will be deceiving yourself to believe that all these will just fly past you, without any effect.'[34] All native dances 'come from the pit of hell'.[35] The masquerade is 'an embodiment of evil spirits'.[36] Customs concerning the placenta are a particular source of evil: 'The problem of placental bondage accounts for most of the problems of the black race', because if your placenta was thrown in the gutter, you will live a life in the gutter; if in the dust-bin, you will be a citizen of the dunghill; if in the toilet, you will spend your life with disposed waste; if it was eaten by a dog, you will be sexually loose; if it was hidden in a crack, you will be the companion of lizards, and so on.[37] Polygamy is the source of untold evils. 'The spirit of polygamy is prevalent in almost every African community... This is not ordinary. There is a spirit behind it. When this kind of spirit comes upon a woman, she will never find a man who has never married before to marry her... A man who has the anointing of polygamy will never be satisfied with one woman.'[38]

It is in the black race that you find promotion of the inferior and demotion of the superior... It is in the black race that you find the young widows factory, that you see many firstborns being used as torchlight, so that they never find their feet. It is in the black race, that you find the trademark of poverty, star-vation and famine, that we have the greatest promoters of polygamy. Here we have plenty of lands of wasted destinies, plenty of sit-tight and confused lead-ers, senseless civil and tribal wars, destructive witchcraft destroying everything and women abuse... This is a land of vultures that attack the seed of God planted into man.[39]

Olukoya talks about these major categories (witches, marine spirits, spiritual spouses, curses) at length and in considerable detail. It may appear that he has a sharply defined cosmology with identifiable causes responsible for particular effects, but this is not so. What he ascribes to a spirit spouse he can on other occasions equally ascribe to a witch or a marine spirit. In fact, almost anything can be ascribed to

[34] D.K. Olukoya, *Power to Shut Satanic Doors*, Lagos: MFM, 2011, 26.

[35] Olukoya, *When the Wicked is on the Rampage*, 68.

[36] Olukoya, *Victory over Satanic Dreams*, 21.

[37] D.K. Olukoya, *Satanic Technology*, Lagos: MFM, 2001, 35–7; 48.

[38] D.K. Olukoya (with Shade Olukoya), *Prayer Strategies for Spinsters and Bachelors*, Lagos: MFM, 1999, 61f.

[39] D.K. Olukoya, *Power against the Enemy Opposed to your Shining*, Lagos: MFM, 2012, 6.

a definite source, but on other occasions those same things can be attributed to another source, equally identified. Witchcraft thinking is a work in progress. It is an *imaginaire* or imaginary, a worldview, a mentality that can flexibly be applied everywhere, rather than a thought-out doctrine with every anomaly eliminated, every inconsistency ironed out.

Olukoya does stress repentance, righteousness and a moral life, and it is a puritan morality, too. At times he can sound like John Chrysostom, Jonathan Edwards, or John Wesley, denouncing sin, pride, stubbornness, anger, envy, selfishness, deceit, impatience, vengeance, adultery, lust, murder, uncleanness, gluttony, gossiping, cursing, ingratitude, vanity, covetousness, laziness—the list goes on and on.[40] A few sermons are completely in this vein, but the Wesleyan/Edwardsian calls to holiness are normally set in an enchanted frame, necessary to combat the spiritual forces that will otherwise overwhelm us. While he is taking this Wesley/Edwards line, the agency of spirits can be temporarily made peripheral—but only temporarily. At times the juxtaposition between the moral and the enchanted can seem rather abrupt: in the midst of outlining the spiritual forces against us, he can move to a totally different register, demanding total repentance and conquest of self; he can just as easily move in the other direction.[41]

Like all Christians, Olukoya anchors his Christianity in the Bible. However, though he can extend himself recounting the stories of Jezebel, Elisha (especially with Naaman and Gehazi), Joseph and Lot, Olukoya is not particularly imaginative. Normally his use of the Bible is atomistic, simply lumping together texts which happen to contain the word he is dealing with (for example, 'dream', 'night', 'fool', 'star', 'blood', 'name'). Likewise, he is given to justifying some point by invoking biblical statistics, that, for example, the Bible contains twenty-eight accounts of dreams, 121 mentions of dreams,[42] and 161 references to curses.[43] He justifies reversing curses sevenfold by noting

---

[40] D.K. Olukoya, *Contending for the Kingdom*, Lagos: Battle Cry, 2005, 42–61.

[41] Compare pages 41–56 of D.K. Olukoya, *Raiding the House of the Strongman*, Lagos: MFM, 2011, which could be by Wesley or Jonathan Edwards, with the rest of the book. A rare quotation from a hymn 'by one man called Wesley' might indicate that Olukoya's familiarity with the Wesleys is slight (D.K. Olukoya, *When the Enemy Hides*, Lagos: MFM, 2011, 28).

[42] Olukoya, *Your Foundation*, 56, 153.

[43] D.K. Olukoya, *Power against Dream Criminals*, Lagos: MFM, 2001, 35.

that God himself performed sixteen executions in the Bible; thus 'God himself is the ultimate killing machine' and 'a holy killer'.[44]

His preoccupations suggest that his Christianity is geared to the less well off rather than to the middle class: avoid television, fashionable clothing, make-up, trousers (for women), false fingernails, perfumes, ear piercing and especially jewellery.[45] His insistence that serious Christians should preach on the buses indicates that this is the mode of transport for many of his listeners. Just as revealing is his singling out Whites as beings from almost a superior level (in a way Nigeria's more consciously cosmopolitan preachers would never do).[46] He makes no effort to impress with cosmopolitan sensibilities. Children should be beaten: 'Sayings such as "I don't believe in beating children" is where the trouble starts'.[47] He seems aware of the criticism that his preoccupation with dreams leaves him open to the charge of 'lack of civilization'.[48]

What essentially characterizes Olukoya's Christianity is spiritual warfare. Spiritual warfare is a better shorthand label for his Christianity than deliverance, because although he talks a great deal about deliverance, and many of his examples describe his delivering those variously afflicted, deliverance is not the prime motif. The essence of his Christianity is prayer—violent prayers of 'holy madness', the 'offensive warfare' of a 'firebrand warrior'—either in church or at home. This prayer is the principal means of thwarting the evil forces arrayed

---

[44] Olukoya, *Overpowering*, 61; D.K. Olukoya, *Stop Them before They Stop You*, Lagos: MFM, 2009, 32 & 37. Olukoya has published his own fascinating (KJV) *Prayer and Deliverance Bible*, Lagos: MFM, 2007, which through his notes, introductions and commentary presents the entire Bible in terms of his preoccupation with demons and spirits; see Paul Gifford, 'A Modern Nigerian Interpretation of the Bible', *Journal of Theology for Southern Africa*, forthcoming.

[45] Jewellery is associated with spirits under the ground and under the waters; 'You are a lot safer without jewellery... If God wanted you to put on jewellery, he would have hung some on your neck and hands and made holes in your ears' (Olukoya, *Contending for the Kingdom*, 9). 'All those involved in "panel beating" of the body, spraying of the body, painting the lips, scraping off hair on the face, painting the face with strange colours are daughters of this woman called Jezebel, because Jezebel is the mother of all demonic painters' (Olukoya, *Criminals*, 53).

[46] See D.K. Olukoya, *The Terrible Agenda*, Lagos: MFM, 2009, 27; Olukoya, *Stop Them Before They Stop You*, 45, 65, 101.

[47] Olukoya, *Criminals*, 59.

[48] Olukoya, *Victory over Satanic Dreams*, 2.

against us and reclaiming our true destiny, and Olukoya's normal understanding is that the Christian can pray himself or herself free, even if often enough Olukoya is needed to identify the particular evil force and specify the proper prayer. These 'prayer points' are the most characteristic feature of MFM. Their typical form is: 'Every satanic padlock fashioned against me, be roasted by fire in Jesus' name', or 'Every evil load programmed into my life in a dream, go back to your sender by fire, in the name of Jesus', or 'Any organ of my body that has been exchanged for another through witchcraft operations, be replaced now, in the name of Jesus'. These prayer points can number fifty or sixty at a time, sometimes over two hundred.[49] They can begin a sermon, end one, or come at any time between—or indeed, all three. In church they are shouted violently in unison—of course, by oneself if at home. The number and nature of these prayer points corroborate my claim that the enchanted imagination pervades his church. Even if they come after an almost Wesleyan exhortation to holiness, the prayer points invariably revert to an enchanted register.

Olukoya's church represents one distinctive form of African Pentecostalism, and is an almost pure example of it. Before considering how widespread this form is, we will consider another prominent subgroup within African Pentecostalism.

---

[49] For whole books of such prayers, see D.K. Olukoya, *Violent Prayers to Disgrace Stubborn Problems*, Lagos: Battle Cry, 1999; D.K. Olukoya, *Deliverance through the Watches from Sexual Perversion*, Lagos: MFM, 2011.

3

# VICTORY

We have seen that Olukoya's religious vision is that humans are born with a glorious destiny (not in an afterlife but in this world), but this destiny is threatened by ubiquitous spiritual forces. All Africa's Pentecostal churches originate from the same idea: a Christian is destined for victory in every aspect of life, which includes material prosperity. Among them are many that place enormous emphasis on material prosperity, and it is one of these that I will discuss as my second example, Living Faith Church Worldwide, better known as Winners' Chapel. It was founded in Lagos in 1983 by David Oyedepo. By 2013 it boasted 6,000 branches in Nigeria, 700 branches in other African countries (sixty-one in Kenya), and thirty in Europe and North America. Winners' boasts in Lagos the biggest church auditorium in the world, seating 50,400, and in Nairobi in April 2013 it opened the biggest church in East and Central Africa at a cost of US$18 million. The senior pastors, at least in the continent's major cities, tend to be Nigerians, well schooled in the founder Oyedepo's teaching and fiercely loyal. They recommend Oyedepo's books and promote the pilgrimage to the annual conference ('Shiloh') at headquarters (the 560 acres of 'Canaan Land', outside Lagos, where their Covenant University is situated).

In this chapter, I will try to give some understanding of what Oyedepo's Christianity is. Over the last twenty years, I have attended Winners' services in various African countries, seen many more on tele-

29

vision, and read a good deal of Oyedepo's material. I will draw on all these data. I will also make use of a considerable number of testimonies, which give a good insight into how his followers understand and experience his ministry. Even if the testimonies in his publications have been doctored for public circulation, that reinforces the case that this is how Oyedepo wishes to be understood and experienced. The examples and excerpts I have chosen are not unrepresentative. The testimonies below accurately reflect my experience of the church across the continent over twenty years.[1]

## Word of Faith

Obviously and unashamedly, Oyedepo's Christianity is about victory, triumph, blessing, dominion. Christians should be 'gloriously distinguished in all spheres of life'.[2] A Christian should 'enjoy victory unlimited and on all sides',[3] because faith 'overcomes all forces of darkness, economic problems, sickness, disease, family disintegration, untimely death, and every obstacle you can possibly imagine on earth'.[4] 'Everyone that is saved is saved to shine, not to suffer frustration. As a matter of fact, the believer can be said to be a celebrity, someone the world should celebrate.'[5] 'There is a land of plenty in the Kingdom of God... a land where there is no lack of any kind, and where you eat bread without scarceness... It's a land full of treasures (Deut 8,7–10)'.[6]

Originally, his Christianity was clearly part of the Word of Faith movement, preaching the faith gospel, or health and wealth gospel. He preserves the essentials. You must think only positive thoughts. 'You are what you think... If you don't think success, you will never have it... Every negative thought you allow to have a grip on you, blocks you from your inheritance.'[7] You must proclaim your belief. 'Poverty

---

[1] I have written of Winners' Chapel before, most notably in Paul Gifford, *Ghana's New Christianity: Pentecostalism in a Globalising African Economy*, London: Hurst, 2004, esp. 51–61, and Paul Gifford, *Christianity, Politics and Public Life in Kenya*, London: Hurst, 2009, esp. 121–5, 185–8.

[2] David O. Oyedepo, *Signs and Wonders Today: a Catalogue of the Amazing Acts of God among Men*, Lagos: Dominion, 2006, 14.

[3] Ibid., 42.

[4] Ibid.

[5] Ibid., 403.

[6] Ibid., 165.

[7] David O. Oyedepo, *Releasing the Supernatural*, Lagos: Dominion, 1995, 132.

and prosperity, health and sickness, fear and security, all lie in the tongue. If you talk health, you will be healthy; if you talk sickness, you will be sick. Talk prosperity and you will be prosperous.'[8] For this reason he refuses to use the marriage formula 'for better or worse', because it allows for the negative.[9] 'A cardinal step in the release of the supernatural is the production of sound. It is the production of sound based on the Word of God revealed to you that will compel supernatural forces to work in your favour... Your mouth is a destiny-moulder.'[10] 'Only the confident loud-mouths command the miraculous in the kingdom'.[11] Absolute faith is required: 'Your actions must agree with your words. You cannot say, "By his stripes I was healed" and continue to patronize the chemist's shops looking for Panadol'.[12] Of course, 'Spiritual laws or principles always work whether you know it or not'.[13]

He often refers to international Pentecostal stars: Fred Price, Derek Prince, D.L. Moody, T.L. Osborn, Dodie Osteen (I've never heard mention of her son Joel Osteen), Lester Sumrall, John Avanzini, David Yonggi Cho, Jerry Savelle, A.A. Allen, Smith Wigglesworth Mike Murdock (with Benson Idahosa and Enoch Adeboye the only Africans I have heard him mention). Those familiar with the Christianity of these celebrities will have no difficulty placing Oyedepo. He is prepared to acknowledge his indebtedness especially to Kenneth Hagin and the Copelands. He learned the 'secrets of kingdom prosperity' on a three-day retreat with two books written by the Copelands. He once slept in a bed in which Kenneth Copeland had slept: 'That contact turned my financial status around, all because I had the correct sense to recognize my superior'.[14] Oyedepo was always near the wealth end of the faith gospel. This is obvious from the account of his calling by God. His experience is obviously modelled on the call of Moses, but whereas Moses in Midian was commanded: 'Go and set my people

---

[8] David O. Oyedepo, *The Miracle Seed*, Lagos: Dominion, 1986, 70.

[9] Ibid.

[10] David O. Oyedepo, *Commanding the Supernatural*, Lagos: Dominion, 2006, 131–36.

[11] Oyedepo, *Releasing the Supernatural*, 70.

[12] David O. Oyedepo, *Born to Win*, Lagos: Dominion, 1986, 124.

[13] Oyedepo, *Releasing the Supernatural*, 32.

[14] David O. Oyedepo, *Walking in Dominion*, Lagos: Dominion, 2008, 175.

free', Oyedepo in the United States in 1987 was simply told: 'Get down home quick and make my people rich'.[15]

Oyedepo consistently argues from biblical texts. Given his preoccupations, certain texts recur. His key text is probably Psalm 82, 6: 'You are gods'.[16] Other recurring texts are Exodus 7, 1 ('See, I have made thee a god to Pharaoh'); John 10, 30 ('I and the Father are one'); Ezekiel 37, 1–10 (the valley of the dry bones); Malachi 3, 10 ('I will open the windows of heaven and pour out a blessing'); Joshua 1, 8 ('In this book... you will have good success'); Proverbs 10, 22 ('make rich without sorrow'); 2 Corinthians 8, 9 ('that through his poverty you might be rich'); Deuteronomy 18, 1–13 ('If thou shalt hearken diligently unto the voice of the Lord... all these blessings'); Deuteronomy 8, 18 ('he that giveth thee power to get wealth'); John 1, 12 ('But as many as received him, to them gave he power'); John 14, 12 ('You will do even greater works'); 3 John 2 ('that you prosper'). His understanding of the Bible enables him to jump indiscriminately from the Gospels to the Psalms, the prophets to Paul, Genesis to Revelation, but he can often argue with considerable ingenuity.

Anyone not born again is a child of darkness. However, becoming born again is less about speaking in tongues than about power. So many who are born again operate with no supernatural power, because they don't know what they have at their disposal. Knowledge and power are thus crucial. Those born again but with hardly anything tangible to show for their Christianity 'are simply victims of ignorance more than anything else'.[17] In fact, 'ignorance is more serious' than sin.[18] Oyedepo claims (in a passage so different from Olukoya): 'You are not suffering because there is a great devil somewhere, but rather because of your great ignorance'.[19] 'Your greatest enemy is not the woman or the man next door or the proverbial village witch, but your ignorance of what you must do to have dominion.'[20] 'Too many

---

[15] David O. Oyedepo, *Breaking Financial Hardship*, Lagos: Dominion, 1995, 51; David O. Oyedepo, *Winning the War against Poverty*, Lagos: Dominion, 2006, 79.

[16] 'As a result, you have the same nature with God the father' (Oyedepo, *Commanding the Supernatural*, 61).

[17] David O. Oyedepo, *Exploring the Riches of Redemption*, Lagos: Dominion, 2004, 54.

[18] Oyedepo, *Born to Win*, 98.

[19] Oyedepo, *Walking in Dominion*, 152.

[20] David O. Oyedepo, *Understanding your Covenant Rights*, Lagos: Dominion, 2003, 9.

Christians focus on spiritual warfare, but there is a place for mental warfare, which is where most people have lost the battle all their lives.'[21] If only we understood, we could walk in power.

What we must understand is the Word. 'The Bible is God's wisdom in print form'.[22] 'It is the depth of your understanding of the truths of scriptures that determines the heights of your triumph in life'.[23] 'Until you find the Word point on any issue, you should not expect any fruit,'[24] but once you have found it, 'Obedience is the key factor to walking in the realm of the miraculous. Whether what the Word says applies to reason or not, go ahead and do it.'[25] 'God will forever back up his Word'.[26] Oyedepo ranges widely in the Bible, and insists our 'redemption package' includes power, riches, wisdom, strength, honour, glory, blessing,[27] but his principal preoccupation is clearly wealth. Likewise, the one essential demand of the Word that we must know and obey is tithing and offering; these are 'the most important thing'.[28] We must give continually: 'Giving is the gateway to wealth'.[29] We must not stop just with the tithe: 'The tithe is fundamental, but not enough'.[30] The resulting covenant wealth is considerable: 'Prophetically, you and I have been packaged and programmed for unusual supernatural prosperity.'[31] 'The Abrahamic covenant of blessings grants you access to an unlimited supply of money until you become the envy of your generation.'[32] 'God has programmed to bring you into a financial dreamland';[33] 'When you agree with the Almighty, you will lay up gold as dust.'[34] By contrast, 'If you will not be an excited giver, you will die in poverty'.[35] This law of seedtime and harvest (see Genesis 8, 22) is

---

[21] Ibid., 9.

[22] Ibid., 45.

[23] David O. Oyedepo, *All you Need to Have All Your Needs Met*, Lagos: Dominion, 2004, 10.

[24] Oyedepo, *Miracle Seed*, 26.

[25] Ibid., 48.

[26] Ibid.

[27] David O. Oyedepo, *Possessing Your Possessions*, Lagos: Dominion, 2006, 66.

[28] Ibid., 151.

[29] David O. Oyedepo, *Anointing for Breakthrough*, Lagos: Dominion, 1992, 154.

[30] Oyedepo, *Possessing your Possessions*, 153.

[31] Oyedepo, *Winning the War*, 75.

[32] Ibid., 68.

[33] Ibid., 139.

[34] Oyedepo, *All you Need*, 5.

[35] Oyedepo, *Releasing the Supernatural*, 89.

immutable: 'Natural laws have no power to subdue spiritual laws'.[36] 'If there must be harvest, there must be seed sown. That is the law, and the scriptures cannot be broken.'[37]

Jesus lived in this covenant blessing; the idea that he was poor is a lie that the church has devised to restrict us to mediocrity. 'The "poor" Jesus had a treasurer, had a bed in his ship or at least enjoyed a first class cabin, where He had a pillow on which to rest His head. He hired the upper room in Jerusalem when He went there for a feast. He had a coat that the Roman army officers fought among themselves to possess.'[38] 'He ate whatever He wanted and whenever He desired it. He lived in a place that commanded envy, because John's disciples who went to see where He lived never returned to their master.' The upper room for the Passover feast 'is what is called the Penthouse in today's language. He was traveling by sea in Mark 11, and had a convoy of other ships with him.'[39]

In recent years, perhaps in response to criticisms made against prosperity preachers like himself, Oyedepo has introduced the idea of giving to others, but such additions do not obscure the fact that the covenant-giving that brings us covenant-blessing is basically giving to God, or (which is essentially the same thing) to the church. 'Your giving is first to God, not to your local government council or to friends. We are not philanthropists. It must be first to God.'[40] He illustrates this with the examples of David and Solomon, those preeminent 'covenant practitioners' and 'biblical success giants', who gave handsomely to God's house, and were spectacularly rewarded. David sowed the equivalent of over US$100 million for the building of the temple: 'If you want the rain, plant the seed first'.[41] Elsewhere Oyedepo gives David's contribution as US$632 million; a true 'kingdom addiction'.[42] 'Solomon loved the Lord and showed it by sacrificing the largest burnt offering in history. No wonder he is still the wealthiest man the world has ever known.'[43] It is clear, too, that the needs of God and the church take

---

[36] Oyedepo, *Understanding your Covenant*, 97–100.
[37] Oyedepo, *Winning the War*, 107.
[38] Oyedepo, *Anointing for Breakthrough*, 149.
[39] Oyedepo, *Winning the War*, 67 and 72.
[40] David O. Oyedepo, *Showers of Blessings*, Lagos: Dominion, 1997, 71.
[41] Oyedepo, *Anointing for Breakthrough*, 163.
[42] Oyedepo, *Winning the War*, 137. The figure is also about US$600 million in Oyedepo, *Breaking Financial Hardship*, 1995, 68.
[43] Oyedepo, *Releasing the Supernatural*, 153.

priority over our own: 'Until Solomon finished building the house of the Lord, he didn't build his own house.'[44] 'It is time to place kingdom budgets as priority over your own budget. Worship God with your means and free yourself from the tension of the hour... This is the big bang that will grant you eternal access into sweatless supplies.'[45]

## Oyedepo's role

But Oyedepo's Christianity is far more than his teaching. His person is essential. In theory this Christianity is for all, because it is simply the outworking of the covenant described in the Bible; anyone with this knowledge can exercise the resultant power. Yet in practice Oyedepo seems essential. The tension is captured here: 'Sometime ago, a woman came to report to me that for some inexplicable reasons, the clothing material she was selling were not being bought. I went to her shop, laid my hands on the merchandise, and said, "Clothes, be gone, now". The following day, some people who came from outside the town bought up everything.'[46] Similarly, Oyedepo laid his hands on the hands of a trader with the same problem: 'To his amazement the following day, at about twelve noon, a man in a trailer reversed into his drive way and purchased every item in the shop!' Oyedepo continues: 'In actual fact, he has access to the same miracle hands that I have, and so does everyone that believes. Unfortunately, however, not all that believe know that there is a miracle in their hands.'[47]

People are cured merely by touching his garments: 'One day I was walking through the congregation to the pulpit and a man who had suffered a spinal injury for seventeen years touched my clothes (a flowing gown) and immediately heard a cracking sound in his lumbar region. That was it! He was instantly healed!'[48] Oyedepo feels he has to add the disclaimer that it was not his power, but God's, because unlike Jesus who felt power leave him (Mark 5, 30), Oyedepo felt nothing. Oyedepo can use this power consciously. One day he hung up his coat, 'instructing anybody looking up to God for healing to touch it'. A woman with bowel problems for thirty-eight years touched it and

---

[44] Oyedepo, *Walking in Dominion*, 91.
[45] Oyedepo, *Winning the War*, 135; see all 65–142.
[46] David O. Oyedepo, *Walking in the Miraculous*, Lagos: Dominion, 1998, 15.
[47] Ibid., 15f.
[48] Oyedepo, *Walking in Dominion*, 77–9.

was immediately healed.[49] At a Victory Celebration, he anointed the *agbada* he was wearing, and passed it around 'with the instruction that everyone that desired a "big bang" miracle should touch their foreheads with it'—again, with predictable results.[50]

A dream featuring the Bishop is sufficient,[51] even just touching his pulpit,[52] and superimposing the Bishop's picture on that of a missing loved one brings him home.[53] Just looking at the Bishop cures brain tumour.[54] A man suffering memory loss, when asked by the Bishop how he was, responded, 'Fine, thank you', and found himself instantly healed.[55]

A soldier threatens to shoot him; Oyedepo simply tells him, 'You are too small', and the gun falls from the soldier's hand, and he abjectly apologizes.[56] Assassins attacked Oyedepo: 'I looked at them right in the face and cried out, "In the name of Jesus!" and the anointing from heaven came and sent them falling backward, as though a wind pushed them down. They began to scream, "He has a gun!" as they took to their heels.'[57] A local government official objected to the disturbance his church was causing to local people: 'I banged hard on his table, warning him not to dare anything, otherwise he would be a dead man, and I walked out with authority.'[58] He simply overrules doctors, even concerning his wife and daughter, on the grounds that diagnoses of ill-health are impossible for members of his family.[59] A doctor monitoring his blood pressure is simply told his reading cannot be correct.[60] A woman has no womb: Oyedepo simply tells her to go ahead and have a baby: 'That settled it'.[61] He overrules doctors' reports,[62] because doc-

---

[49] Oyedepo, *Commanding the Supernatural*, 127.

[50] Oyedepo, *Anointing for Breakthrough*, 250.

[51] Oyedepo, *Signs and Wonders*, 539.

[52] Ibid., 175.

[53] Ibid., 375.

[54] Ibid., 271.

[55] Ibid., 431.

[56] David O. Oyedepo, *Winning Invisible Battles*, Lagos: Dominion, 2006, 54.

[57] Oyedepo, *Anointing for Breakthrough*, 115.

[58] Oyedepo, *Winning Invisible Battles*, 53.

[59] Oyedepo, *Releasing the Supernatural*, 37, 43; some of these cases raise serious legal issues; in the USA exponents of the faith gospel have been prosecuted for not taking reasonable care of dependents.

[60] Oyedepo, *Exploring the Riches*, 41.

[61] Oyedepo, *Winning Invisible Battles*, 98.

[62] Oyedepo, *Signs and Wonders*, 535.

tors deal in facts, not (covenant) truth.[63] In that sense he can call science 'an enemy of faith'.[64]

His status determines his wealth. 'I have not found any reason why anybody in the church I pastor should be richer than me because it was *Jesus* who rode on the colt. The disciples were following him on foot!'[65]

One's response to him determines one's situation in life. On one outreach, he told his colleagues: 'Friends, the Lord just spoke these words to me: "Bring everything in your pockets out, and don't worry about what you will eat, I will take care of it".' Oyedepo remarks: 'I don't think the others brought out all they had. Some did not understand it. How do I know? Some eleven years after, those who did not fully understand are yet to find their footing in life! But I gave all I had in my pocket, which was about 120 naira. That's why my showers haven't stopped falling.'[66]

Oyedepo also claims to have 'creative breath'. 'The Father has creative life in His breath, so does the Son. And because the Son says He has sent us as the Father sent Him, therefore, I have creative life in my breath also. And because the Son quickens whomsoever He wills (Jn 5, 21), I too can quicken whomsoever I will by that same breath of life.'[67] He recounts that he breathed on a child with polio, and 'instantly, the legs straightened out'.[68] He claims to have cured many of HIV/AIDS this way.[69] Testimonies tell of this miraculous breath, too: 'At the November "Breakthrough Night", the Bishop called some people out for special ministration. I went out and he breathed into my mouth. On getting back to my seat, I started feeling the power of God inside me. My body was chilled' and the cure (from severe constipation) effected.[70] A woman unable to conceive testifies: 'As the Bishop breathed into me, something cleansed me, and I became pregnant'.[71]

---

[63] Ibid., 521.
[64] Ibid., 518.
[65] Oyedepo, *Releasing the Supernatural*, 94.
[66] Oyedepo, *Showers of Blessing*, 75f. The value of the naira has changed from about parity to the US dollar in 1985, to 8 to the US$1 in 1990 (on parallel market 11), 22 in 1995 (on parallel market 70), 86 in 2000 (on parallel market 105), 120 in 2003 (on parallel market 135), 128 in 2006, 150 in 2011.
[67] Oyedepo, *Signs and Wonders*, 161.
[68] Ibid.
[69] Ibid.
[70] Ibid., 303.
[71] Ibid., 527. See also Oyedepo, *Walking in Dominion*, 155.

I noted that he began his ministry clearly as a Word of Faith preacher, but over time, he has come to place more stress on his 'prophetic anointing'. He has become the quintessential prophet, claiming crucial significance in the victorious living of his followers. His ministry actually brings this about. God speaks to him clearly. What God has revealed, Oyedepo can pronounce and actually bring about. The implications of such a claim cannot be exaggerated:

Prophetic verdicts are divine verdicts; they are heavenly verdicts. They are God's commands given expression to through mortal lips... Every time the prophet says, 'Thus saith the Lord', it is actually the Lord Himself speaking. He is only using the prophet's vocal system as a microphone... Prophetic verdicts will cause your daystar to rise. It will always bring a change of position, as mountains and hopeless situations bow to it. It gives life to any dead situation, and turns worthlessness to exceeding greatness.[72]

His status is thus further enhanced: 'Prophets are the carriers of God's power, and this power is like a river. One characteristic of rivers is that they flow downhill, not uphill... If you must partake of what the prophets carry, you must accept them as being placed above you.'[73]

He is not loath to exercise his prophetic calling. He prophesies that there will arise five women shipping magnates in his congregation. One testifies to how the Bishop miraculously brought this about.[74] He declares that everyone wanting to marry in the course of a particular year will do so.[75] He prophesies that no family member will die that particular year;[76] also that 'this year is your year of laughter; no sorrow is permitted in your lives. Nothing will die in your hands this year.'[77] He proclaims: 'Within seven weeks, you will get whatever you are asking for.'[78] At the dedication of the faith tabernacle (the 40,000 seating headquarters), he declared: 'You will not go home with any problem you came here with'.[79]

---

[72] Oyedepo, *Signs and Wonders*, 153.
[73] David O. Oyedepo, *Riding on Prophetic Wings*, Lagos: Dominion, 2000, 120.
[74] Oyedepo, *Signs and Wonders*, 344.
[75] Ibid., 467.
[76] Ibid., 297.
[77] Ibid., 589, similarly 591.
[78] Ibid., 472.
[79] Ibid., 301.

## Oyedepo's rituals

Oyedepo began as a standard Word of Faith preacher and transformed himself into a prophet. He claims genuine originality, and to have introduced important innovations into Christianity:

The Holy Ghost has sent me to open a new chapter to this generation. He has sent me with the powerful Word of Faith, and has also delivered into my hands mysterious instruments that have been used over the years to raise the dead, destroy HIV/AIDS, dissolve cancers, establish liberty, provoke success, and command favour, all for the uplift of Zion! We are grateful to God for counting us privileged to know these things which hitherto had been hidden, but which are now revealed to us by His Spirit. God has delivered into our hands divine instruments for victory. Through their use, the lame have walked, withered limbs have been cured, the mad have been restored back to sanity, and the barren have become joyful mothers of children. It's been signs and wonders galore! (These) biblical instruments of power ... were delivered (to me) purely by revelation.[80]

His main instrument of victory is the oil of anointing which will 'give a man or any object on which it is poured, immunity against any form of evil... it is able to raise up any dying business, resurrect any collapsing career, and reverse any ancestral family curse. It makes a way for the plan of God for your life to find fulfilment.'[81] It is an 'all-purpose drug for any ailment of life',[82] bringing 'honour and respect'.[83] Oil 'destroys all the discomforts of life'.[84] He is said to have prophesied that on drinking 'a shot of the anointing oil... every affliction in (listeners') bodies would vanish'.[85] Oyedepo recounts that a fibroid in a woman's womb was transformed into a baby by anointing, and when born this baby had an oil mark on its head.[86] A woman's husband had been straying, but she anointed the sinful bed, with the result that the sinning couple quarrelled, and the husband got rid of the new woman.[87] A man whose business was ailing anointed his signs, 'and people started flooding into his office'.[88] 'A brother received a letter

---

[80] Ibid., 58.
[81] Ibid., 101f.
[82] Ibid., 113.
[83] Ibid., 104.
[84] Ibid., 108.
[85] Ibid., 304.
[86] Oyedepo, *Riding on Prophetic Wings*, 75.
[87] Oyedepo, *Winning Invisible Battles*, 190.
[88] Ibid.

terminating his appointment. He anointed the letter and went back to the office. The same people started apologizing to him for sending him such a letter, and gave him a promotion instead!'[89] A chemical engineer tried to get a paper-manufacturing company to accept a new glue he had devised, but without success; he was moved to stir 'some anointing oil into the glue', and won the order.[90]

Another special instrument is footwashing:

> Jesus, by this mystery, was restoring to the redeemed the dominion that was lost in the first Adam. Jesus washed His disciples' feet so that they too could enter the realm where the father had put him. Something was being transferred to Jesus' disciples as he washed their feet. Evidently dominion was passed unto them through this mystery of divine transference, such that when Jesus left, His disciples represented Him spirit, soul and body. Everything bowed to them. As your feet are dipped into the water you are empowered to walk in the realm of dominion.[91]

Footwashing 'provides access into our enviable inheritance. And what is this inheritance all about? Mysterious dominion for mysterious triumphs.'[92] Among its benefits, it 'empowers for access into realms of supernatural fortunes'.[93] I have attended Winners' footwashings where the stress has been explicitly placed on Joshua 14, 9: 'Whatsoever your feet tread upon shall be given unto you for a possession'. This makes the ritual, performed by the man of God, one more assurance of owning property.

Another instrument is the blood of Jesus. Merely by proclamation, one can turn almost anything—one's bathwater,[94] or breast milk[95]—into the blood of Jesus with the promised miraculous effects. 'Through his blood, we are presented holy, unblamable, and unreprovable in His sight. And by that placement, all things come under our authority. All things that are under His authority automatically come under us.'[96] 'Man was made to have dominion over every other creation of God. He was also designed for blessings. This is the original inheritance of

---

[89] Ibid.
[90] Oyedepo, *Anointing for Breakthrough*, 250.
[91] Oyedepo, *Signs and Wonders*, 147; Oyedepo, *Walking in Dominion*, 85.
[92] Oyedepo, *Signs and Wonders*, 149.
[93] Ibid.
[94] Ibid., 266.
[95] Ibid., 273.
[96] Ibid., 125.

man that was lost to sin, but which the blood of Jesus has re-purchased for us.'[97] 'Power is available to you by the blood, so you do not have to be a weakling anymore... Pharaoh surrendered power after the Passover blood came on the scene. Then God gave Israel favour, and they spoiled the Egyptians. The Israelites were decked with riches at the expense of the Egyptians... By the blood, the wisdom of God is available for us in every conflict of life... The blood is able to give you instant, on-the-spot deliverance from any form of sickness and disease... The blood of Jesus has justified you, so you can live a glorious life... You have been restored back to blessing, which makes rich with no sorrow added to it... We have access to greatness through the blood of Jesus.'[98] 'The blood of Jesus is the seal of our victory in every conflict in life.'[99]

Another instrument is the anointing diffused through his innovation of 'the mantle'. He cites Elijah (2 Kings 2), Aaron (Ps 133, 1f), the woman with issue of blood (Mt 9, 20ff) and Paul (Acts 19, 11f) to show that 'any material that has come in contact with the anointed of God carries with it the unction' for dominion.[100] God has not changed in his way of working: 'He is working though men sent for the deliverance of mankind... these men carry transferable unction... God gave me this mantle ministry for the liberation of mankind... It is a ministry of transmission of unction... It is a mantle for exploits. It is the end-time prophetic mystery in the hand of the carrier, for amazing results, signs and wonders. It is a carrier of divine energy and heavenly virtue.'[101] So a handkerchief, say, touched by Oyedepo can effect wonders. One of his Bible students was taken to a dead man: 'He struck the dead with his mantle seven times, saying, "The God of Bishop David Oyedepo shall bring you back to life". And the dead man jerked back to life.'[102] A woman became insane; Oyedepo couldn't visit her personally, but gave his handkerchief to her husband telling him to wipe her face with it. On seeing the husband, the mad woman 'ran to grab the handkerchief, but he wiped her face with it, and the madness vanished

[97] Ibid., 128.
[98] Ibid., 131f.
[99] Ibid., 141.
[100] Ibid., 155.
[101] Ibid., 158f.
[102] Oyedepo, *Walking in Dominion*, 18.

instantly.'[103] A barren woman managed to wipe the bishop's face with her handkerchief: 'I then went to a corridor and used the mantle to rub my body all over,' and was soon pregnant.[104] The mantle even helps with exams. A woman recounts that her three children were 'dullards' at school. The bishop had an impartation service, instructing 'that every man should come with his or her mantle, that would later be placed on our children's head for excellence'. The next year, 'all three of them came first in their various classes.'[105]

Although he cannot claim the eucharist as new or special to him, he can reinterpret it in his own special way. In Oyedepo's understanding, the eucharist 'is designed for strength, health and longevity... It swallows up everything that is tying down your system or ravaging your body.'[106] 'After an encounter with the blood of Jesus in the miracle meal, none of the diseases ravaging the world will ever be able to follow you... It is the seal of our covenant exemption from all satanic assaults.'[107] 'Every zero sperm count, dead womb, dead ovaries, whatever is called dead will be quickened back to life by the power in the blood contained in this miracle meal.'[108] 'The miracle meal is one of the Great Physician's covenant provisions for ensuring that you be in health and prosper in your spirit, soul and body.'[109] 'When you partake of the communion... expect every benefit of redemption to be brought your way.'[110] This is a reworking of a central institution of Christianity to fit his message of abundance, success, prosperity.

[103] Oyedepo, *Winning Invisible Battles*, 215.
[104] Ibid., 233.
[105] Ibid., 230.
[106] Ibid., 63f.
[107] Ibid., 71.
[108] Ibid., 73.
[109] Ibid., 80.
[110] Ibid., 92. See also David O. Oyedepo, *The Miracle Meal*, Lagos: Dominion, 2002, 79. In this book specifically on the eucharist, Oyedepo insists that the eucharist is 'designed to actualise the flow of eternal life in your system. It is designed to renew the flow of that life that is immune to all forms of sickness and disease' (ibid., 16). In reference to the blood smeared on doorposts before the Exodus (Ex 12, 7): 'Whenever the angel of death saw the blood he passed over. In that situation, the blood of the lamb was for the exemption of God's people from the evil befalling others around them' (ibid., 29). Another OT text reinforces this: 'by the blood of thy covenant... I declare that I will render double unto thee' (Zech 9, 9–12) (ibid., 30f). When Jesus died on the cross, 'the earth

## Conclusion

Winners' is more self-confident than MFM, and with a more public profile. In Nigeria, Oyedepo is a national figure, and internet clips show Presidents Obasanjo and Jonathan attending his church. This does not mean that Oyedepo attracts only the middle classes or the well off. Winners' policy is to have only one church in any one city or town, to which the church provides free or subsidized buses. Provision of transport means that Winners' clientele is far more heterogeneous than that of most churches; besides the many SUVs and Mercedes in the car park, there is a large percentage of the congregation bussed in from slums. Oyedepo's message has a wide appeal.

Oyedepo does talk of righteousness, repentance and morality, but for the most part this dimension is simply presumed; it certainly takes up a surprisingly small part of proceedings, in comparison with the incessant insistence on giving to the church and on the Bishop's anointing. Oyedepo is far less given to denouncing the world; worldly success is what he preaches and embodies, and the world is the proper stage for the Christian's glorious victory.

We noted the denunciation of so much that is African in Olukoya's MFM. Oyedepo can occasionally criticize Africa. He can mention that Africans are always looking for someone else to blame; also, that the 'undoing of the black race' is the attitude of seeking what one can get out of something, rather than what one can put in.[111] He can refer to idleness as 'the bane of the African man',[112] and can also refer to the black man's 'poverty mentality' which blocks prosperity, and his tendency to blame one's poverty on blackness rather than focus on the covenant promises.[113] However, as one would expect in a ministry

---

quaked, the rocks rent, graves were opened and many dead—the saints which slept—arose (Mt 27, 50–52). Similarly, as that blood gets into your body, everything holding you down will quake, everything trying to pull you to the grave will be destroyed, anything dead in your system will be fully restored to life by the power of the blood' (ibid., 32). 'The communion is not some form of religious snack, it is what grafts you to the eternal dimension of life where the challenges of this world have no more power over you, where the enemy can reach you no more', so the believer should not die of sickness or disease (ibid., 50). A believer can use any materials for a private eucharist, and on any occasion, even at home.

[111] David O. Oyedepo, *Success Strategies*, Lagos: Dominion, 2003, 81 and 102.
[112] Oyedepo, *Signs and Wonders*, 433f.
[113] Oyedepo, *Winning the War*, 16 and 153.

stressing its internationalism, denigrating Africa is hardly characteristic of Oyedepo's Winners' Chapel.

Oyedepo mentions Satan a good deal, and to that extent is much more recognizably 'Christian' than Olukoya's stress on marine spirits, spirit spouses and witches. Oyedepo does mention 'witches and wizards', sometimes adding curses and 'Ogboni cults' (a Yoruba secret society associated with mystical powers), but it is usually in passing, and not elaborated at any length.[114] However, even if he seldom expands on Satan's 'agents and agencies', these, as we shall see in the next chapter, are often understood in an enchanted sense.

Oyedepo began as a faith preacher, has come increasingly to stress the prophetic dimension, and is concerned primarily with prosperity—enormous prosperity, which he in person flamboyantly embodies. In theory, such covenant success is available to anyone who knows the Word, but in practice Oyedepo has become essential in prospering his followers. His preaching, his anointing, his rituals—his mere appearance, presence or breath—can effect any desired transformation. It is no surprise that Oyedepo feels he must provide a disclaimer that he is a mere mortal, and that the power is God's, not his.[115] Nevertheless, only a few testimonies of his followers are to God himself. Testimonies are overwhelmingly to Oyedepo's power, often to the 'God of David Oyedepo',[116] or to what 'God does through his servant, Bishop David Oyedepo'.[117] 'Nothing is impossible for the God of Bishop David Oyedepo.'[118]

---

[114] In David O. Oyedepo, *The Blood Triumph*, Lagos: Dominion, 1995, 21, he remarks, 'There are accidents happening now in more than 1,000 places on earth, personally caused by Satan', but in my experience that is quite uncharacteristic. His normal position is essentially that Satan has been routed. A Christian has no need to give Satan a thought, as Oyedepo insists he never does; see David O. Oyedepo, *Satan get Lost: Outstanding Breakthroughs in Spite of the Devil*, Lagos: Dominion, 1995.

[115] Oyedepo, *Signs and Wonders*, 647f.

[116] Ibid., 269, 596.

[117] Ibid., 383.

[118] Ibid., 518. To be quite clear, one can find an occasional element of do-it-yourself transformation, of effecting prophecies oneself without the agency of the Bishop. In theory, anyone can use the oil, invoke the blood of Jesus (ibid., 70, 83), consecrate the eucharist at home (ibid., 90f), with all their miraculous consequences. A few testimonies reveal this. 'The Bishop had instructed that those of us going for interviews should take off our shoes and claim our victory. In obedience to his command, when I got to the NNPC [Nigerian National

Petroleum Corporation], I took off my shoes and prophesied. To God be the glory, I got the job.' (ibid., 454). One woman, desiring marriage, read a church bulletin that 'talked about the creative wisdom of God', was led to collect some sand, and said: '"God, you who made Adam and Eve from sand are going to create my husband today". I started prophesying to that sand.' The very next day she met her future husband (ibid., 475f). However, at Winners' testimonies are overwhelmingly to Oyedepo and his power.

4

# PENTECOSTALISM AND MODERNITY

Obviously, African Pentecostalism is a diverse phenomenon. Of the two examples we have studied, both are concerned with a glorious this-worldly destiny, but Olukoya's Pentecostalism is primarily concerned with combating the evil forces threatening that destiny; Odeyepo's almost exclusively with effecting that destiny through tithes and offerings, and through his own anointing.

## The six registers of victorious living

It is the vision of *this-worldly victory* that is common to all African Pentecostalism. This emphasis is seen in the names of the churches ('Victory Bible Church', 'Jesus Breakthrough Assembly', 'Triumphant Christian Centre'). The titles and themes of conventions, crusades and conferences repeat this emphasis ('Living a Life of Abundance', 'Taking your Territories', 'Stepping into Greatness'). In talking to these Christians, attending their services, studying their sermons, testimonies, and literature, the winning motif is characteristic.

I have distinguished six different registers on which this success refrain is played. The six ways in which Christianity is linked to success and wealth are not necessarily incompatible. Many churches combine many, even all of them. Other churches, as we have just seen, are more associated with one or two ways, less with others. Let me outline these six ways.

First, motivation. In these churches the emphasis is to get on, to succeed, to prosper, to be important, to take control. Moreover, they say, these things are your right and inheritance as a Christian, which you should expect and can demand. Sometimes a racial element enters into this: you can succeed like Whites, and being African does not mean subservience and poverty.

Second, entrepreneurship. I first encountered it at Winners', but it now seems widespread, that at least once every service you will be invited to turn to your neighbour and ask: 'Have you started your own business yet?' Business skills are explicitly lauded, and in bigger churches businessmen's fellowships are formed, and workshops for businessmen provided, even business fairs. Established businessmen in the congregation can be asked to assist those starting out.

Third, practical skills for personal living and business success— like hard work, organizing time, avoiding drink, budgeting, saving, investing.

Fourth, the faith gospel, or the belief that faith is what you need to share in the victory of Christ over sin, sickness and poverty. In faith you simply claim what is already yours. This swiftly became linked to the idea of 'seed-faith', that by planting seed you determine your harvest. I have shown how Oyedepo exemplifies this aspect.

Fifth, the 'anointing' of the pastor. Increasingly, success and prosperity are thought to come through the powers of the 'man of God'. Pastors now frequently make themselves indispensible. A church can come to centre on its leader's 'prophetic declarations' or 'prophetic word'. Testimonies, too, increasingly attribute blessings not so much to God as to the 'Man of God', or to God through the anointing of his servant. Oyedepo is a perfect illustration of this element, too.

Sixth, defeating the spirits blocking one's advance, which I have illustrated through Olukoya's MFM.

*Their common features*

At Olukoya's MFM, the enchanted imagination is inescapable. It is nowhere near as prominent in Oyedepo, but the point to note is that it is not absent. Consider these testimonies from Winners'.

One couple who had flourished individually before their marriage, afterwards immediately experienced problems. The husband explains: 'I killed a snake in the room where we kept our wedding gifts. And that was how our problems started.' He continues: Oyedepo had 'placed a curse on anyone who steals other people's things from the Shiloh [annual pilgrimage] ground, declaring that they would carry whatever curse the owner of the stolen property came to Shiloh with.' This couple came to Shiloh where they had their cellphone stolen. The wife 'then began to dance, rejoicing that our problems were all over, as they had been transferred to the thief'—and indeed her good fortune returned immediately. The husband, however, continued to suffer all manner of ills. They returned to the Shiloh gathering the following year, where before going to bed, the husband

prayed, 'God make me to fly, make me to work again'. And lo, I woke up the following morning to find a dead bird under my pillow. We shared the testimony in church that day, after which the Bishop called us back and decreed, saying, 'Exactly a month from now, whoever is responsible for this will go down [die]'... And just as he had said, exactly a month later we got the news that the person behind all our problems was dead! And two weeks after his death, I got a job, and was started off with a very good package. Also I was called to come for my visa to Europe... God used this church and His Word to restore us.[1]

A woman attended the 1998 Winners' Covenant Family Day 'in which family and generational curses were broken', after which 'the spirit husband that had been having affairs with me in the dream (left me). All the covenants and curses tormenting my life are now broken, and the snake that used to move about in my stomach has miraculously left me.'[2]

A woman died in the labour room. A Winners' member anointed her back to life. But the baby was stillborn. So the member 'anointed the child and it came back to life. But something more happened. When the child came to life, lo and behold, it had a chimpanzee's face.' She proclaimed that the baby's face be changed, took a photo 'of the child's parents and said: "Lord, every child must have a resemblance of either one of the parents or both of them"'. Within two hours, 'the fresh face of a baby came out.'[3]

A woman, hitherto a tither, decided not to pay. 'Consequently, mysterious rats invaded the bonnet of her car and ate up all the wires. She

---

[1] David O. Oyedepo, *Signs and Wonders Today: a Catalogue of the Amazing Acts of God among Men*, Lagos: Dominion Press, 2006, 318–21.

[2] David O. Oyedepo, *Exploring the Riches of Redemption*, Lagos: Dominion, 2004, 114.

[3] David O. Oyedepo, *Winning Invisible Battles*, Lagos: Dominion, 2006, 231.

49

had the car fixed, but the rats appeared again and ate up all the new wires. This continued, until her eyes were opened. She rushed to the office to pay her tithes and rats mysteriously disappeared!'[4]

Oyedepo casts an 'engine-knocking demon' out of his car, which goes into the car of a neighbour, whose car is out of action for six months.[5] He can turn back a swarm of praying mantises bothering a follower.[6] A broken alarm clock, anointed with oil, begins to work perfectly.[7]

Oyedepo can talk of spells[8] and family curses,[9] and can reverse curses as well as anyone, even to death, as we have just seen. As another example, one woman's 'legs became swollen as though I had elephantiasis... There was no medical solution to it; no name for it. The enemy wanted to paralyse my legs.' The woman came to Oyedepo's footwashing ritual, with immediate cure. 'The daughter of the person that charmed me is now paralysed in one hand; she can't hold anything with it. I thank the God of this commission [a term frequently used by members to refer to Winners'] who has been especially faithful to me.'[10] Oyedepo was in danger of becoming world famous in April 2012 for a lawsuit and demand for the equivalent of US$1.3 million in damages for striking during a service a young woman whom he called a witch, although she insisted she was not.[11] In Winners' Sunday services, announcements will be made of deliverance services during the week. Enchanted considerations are never far below the surface, though they are peripheral in comparison with Oyedepo's emphasis on tithes and offerings and his special anointing.

I am not claiming that every single Pentecostal church in Africa foregrounds the enchanted world, and certainly not to the extent of Olukoya. I have written extensively about one Pentecostal church, Mensa Otabil's International Central Gospel Church in Accra, which even denounces this mindset as dysfunctional and to be transcended.

---

[4] David O. Oyedepo, *Winning the War against Poverty*, Lagos: Dominion, 2006, 267.

[5] David O. Oyedepo, *Releasing the Supernatural: an Adventure into the Spirit World*, Lagos: Dominion, 1993, 26.

[6] Ibid., 53.

[7] David O. Oyedepo, *Anointing for Breakthrough*, Lagos: Dominion, 1992, 252.

[8] Ibid., 460.

[9] Ibid., 102, 342, 559.

[10] Ibid., 253.

[11] In July 2012 the Ogun State High Court dismissed the case as 'lacking merit'.

Otabil preaches that there is no future for Africa unless people stop thinking in this enchanted way.[12] But Otabil, in my experience, is virtually unique, and besides, even Otabil's church, at least when I was last in Ghana, conducted exorcism sessions on Saturday mornings; they were not called that (they were called 'problem solving'), and Otabil himself never attended (he left it to junior pastors), but this seems to be grudging acknowledgement that an African Pentecostal church *has* to cater for this mindset. For those whose primary, immediate and natural mode of experiencing reality is in terms of pervasive spiritual forces, Pentecostal churches are a natural home. I would argue that the enchanted imagination that Olukoya focuses on almost exclusively, and to an almost unsurpassable degree, is present in all African Pentecostalism, on a spectrum from aggressively unavoidable to gently unobtrusive.

When we turn from the enchanted imagination exemplified by Olukoya to the divine enrichment of Oyedepo, we discover considerable common ground as well. Not all are as aggressive as Oyedepo, but the faith gospel is pervasive in African Pentecostalism, at least its 'seed faith' or 'plant-so-you-may-reap' idea. This 'seed-faith' theology is not an incidental or optional extra to Africa's Pentecostalism, but has been indispensable, for this has been the motor that has powered this entire explosion. Of course, it is great to have overseas sponsors, but for most churches this remains a dream. Yet all these buildings, programmes, vehicles, musical instruments and sound systems have had to be paid for, in economically straitened circumstances, along with an entire new class of religious professionals. For this, seed-faith theology has proved extremely functional. Oyedepo perfectly exemplifies this, but the faith gospel is not foreign to Olukoya either. For Olukoya, too, a Christian should be rich; and God has even revealed to Olukoya that MFM Christians 'will be the richest and most prosperous of all believers all over the world'.[13] Olukoya includes the motivation and ambition of the faith preachers: 'Hate your present position with a perfect hatred'.[14] He can use the faith gospel motifs of speaking good things into existence, and refusing to harbour negative thoughts. In accor-

---

[12] Paul Gifford, *Ghana's New Christianity: Pentecostalism in a Globalising African Economy*, London: Hurst, 2004 113–39.

[13] D.K. Olukoya, *The Mystery of First Fruit Offering*, Lagos: Battle Cry, 2007, 6, 50.

[14] D.K. Olukoya, *Deliverance from Limiting Powers*, Lagos: Battle Cry, 2005, 26.

dance with his atomistic use of the Bible mentioned above, he notes that whereas faith is mentioned in the Bible fewer than 500 times, giving is mentioned over 2,000 times; and 'out of the 38 parables of Jesus, 16 dealt with giving'.[15] Olukoya teaches the need to tithe, and gives this his particular twist—failure to do so entraps one in satanic financial chains. But tithes and offerings are not as prominent for Olukoya as for most prosperity churches, certainly in comparison with fully-fledged prosperity churches of the likes of Oyedepo. Olukoya frequently denounces other churches, prosperity churches above all (in general, not by name). He goes out of his way to separate himself from self-aggrandizing pastors by, for example, insisting he will not accept gifts from dubious Christians. However, combining the prosperity motifs with hard-core enchantment is not without difficulties, because the two operate on different planes. For example, the faith movement's idea that giving to God automatically brings wealth Olukoya must neutralize by observing that if you have been tithing to an unworthy pastor, it is just pouring money down the drain.

We can obtain a clear illustration of their similarities and differences from the example of curses. In chapter two, we noted that curses are an integral part of Olukoya's enchanted universe. Oyedepo too has specifically addressed the topic, and his treatment reveals that he does believe in curses in Olukoya's sense. Thus a souvenir bought on a trip to Israel turned out to be an idol that had to be burnt before the demonic hold was broken.[16] So, too, American Indians cursed the American government centuries ago for their inhuman mistreatment; this (he argued) caused American presidents to be assassinated every twenty years until the curse was identified and broken—'and that's how President Reagan narrowly escaped being assassinated'.[17] But Oyedepo has adapted the notion of curses to his preoccupations, namely to tithes, offerings, and his own special anointing. Unlike Olukoya who is concerned with the curses inflicted on us by others, Oyedepo is concerned with curses brought on the believer through disobedience. Failing to pay the tithe brings down a curse (Mal 3, 9). 'And because it is a curse of the Lord, no prophet can break it.'[18]

---

[15] Olukoya, *The Mystery of First Fruit Offering*, 58.

[16] David O. Oyedepo, *Breaking the Curses of Life*, Lagos: Dominion, 1997, 15.

[17] Ibid., 17.

[18] Ibid., 41. It may even be fatal to pray over someone who doesn't pay his tithe: 'If

Similarly, to resist a spiritual father will bring a curse: 'Never sit down or gather against someone God has anointed. Never!'[19] Many have died like that. 'You don't look at your spiritual father and think he's your equal; you may just die in captivity! Don't do it!'[20] 'God sent me; and all that receive me, receive the One who sent me. Then the rewards and blessings that I am sent to convey become available to such.' One woman came to Winners', but was displeased by something anti-Catholic that Oyedepo said: 'So she hissed and went out of the service.' God punished her with a stone in her stomach; 'As a result, sexual intercourse with her husband became an unbearable experience.' It was revealed to her that she had come under a curse, for two years, and had to have it lifted by Oyedepo, to whom she came begging for forgiveness.[21] We are fortunate that 'every curse of the Lord demands nothing but absolute obedience, to be averted'.[22] More specifically: 'You can break them through this covenant of giving'.[23]

In summary, then, in essentials they overlap. The enchanted imagination lies not far below the surface at Oyedepo's Winners' Chapel, though it is nowhere near as obtrusive as in Olukoya's MFM. Likewise, although far less aggressively than Oyedepo, Olukoya does depend on the faith gospel, as does virtually every other Pentecostal pastor in Africa.

### Pentecostalism and modernity

For many observers it is almost axiomatic that African Pentecostalism is a major vehicle of modernity. For Peter Berger, the spread of Pentecostalism is probably the best thing to happen to the developing world. With its stress on motivation, entrepreneurship and discipline, this is the Protestant work ethic reaching the Third World. It will do for the developing world what Calvinism did for Europe in the eighteenth century.

---

you don't stop that prayer on time, God can stop you from breathing!' (ibid., 42).

[19] Ibid., 55.

[20] Ibid., 59.

[21] Ibid., 109f.

[22] Ibid., 124.

[23] David O. Oyedepo, *All You Need to Have All Your Needs Met*, Lagos: Dominion, 2004, 116.

Hence the revealing title Peter Berger gave to an article on Pentecostalism: 'Max Weber is alive and well and living in Guatemala'.[24]

In 2008, South Africa's Centre for Development and Enterprise, much influenced by Berger, produced a report on Pentecostalism entitled *Under the Radar* which makes great claims for the public effects of Pentecostalism. The report is influenced by 'the claims of sociologists of religion that Pentecostalism has a special affinity with market-based development, and a kinship with what historians call the "Protestant ethic"; a cluster of beliefs, attitudes and habits that underpinned the spectacular economic growth of north-west Europe during the industrial revolution.'[25] Pentecostalism is said to comprise features like intense spirituality, centring on rebirth experience and the supernatural (faith healing, speaking in tongues); relatively unhierarchical and decentralized organization, reflecting a high level of local and even individual initiative and strongly entrepreneurial motivations; relative accessibility and informality in terms of ordination and leadership. However, encouraging entrepreneurship is considered the main characteristic, so much so that the South African state is urged to promote Pentecostalism.[26]

David Martin can conclude his study of African Pentecostalism by saying, 'Pentecostalism in Africa is a collective raft pointed with determination towards modernity'.[27] Elsewhere he has spelt it out fully: 'The lineage running from Pietism to Pentecostalism is linked positively to modernity in respect of the domains of gender, secular law, transnationalism, voluntarism, pluralism, the nuclear family, peaceability, personal release and personal work discipline, consumption, modern communication, social and geographical mobility—as well as changes in mediation, authority, and participation.'[28] In other words, in all these

[24] Peter L. Berger, 'Max Weber is Alive and Well, and Living in Guatemala: The Protestant Ethic Today', *The Review of Faith and International Affairs*, 8, 4 (2010), 3–9.

[25] *Under the Radar: Pentecostalism in South Africa and its Potential Social and Economic Role*, Johannesburg: Centre for Development and Enterprise, CDE In Depth no 7, 2008, 9.

[26] Ibid., 34.

[27] David Martin, *Pentecostalism: the World their Parish*, Oxford: Blackwell, 2002, 152.

[28] David Martin, 'Pentecostalism: a Major Narrative of Modernity', in his *On Secularisation: towards a Revised General Theory*, London: Ashgate, 2005, 144.

areas, from gender to law, from work ethic to exercise of authority, Pentecostalism is bringing Africa into the modern world.

I am less positive. I think these positive assessments require that one focuses on the first three of the six registers of victory outlined at the beginning of this chapter. If one considers only motivation, entrepreneurship and personal life skills, the effects of Pentecostalism must of course be positive. But these positive evaluations hardly advert to the fourth, fifth and sixth of the registers I have distinguished, and which I regard as much more widespread and significant. To the extent that African Pentecostalism builds on the faith gospel, a pastor's anointing, and the enchanted religious imagination, the effects seem far less positive.

## Spiritual warfare and modernity

Consider Olukoya's MFM and modernity. First, take the idea of human agency or responsibility. There is a genuine tension in Olukoya's Christianity. On the one hand, no demon can touch you if you are a child of God.[29] However, this sits very ill with his emphasis on blind witches, unsuspected spirit spouses, and ancestral curses as sources of problems. Sometimes the tension arises quite starkly. He writes: 'Without your consent, no enemy can tamper with your destiny', but on the very next page he recounts the story of a man whose parents at his birth used a witchdoctor and his placenta to ensure that he lived in penury.[30] At the age of seventy-two this man was lucky enough to find Olukoya who delivered him from his affliction, but without that good fortune he was apparently helpless. This idea of forces of which we have no knowledge recurs incessantly. How can you know everything your ancestors did, and therefore what ancestral curses you labour under?[31] How can you know all the spiritual forces controlling your

[29] 'The Lord has given us all the weapons he could ever need for the battle of life' (D.K. Olukoya, *Victory over Satanic Dreams*, Lagos: MFM, 1996, 20); 'No problem can stay where Jesus is' (D.K. Olukoya, *When the Enemy Hides*, Lagos: MFM, 2011, 22). Also D.K. Olokoya, *The Terrible Agenda*, Lagos: MFM, 2009, 21 and 64; D.K. Olukoya, *Dining Table of Darkness*, Lagos: Battle Cry, 2005, 49.
[30] D.K. Olokoya, *Destiny Clinic*, Lagos: MFM, 2005, 32.
[31] 'Whatever evil practices they engaged in even hundreds of years ago, you partook with them. Of course the consequence of such events are affecting your destiny to date' (Olukoya, *Destiny Clinic*, 24).

village or region? If you are an orphan ignorant of your origins or parentage, how can you know the forces oppressing you? Perhaps you don't know the meaning of your name. Perhaps you don't know what happened to your placenta, which he claims can be so extensively manipulated to your disadvantage.[32] How can you know the complete history of the clothes, jewellery and shoes you wear? How can you know if your underwear has been stolen and then returned bewitched? How can you know if your mother or children or spouse or colleagues or friends are witches?[33] They may not know themselves. If you are a 'blind witch' yourself, by definition you are unaware of the fact. Who knows what activities enthroning demonic forces took place in your house before you came to live there? How much moral responsibility can one have in such a universe?

In fact, how can one succeed against such odds? There are twenty-six star-arresters (from drinkers of blood, dream manipulators, counterfeit angels, to satanic caterers) at large. There are twenty-four different kinds of Night Raiders (including marine powers, forest demons, ancestral strongmen, counterfeit angels, dream manipulators, night caterers), and 'very few people are victorious over' them.[34] There are twenty places of intensified 'demonic traffic' (ranging from market places to crossroads, beaches to cemeteries, forests to festivals) where it is impossible to remain for any length of time 'without getting demonically infected or polluted'.[35] There are ten different 'local' satanic strategies (covering everything from killer dolls, evil cauldrons, spiritual burials, counterfeit bodies and satanic blood banks).[36] Olukoya lists forty different weapons that satanic spirits wield against us.[37] There are twenty-

---

[32] 'People go around clinics asking for placentas to buy, and once they are given to them, they can permanently destroy the baby's life through that means' (D.K. Olukoya, *Power to Shut Satanic Doors*, Lagos: Battle Cry, 2011, 34).

[33] 'If you have a wicked mother or grandmother who belongs to the spirit world, such a parent may decide to give your hand in marriage and collect your bride price in the spiritual realm. That means that you have been married in the spiritual realm. Unfortunately, most people are not aware of the payment of such a dowry' (D.K. Olukoya (with Shade Olukoya), *Prayer Strategies for Spinsters and Bachelors*, Lagos: MFM, 1999, 60f).

[34] D.K. Olukoya, *Power against Dream Criminals*, Lagos: MFM, 2001, 114f.

[35] Olukoya, *When the Enemy Hides*, 43–7.

[36] D.K. Olukoya, *Satanic Technology*, Lagos: MFM, 2001, 158–66.

[37] D.K. Olukoya, *Your Foundation and Your Destiny*, Lagos: Battle Cry, 2001, 255.

one idol chains (from financial chains, to nightmares, stagnation and marital bondage); twenty chains of closed heavens (from divorce to hatred and failure); ten weapons of oppression (from star-hunters to money swallowers, progress arresters and poverty activators); fourteen hidden weapons of Satan (from vagabond anointing to witchcraft handwriting and desert spirits); seven serpents and scorpions (from devourers to fowlers, oppressors and tormentors); thirty powers of the night (from familiar spirits to household pursuers and dream manipulators); twenty-one floating spirits (from the spirit of discouragement to the spirits of torment, of infirmity and spiritual blindness; the presence of a floating spirit is evident if you went to bed with no problem but woke up with heaviness); twenty-one African 'doors' or entry points for satanic possession (from idolatry to chieftaincy titles, incense, pilgrimages and libations). The forces against us are simply innumerable. Despair or at least resignation to fate seems the most appropriate response.

Second, his Christianity militates against any form of community or social capital; it breeds fear and distrust. 'Most of the people who pretend to be your friends are hidden enemies';[38] don't accept gifts from others, because all too often they are entry points for the enemy;[39] for the same reason, avoid food sold along the roadside, especially by women wearing make-up and jewellery. Above all, his Christianity creates division within families. Olukoya insists that most ills come from members of one's own family. His sermons are full of illustrations. A woman saw a frog on the yam she was pounding; when she struck it she became paralyzed in an arm and a leg; on praying a 'return to sender', she was cured but her sister became paralyzed immediately, revealing that the sister was responsible. A father who was determined that none of his sons would surpass him in wealth mystically killed one son's very astute wife who was in the process of bringing this about. A very intelligent man was bound in poverty; praying revealed that his parents had taken him to a witchdoctor at birth, who had prophesied that the son would be so successful he would control white men. Since this would entail his leaving the country, the parents, through the

---

[38] D.K. Olukoya, *The Serpentine Enemies*, Lagos: MFM, 2001, 19.
[39] Because there are mass initiations at schools, children should reject any sweets or biscuits offered on the supposed occasion of a birthday; 'lots of children have been, unconsciously, initiated this way' (Olukoya, *Power to Shut Satanic Doors*, 35).

witchdoctor and a ritual with his placenta, ensured the man would never achieve his destiny.[40] A man owning several businesses, including a bank and buses, lost everything; Olukoya established that it was a wicked maid who had kept the bank and the buses 'under water' on the instructions of the man's mother. A woman showed Olukoya two doctor's reports: one showed she was five months pregnant, the other revealed no trace of a baby. Olukoya established that her family had promised an idol that they would supply a specific number of babies every year, and that that year's quota had not been met. So the family had removed the baby, with plans to remove three more.[41]

A woman due for promotion faced the resentment and manipulation of her colleagues. Sitting in her office on the fifteenth floor, she felt something cold around her legs. She looked down and saw a snake coiled around her. Since an ordinary snake had no place on the fifteenth floor, she realized immediately that this was a satanic agent. She stood firm on God's promises, and called on the Holy Spirit to kill the snake, which quickly died. On going home later, she discovered her husband lifeless on the bed. Only then did she realize that it was her husband who had been her enemy all along.[42] A family of sisters all had broken marriages. Led by God, one embarked on a twenty-one-night vigil. By the fourth day, her grandmother could not come out of her room, which revealed that she was responsible; the granddaughter redoubled her prayers, and by the seventh day the grandmother was dead, leaving behind strands of hair of the granddaughter, who burned them, and within four more days her husband was begging her to come back to him. A young girl with seventeen padlocks revealed that she had through witchcraft used twelve to lock up all the riches her father would ever have. A woman with a good salary who nevertheless remained desperately poor was inspired one night to take up a cutlass 'to cut off every hand of poverty that is against my life'. The next morning she was informed that her grandmother had woken up with bleeding stumps and her hands cut off—'Right from that day, the agenda of wealth that the Lord had for her began to manifest'.[43]

---

[40] Olukoya, *Terrible Agenda*, 27; D.K. Olukoya, *The Star Hunters*, Lagos: MFM, 2002, 5; and Olukoya, *Prayer Strategies*, 34; in this last, placenta becomes umbilical cord.

[41] Olukoya, *Power to Shut Satanic Doors*, 25.

[42] D.K. Olukoya, *Overpowering Witchcraft*, Lagos: Battle Cry, 1999, 139.

[43] D.K. Olokoya, *Raiding the House of the Strongman*, Lagos: MFM, 2011, 9.

Third, and most importantly, consider the scientific rationality that is required by modernity. This aspect is particularly relevant in considering Olukoya's church, for all his publicity stresses the fact that he has a PhD in molecular genetics from Britain's University of Reading. Yet he seems untouched by scientific rationality. He warns against astrology, yet he believes in the power of 'the heavenlies' to influence us. Satanic forces are responsible for 'imbecile and delinquent children'.[44] Deaths in childbirth (all? some?) seem to be the work of spirit husbands.[45] A child born from the sexual act between a physical mother and a spiritual father 'becomes a hermaphrodite'.[46] The findings of his thirty years of research into ancestral curses show, among other things, that those from polygamous homes have wives suffering from 'general backwardness', those whose ancestors were thieves suffer from incurable diseases, those descended from hunters 'end up fishing and catching nothing in life', those descended from adulterers suffer chronic diseases, those whose ancestors participated in tribal dancing 'experience a vagrant or vagabond lifestyle'.[47] In my opinion, Olukoya has not reconciled two forms of rationality, but has rather turned his back on the particular rationality which underpins modern science.

## Covenant wealth and modernity

Undoubtedly, Oyedepo's relentless stress on achievement must encourage ambition. Each year, each month, even every week, a Winners' church is blazoned with new banners, with slogans like 'Fruitfulness all Round', 'I am a Child of Destiny', 'Success is my Birthright', 'All Things are Possible', 'I am Destined for Exploits', or 'More than a Conqueror'. Talking to members after services and functions, one cannot miss the sense of determination and confidence many have derived from the church. Many will freely talk of the 'vision' they have caught

[44] D.K. Olukoya, *The Chain Breaker*, Lagos: Battle Cry, 2010, 91; Olukoya, *Deliverance from Limiting Powers*, 85, 158; Olukoya, *Overpowering Witchcraft*, 156.

[45] Olukoya, *Prayer Strategies*, 52.

[46] Olukoya, *Raiding the House of the Strongman*, 26.

[47] Olukoya, *Your Foundation*, 76–81. He seems a biblical fundamentalist. He takes his cosmology from the Bible, the firmament above man and the sea below. He appears to think creation happened in 4000 BC, since Satan 'has dealt with men and women for more than six thousand years' (Olukoya, *Prayer Strategies*, 40).

which has given purpose to their lives. Even if it is not permanent, the commitment is often palpable. Oyedepo presents himself as the quintessential entrepreneur. He is effectively the CEO of a massive multinational enterprise, and is listed in Forbes as Nigeria's richest pastor, with an estimated wealth of US$150 million.[48] The church is a family concern. His wife runs their Faith Academies across Nigeria, and about ninety Kingdom Heritage nursery and primary schools. Two of his sons run Winners' operations in Britain and South Africa.

Yet wealth and success through the logic of seed-faith could not be further from Weber's spirit of capitalism. Oyedepo stresses the need to work, but victory and success in business, in getting jobs, in health and in life, do not depend on work. 'Remember (prosperity) is a supernatural act of God. It is not something to labour for.'[49] Again: 'You never get rich through sweat, at least not in the kingdom… We are commanded not to be idle, but your strength is inadequate to guarantee you riches; so don't sweat over it, the sinners are the ones sweating over it.'[50] 'If we join the world in the struggle for survival, we will fail the way they fail. The knowledge and the practice of the truth make you a sweatless winner… Not all winners sweat to win. Sweating is a curse. It symbolizes struggle… It is the blessing of God that make rich without adding any sorrow. They are released through obedience. Your expertise will not make rich.'[51] He cites the Bible in support: 'I send you to reap where you bestowed no labour; other men laboured and ye entered into their labours.'[52]

His 'sorrow-free kingdom prosperity' comes primarily from giving money to him—in Oyedepo's words, from being a 'covenant practitioner',[53] for 'prosperity is a covenant'.[54] Oyedepo is quite clear: 'Riches

---

[48] http://www.forbes.com/sites/mfonobongnsehe/2011/06/07/the-five-richest-pastors-in-nigeria, accessed 17 May 2012.

[49] David O. Oyedepo, *Covenant Wealth*, Lagos: Dominion, 1992, 78.

[50] Ibid., 81.

[51] David O. Oyedepo, *Breaking Financial Hardship*, Lagos: Dominion, 1995, 81f. 'Everything depends on the Lord's mercy which is only enjoyed by them who are at rest in the Lord… Rest implies that you have ceased from doing it yourself, you have ceased from your own efforts' (Oyedepo, *Releasing the Supernatural*, 127f).

[52] See his 'Double Portion Flight 2013' (his home page accessed 27 June 2013).

[53] Oyedepo, *Signs and Wonders*, 439 & 479.

[54] Ibid., 565.

is God's will for you... the covenant is your access to it... What is the guiding law of the covenant, and how do we access it? ... There is a law that connects you to the source of covenant wealth... It is the law of seedtime and harvest.'[55] Oyedepo has told of the moment when this was revealed to him: 'For the first time in my life, I knew that God deals with people on covenant terms. From that time the yoke of poverty was broken in my life and I knew I can never be poor. I am not in any trade, neither have I ever invested any dime into any business, yet I will never beg till my time on earth is over. Why? Because I favour His Kingdom.'[56] He trumpets that the origins of his wealth are not in any capitalist dynamic but in a biblical one. 'Having laboured (at the Word), I have "ceased from my own works", as God ceased from His. Abundance now attends to me naturally.'[57] It is far from obvious how a 'Christianity of covenant favour' will usher in a new economic dispensation.

To repeat, Oyedepo obviously believes in work. Introducing a number of testimonies in a chapter in his *Signs and Wonders* entitled 'Miracle Jobs', he says as much: 'There is no substitute for hard work'.[58] 'Hard work is the key to distinction. Without hard work, your destiny will decay. So, go and work!'[59] The Bishop even holds himself up as a model, working eighteen hours a day. Yet the striking thing in his publications and in services is just how little or seldom work features. The very first testimony in this 'Miracle Jobs' section is not about work at all; it is from a man who increases his tithes, and 'to cut the story short, I am now a General Manager of a company, with over 200 staff under me... This was a job I didn't apply for!'[60] A few pages later, we have the same logic. One 'believed God for a mega bank job', and submitted his CV to a bank. The Bishop called for another sacrificial offering for Covenant University:

I wanted to pledge 40,000 naira but ... I did not have that amount, but I had a CD three-changer in my room, which I laid on the altar as my Isaac. After my morning devotion, I was thanking God for all this grace in my life and my

---

[55] Ibid., 166f.
[56] David O. Oyedepo, *Force of Freedom*, Lagos: Dominion, 1996 83.
[57] David. O. Oyedepo, *Commanding the Supernatural*, Lagos: Dominion, 2006, 116.
[58] Oyedepo, *Signs and Wonders*, 433.
[59] Ibid., 436.
[60] Ibid., 440.

career throughout 2004. At about 9.30 am a call came in from the bank, saying I should come for my appointment letter! This is my turning-point proof. I don't know anybody there; and I'm starting with a supervisor post, without any experience in a banking set-up. I don't merit it, but God made it possible.[61]

This is the logic of the overwhelming majority of testimonies at Winners'. The following are representative. 'I joined this commission in 1996, and in that same year the Bishop called for a sacrifice offering for 20-years covenant rest... I brought my colour TV, video and sound system. Those were the only things I had then... Two weeks after I gave the sacrifice, the Lord gave me another shop.'[62] Another: 'I paid my tithe, redeemed my pledge, and paid my foreign missions and Canaan Land subscriptions, and the heavens opened again.'[63] Another records that the Bishop 'told us to give the most precious thing we had.' He and his wife took their 21-inch colour TV to the front during the service. 'Between January and now, I've not only replaced that TV set with another beautiful one, I've paid a six-figure amount as tithe! I used to pay a four-figure amount last year... but this year I increased it to a five-figure amount, and have paid till April. I've also acquired a vehicle worth half a million naira.'[64] Another: 'In July... the Bishop taught on sacrificial giving... I sowed all my dollars and naira into the building projects. It may not be very much but I gave all! I even had to borrow some money to feed my family that month. Thereafter it started raining, and harvest time began! Within two and a half months, I made about one million naira net!'[65] Another reports that at Shiloh 2004, 'there was a call for sacrificial offering, and we were enjoined to give our best. I had just finished a small building then that I wanted to put tenants in. But right in the church my wife and I gave it to God. I want to appreciate God that this year 2005, we have two houses!'[66]

Another had read Oyedepo's 1995 book *Breaking Financial Hardship* (which stresses seed-faith). As a result, '(I gave) all that I earned that month to God despite all the enormous bills I had to pay. Immediately after I dropped that money I got an invitation to be inter-

[61] Ibid., 445.
[62] Ibid., 173.
[63] Ibid., 191.
[64] Ibid., 187.
[65] Ibid., 200.
[66] Ibid., 208.

viewed for a Chief Executive job.'[67] Another reports that 'the first day I came to church, the Bishop preached on sacrificial giving. After the service I asked my wife the meaning of sacrificial offering, and what we could give... My wife then advised that we give our television and video set... and I willingly agreed... and dropped them in church as our sacrificial offering. And from then, my situation turned around!'[68] Similarly, 'When the Bishop made a call for the aircraft seed [to buy the bishop's first private jet], I looked around for what to give as a sacrificial offering, as almost everything in the house had packed up; the radio and television had to be knocked on the head before they started working. I decided to give the video player that was at least in a fair condition. It was after that offering that things started to change...'[69]

Another reports that after calling for a sacrifice for Winners' Covenant University, 'the Bishop said, "if you want to see God in an unusual way, then sow an unusual seed". Therefore I decided to sow my annual housing allowance for the year 2004 instead. That same year, God brought me from obscurity into limelight.'[70] Another joined the church in 1996. Soon, he reports, 'I had heard teachings on giving, so I decided not to sell the brand new photocopy machine but to give it to the Lord. The machine was worth 200,000 naira. I brought it to the church as a seed, and from then on, there was a turn-around! First I got a four million naira contract in June 1998. Then in November of the same year, I got another contract worth 18 million naira.'[71]

If it is striking just how little or seldom work features, it is just as striking how often the 'sweatless success' refrain makes it perfectly clear that success is not a product of human effort. Success or victory arises from a totally different dynamic. As we have seen, most victory stems from giving, but testimonies also attest how important Oyedepo's special rituals are. Victory comes from the use of oil, blood, or impartation (the ritual to access a share of the Bishop's own anointing). Consider the case of oil. The Bishop insists, 'When the oil touches just the mirror of your car, it becomes immune to accidents and scratches. When you anoint the gates of your house, no devil, burglar or armed

[67] Ibid., 212.
[68] Ibid., 326.
[69] Ibid., 329.
[70] Ibid., 347.
[71] Ibid., 350.

robber will dare come near it.'[72] Testimonies make the same point. Thus, one person woke one day to find his video player gone. 'He anointed the space where the video player used to be with the anointing oil, and called back his video player. It was restored, along with the thief, in a matter of weeks.'[73] Another anointed his TV set that had long broken down: 'He turned it on, and the television showed clear pictures and produced a clear sound!'[74] Another applied anointing oil to her farm instead of fertilizer. 'To the glory of God, that same year, she harvested the biggest tubers of yam ever, bigger than those of her colleagues.'[75] Another, realizing that though God was blessing him, he was still borrowing, 'got angry, grabbed my bottle of anointing oil, poured out a handful and made some dangerous scriptural pronouncements [that is, dangerous to enemy forces]. I then splashed the anointing oil where we normally kept our money in anger, casting out whatever the devil had placed there. From that day on, we began enjoying a ceaseless flow of abundance! We have paid up all our debts, bought some new household items, and are living in supernatural abundance.'[76]

It is worth noting, since it constitutes something of a subtheme, how often success, after giving, results from miraculous provision on the part of others whom God brings to one's aid—sometimes this is linked to God's bringing the gift-bearing Magi to the infant Jesus (Matt 2, 1–12). One testifies: 'I took the anointing oil one fine morning and anointed my pocket, in obedience to the counsel of God's servant, Bishop Oyedepo. At the close of work that day, someone called me and gave me a fat sum of money. Again, on the Saturday of that week, we went somewhere, and as we were leaving someone handed me a fat envelope, loaded with a fat sum of money.'[77] Another, after the Bishop's teaching on 'covenant responsibility to parents', made up with

[72] Ibid., 112.
[73] Ibid., 106.
[74] Ibid., 107.
[75] Ibid., 108.
[76] Ibid., 331. Sometimes victory comes from the power of proclamation, a key element of the faith gospel. One testifies that the Bishop had preached on significance of names for Christians. He changed the name of his business to 'Higher Altitudes Ventures Enterprises. Today, barely a month after, I have more properties than I can ever sell, and many beautiful offers are still pouring in!' (ibid., 324).
[77] Ibid., 105.

his father. '(The father) immediately stood up, went to his room and brought out packets of 50 naira notes, and gave them to me. He prayed for me to go and start my business (which I had been trying to start for the past five years). When I counted the money, it was 20,000 naira. I was dazed, because my father had never given me that kind of amount of money before. He always said he didn't have money. The covenant really works!'[78]

Another's business was suffering from 'devourers' (Mal 3, 11). But after a teaching at a Winners' Business Fellowship, 'I learnt that tithes and offerings should not be mixed up or interchanged with one another. So I went back to God, asking for money, and He opened the way for me again. Three weeks ago, I was led to sow a seed... and a week later, a brother gave me a car!'[79] Another 'victim of inconsistency in business' received a 'powerful miracle through the blood of sprinkling' at a Breakthrough Seminar. 'Today I have a reputable business, and a God-blessed family with no want at all, for the scripture says that those who seek the Lord shall lack nothing (Ps 34, 9–10). In July 1996, God blessed me with an eight-figure favour from a relation, just by the sprinkling of the blood of Jesus.'[80] Another, a former Muslim, gave a sacrificial offering, and 'from then, my situation turned around! ... God has also miraculously completed a building project I had abandoned for six years. People just started blessing me with building materials, and before I knew what was happening, the house was completed... God also used a friend of mine to give me a car free of charge... a Volvo 740.'[81] Another testifies that the Bishop had invited the congregation to ask God for whatever virtue they prized in Oyedepo's life. 'I had always heard the Bishop say, "I can never be poor". So I asked God to remove the spirit of poverty and failure from my life. I knew I was free as soon as the Bishop laid his hands on me! The following day, my younger sister gave me some money with which to start a little business.'[82]

---

[78] Ibid., 177f.
[79] Ibid., 216.
[80] Ibid., 322.
[81] Ibid., 327.
[82] Ibid., 330. For more examples, see ibid., 176, 199, 203, 204, 250, 277f, 576.

*Conclusion*

Neither Olukoya nor Oyedepo has much interest in the wider world. Olukoya's Christianity concerns the individual, and is geared to bring about the personal victory that should be his or hers. Beyond this, Olukoya has virtually nothing to say. His attitude to the world is typically summed up:

> The kingdom of man is now running to a close. It is the kingdom of human beings. You can see how confused and disorderly it is. The economists are sweating under a system that is no longer obeying their rules. The politicians are confused; they do not know which system will work. Thieves are being released, justice is being murdered; this is the kingdom of man. It is there that one would find human beings fighting each other, causing problems for each other and challenging the Almighty. That kingdom is closing. A lot of things will close with the realization that all man is struggling for here is vanity. It is of no value, as far as God is concerned.[83]

For Oyedepo, it is the church that must flourish. Up until Luther, the world was covered in darkness. Luther's Reformation sparked the technological revolution of the West. The birth of Pentecostalism in Los Angeles has given birth to Silicon Valley. The 'end-time church' is coming into its own, 'the season of the dominion of the church', which will bring 'waves of inventions these last days in the body of Christ'.[84] 'God has an agenda to deck the last days' church with honour, riches and glory such as eyes have never seen, nor ears heard... Heaven has budgeted all the finances necessary for the building of the latter day house.'[85] The new wealth of Nigeria's churches is proof of the movement of God.[86] 'The church is taking her rightful position, and Christianity is now very attractive. Everyone identified with it has become enviable personalities.'[87] 'Many strong nations will bow to the divine authority that God will confer on the Church... Soon the church will control the socio-economic life of the entire world.'[88]

[83] D.K. Olukoya, *Contending for the Kingdom*, Lagos: MFM, 2005, 20.

[84] David O. Oyedepo, *Walking in Dominion*, Lagos: Dominion, 2006, 130.

[85] David O. Oyedepo, *Showers of Blessings: Rains of the Spirit*, Lagos: Dominion, 1997, 47.

[86] David O. Oyedepo, *Wining the War against Poverty*, Lagos: Dominion, 2006, 28.

[87] Oyedepo, *Walking in Dominion*, 15.

[88] David O. Oyedepo, *Success Strategies: Putting your Hand on the Scriptural Password to Unending Success*, Lagos: Dominion, 2003, 44.

Oyedepo's explicitly political vision extends no further than the belief that if Nigeria normalizes relations with Israel, still the inheritors of God's promises, 'she will be healed of her economic and political problems'.[89]

The laws of economics, too, simply don't hold for a 'covenant practitioner' with 'Kingdom immunity'. 'The environment is irrelevant... For the upright, no matter how terrible the situation around him may be, no matter how terrible the economic condition of that country, God will single him out for a blessing.'[90] 'Your business is not failing because there is a slump in your nation's economy, but because there's a problem with your covenant walk!'[91] Let there be no misunderstanding; for Oyedepo, that means you have failed to pay your tithe and make your offerings.

Even if neither has much interest in the world beyond the church, their Christianities have inevitably a public effect. I have argued that Olukoya's undermining of social capital, diminishing of personal agency and discounting of scientific rationality do not advance modernity. I think Oyedepo's Christianity is just as dysfunctional. 'Covenant riches' resulting from tithes and offerings cannot be confused with the Protestant ethic and the spirit of capitalism. Just as importantly, the public effects of Oyedepo's increasing emphasis on 'prophetic anointing' are equally dubious. 'Big Man Syndrome' is the curse of Africa. In August 2000, the same month as the President of Nigeria's Senate was impeached for, among other things, bringing the total of his official vehicles to thirty-two, the Winners' newsletter carried an article about Oyedepo's acquisition of a private jet. Oyedepo now has four private jets, in 2011 adding a US$35 million Gulfstream V jet to his other three. One might argue that Oyedepo and his jets, far from illustrating God's faithfulness to his chosen, is merely the Nigerian Big Man syndrome transposed onto a Christian plane.

Oyedepo makes much of the fact that he is not a businessman; 'I have never had any business transaction of any kind in well over two decades... It is not my area. I belong to the altar. I am addicted to the

[89] David O. Oyedepo, *Born to Win*, Lagos: Dominion, 1986, 76, an early book, and although it has been continually reprinted, I haven't heard this motif in recent years.
[90] Oyedepo, *Showers of Blessings*, 57f.
[91] Oyedepo, *Commanding the Supernatural*, 90.

Word.'[92] Again, 'I'm not in any business at all'.[93] However, this seems rather disingenuous, for in a very real sense business is exactly what he is in. He boasts he has never asked for money for himself, but it is not lost on observers that services are one long demand for money, if not for himself personally, for the church of which he is the CEO and whose four private jets are predominantly for his use and status.[94] He claims no pressure is exerted on anyone: 'We didn't go around begging people to give for the building; neither did we put pressure on them. Everyone in our church is very comfortable, because there is no pressure on them to give.'[95] However, insistence that one can become truly rich only by obeying the Word (as interpreted by Oyedepo), which often amounts to donating huge sums to his enterprises, is in many ways the ultimate pressure. Especially when it is accompanied by warnings: 'Don't curse God's anointed. You have to follow them to the end, without any reservations.'[96] And in some trepidation, since God has been known to kill those who dare challenge Oyedepo.[97]

We will return to this question of Pentecostalism and modernity below, but it is now time to develop our comparison with Catholicism.

---

[92] Oyedepo, *Success Strategies*, 114.

[93] Oyedepo, *Walking in Dominion*, 176.

[94] Oyedepo, *Showers of Blessings*, 50. Personally I have encountered the following calls for funds: sacrificial offering, covenant seed, kingdom investment, prophetic offering, violent offering, chair offering, unlimited favour sacrifice, facility upgrade sacrifice, provoking-open-heaven sacrifice, Covenant University sacrifice and what is called AGIP commitment (Africa Gospel Invasion Programme, Winners' thrust into Africa after 1994).

[95] David O. Oyedepo, *Possessing Your Possessions*, Lagos: Dominion, 2006, 78.

[96] Oyedepo, *Anointing for Breakthrough*, 238.

[97] Oyedepo, *All You Need*, 105–7. A group opposed Oyedepo's plan to move the church from its original site in Lagos to its present location at 'Canaan Land' a little outside. Two adults in the ringleader's family died in a short space of time, before God killed the ringleader himself in a car accident.

5

# GLOBAL CATHOLICISM

Pentecostalism is a global form of Christianity. Olukoya's enchanted Christianity is, as I have argued, thoroughly grounded in traditional religion, but it often enough attempts to anchor itself in Western gurus like Derek Prince, Peter Wagner and Rebecca Brown.[1] Although, as outlined, Oyedepo makes claims to substantial originality, he openly acknowledges his debt to the faith gospel of Kenneth Hagin and Kenneth and Gloria Copeland, even referring to Hagin's understanding of Mark 11, 23f which is often said to be the origin of the 'Word of Faith' movement.[2] Oyedepo cheerfully admits: '(My) commission is clearly a Word of Faith ministry'.[3] He acknowledges his debt to Oswald J. Smith, Smith Wigglesworth and T.L. Osborn. He hosts at headquarters preachers like Mike Murdock and Myles Munroe, of whose gospel he obviously approves. Others in their testimonies (with his evident support) link him to Joyce Meyer, John Avanzini, and the

---

[1] For a time in the mid-1990s, Rebecca Brown and the equally demon-focused Mark I. Bubeck were the best selling authors in Accra's evangelical bookshop; see Paul Gifford, *African Christianity: its Public Role*, London: Hurst, 1998, 103.

[2] David O. Oyedepo, *Keys to Answered Prayer*, Lagos: Dominion, 1986, 18: Hagin translated: 'When you pray, believe *that it has already been done...*'

[3] Ibid., 25. Oyedepo acknowledges his debt to Hagin and Copeland also in David O. Oyedepo, *Riding on Prophetic Wings*, Lagos: Dominion, 2000, 103, 121, 124; and Winners' newsletter *Winners World*, May 2006, 11.

London-based Nigerian Matthew Ashimolowo.[4] The global influence of such (mainly North American) Pentecostal luminaries is often not just acknowledged in Africa but trumpeted. Globalizing processes have tended to bypass Africa, but Pentecostalism is one global phenomenon in which Africa can participate as an equal. Oyedepo proudly takes his place at crusades, conferences and conventions with his peers from other continents, and has no difficulty in bringing them to his celebrations. On Africa's burgeoning Christian channels, his media productions are screened with theirs.

The Catholic Church, however, is international in another sense altogether. It has a hierarchical organizational structure, with an apex in Rome which all local churches look to.

The contemporary Catholic Church, in all its different national expressions, has been shaped by its struggle against modernity. Before the French Revolution, the norm was an established church and a state religion. All that changed with the rise of liberalism, socialism, nationalism, democracy, the secular nation state and other facets of modernity. Catholicism opposed these with all its power. It was the issue of the Papal States that focused the struggle. Those unifying Italy would not contemplate a united Italy without Rome as capital. The Pope insisted on his control of Rome, because a Pope could be no one's subject. The Pope forbade Catholics to have anything to do with the Italy that was trying to dispossess him, and did dispossess him in 1870. The papal theological-institutional project of opposition to modernity is called Ultramontanism.

'The Church was in conflict with the modern world. Everyone admitted it. Popes made the conflict a matter of faith.'[5] Gregory XVI in his encyclical *Mirari Vos* (1832) condemned freedom of conscience, freedom of the press, the doctrine that the church and state should be separated and the doctrine that power comes from the people. Pius IX in his 1864 encyclical *Quanta Cura* and its attached *Syllabus of Errors* proclaimed that it is always wrong to rebel against lawful governments; it is always wrong to allow divorce; it is wrong to believe that nowadays Catholicism should not be the only authorized religion in a state; it is

[4] For Murdock, Munroe, Meyer and Ashimolowo, respectively, see Gifford, *Ghana's New Christianity*, 65–9; 53–5; 50; 67–74.
[5] Owen Chadwick, *A History of the Popes 1830–1914*, New York: Oxford University Press, 1998, 348.

wrong to believe that a Catholic state ought to give the right of public worship to immigrants of a different religion, or to think that freedom of the press, and of the expression of opinion, does not lead to decline in public morality. And finally, 'the only proposition that most of Europe noticed—and at which it laughed: it is wrong to believe that the pope can and ought to reconcile himself with progress, liberalism, and modern civilization'. Chadwick comments: 'No sentence ever did more to dig a chasm between the pope and modern European society'.[6]

Rome outlawed the historical study of the Bible. In 1879 Pope Leo XIII imposed Thomism as the required philosophy of Catholicism and 'the truest philosophy for the modern age'; Thomism was the intellectual arm of Ultramontanism. Local rites were largely supplanted by the one Latin Rite. Above all, Rome was centralizing power on itself. For example, in 1829 there were 646 diocesan bishops in the Latin church. Of those outside the Papal States (within which there were seventy) only twenty-four had been appointed by the pope; the rest were appointed either by state authorities or by diocesan chapters. It was only in 1917 that canon law (canon 329.2) declared: 'The Pope nominates bishops freely'. Chadwick comments: 'For most of the history of the Church the pope did no such thing, and in many countries still did no such thing. But throughout the nineteenth century popes sought to acquire this right. The canon in the codex was aspiration more than reality. But it was now a law of the Church to which popes and curias afterwards appealed at need, in conflicts over the choice of bishops.'[7] By the year 2000 there were only about twenty-four bishops that Rome did not appoint.

Yet Ultramontanism was not all driven from the centre. Often the centring on Rome was driven by local bishops attempting to escape the control of the state, and even at times by lower clergy to escape the authoritarianism of local bishops. Much of it was emotional. Although they were theoretically the focal point of Catholicism, popes before the nineteenth century were remote, faceless figures; local churches were enmeshed in local society, linked to and often largely controlled by state authorities. The age of the railway, telegraph, wireless, photography and newspapers changed all that. The words and faces of the popes became known. The more they were harassed, pilloried, deprived

[6] Ibid., 176.
[7] Ibid., 360.

of their lands, the more they were hailed as martyrs in the eyes of Catholics worldwide. The papal stance of no compromise drew the hearts of Catholics towards Rome, eliciting their protective instincts to the office and personal devotion to the holder. 'This wave of emotion was almost the final influence necessary to bring modern popes to a greater authority in the world-wide church than any of their predecessors were able to exercise.'[8]

Defining oneself so sharply against hostile modern forces gave a strong identity to Catholic culture. Ultramontanism was distinguished for its popular devotions: to the Sacred Heart, the miraculous medal, the scapular, and above all to Mary (her Immaculate Conception was defined in 1854 and Bodily Assumption into heaven in 1950). Processions and pilgrimages were frequent. Pilgrimages honouring the 1858 Marian apparitions to St Bernadette at Lourdes drew half a million pilgrims annually by the end of the century. Many of these devotions furthered the anti-modernity agenda; cults like that of St Thérèse of Lisieux (1873–97) made plain that obedience to religious authority was far more important to God than all the so-called scientific and social advance of modernity.

Ultramontane Catholicism also saw the flourishing of religious congregations: 'The expansion of the religious communities was the most remarkable feature of Catholicism during (the nineteenth century).'[9] Women were particularly attracted to them, obviously from a genuine sense of piety and vocation, but other attractions have been suggested too: the chance of a career and adventure denied in the secular world; to take a stand against a corrupt world (women had little scope for direct political involvement); the promise of care in old age; escape from the dangers of childbirth and the sexual demands of men.[10]

This focus on the pope and rejection of modernity might be said to have peaked during the papacy of Pius XII (1939–58). He pontificated on almost every imaginable question, in discourses to groups as diverse as Catholic midwives or the Italian Association of Cornea Donors and the Italian Union for the Blind, his pronouncements immediately establishing 'Catholic doctrine'. But no sooner did Ultramontanism peak

[8] Ibid., 145.

[9] Ibid., 487.

[10] Nicholas Atkin and Frank Tallet, *Priests, Prelates and People*, New York: Oxford University Press, 2003, 113f.

than it collapsed. This collapse is normally associated with the Second Vatican Council (1962–65), at which the Catholic Church finally (not without some ambiguity) aligned itself to the modern world which it had been fighting so bitterly for so long. From one point of view, the Vatican Council was merely bowing to the inevitable; far from the council opening the windows of the church onto the modern world, those windows had all been blown out by the storms of previous decades and even centuries.

Different aspects of Catholicism's enormously messy alignment with modernity have bearing on our study of African Catholicism.

## *Disenchantment/secularization*

We have illustrated enchanted Christianity in discussing Olukoya. All religions seem initially to have conceived the natural-human-divine as fused together. The Mesopotamian, Egyptian and Greco/Roman religions conceived a cosmic order which made little distinction between the human and non-human, and natural and supernatural worlds: gods had sex with humans and produced demi-gods. Judaism transcended this worldview by conceiving God as totally other, and humankind as different from creation. God had created the world and would eventually end it, and he visited it periodically, but his otherness made it possible to view the world as having its own structure and logic. He made consistent ethical demands, and was beyond magical manipulation. We could obey his laws, but could not bribe or cheat him. Christianity largely adopted this understanding, though 'magic, miracle and mystery' partly remythologized the cosmos, and rituals, penance and indulgences reintroduced some divine manipulation and partly undermined a standard ethical code. The Protestant Reformation, however, intensified the affirmation of the absolute otherness of God, and human uniqueness.[11]

Keith Thomas has traced the decline of magic in England between the Reformation and about 1700. He notes that in those years the link between misfortune and guilt was broken.[12] The hardships of life came to be attributed to impersonal social causes rather than one's personal

[11] Peter L. Berger, *The Sacred Canopy: Elements of a Sociological Theory of Religion*, New York: Anchor, 1967, 111–14; Steve Bruce, *Secularization*, Oxford University Press, 2011, 28.

[12] Keith Thomas, *Religion and the Decline of Magic*, London: Penguin, 1973, 713.

failings or those of other people. Theologians became quite ready to accept the frequency of unmerited suffering. Stoicism became the basic religious message for those in misfortune, and 'the prospect of material relief by divine means was only intermittently upheld outside sectarian circles after the seventeenth century'.[13] The 'animistic conception of the universe which had constituted the basic rationale for magical thinking' simply fell away, in the process of 'disenchantment' made famous by Weber, and was replaced by a conception of an orderly and rational universe in which effect follows cause in a predictable manner.[14] Accusations of witchcraft 'were thus rejected not because they had been closely scrutinized and found defective in some particular respect, but because they implied a conception of nature which now appeared inherently absurd'.[15] As a result, by the end of this period, the nature of religion had changed. A distinction could be made between religion and magic, which would not have been possible two centuries earlier. Thomas notes, 'religion which survived the decline of magic was not the religion of Tudor England... The official religion of industrial England was one from which the primitive "magical" elements had been very largely shorn'.[16]

'Disenchantment' describes that shift away from a spirit-pervaded cosmos, a shift which has come to characterize all Western Christianity. But there is a subsequent, obviously related but distinct process of secularization which has nothing to do with the transcending of enchanted religion, but with the marginalization of religion of any kind.

In its simplest form, the secularization thesis states that 'modernization undermines the power, popularity, and prestige of religious beliefs, behaviour and institutions'.[17] Modernity brings diversity, urbanization, economic growth and affluence, individualism, egalitarianism and a new cognitive consciousness. Diversity has led to separation of church and state. Diversity has also called into question the certainty that believers can accord their religion. 'Ideas are most convincing when they are universally shared. If everyone shares the same

---

[13] Ibid., 766.
[14] Ibid., 771, 786.
[15] Ibid., 690.
[16] Ibid., 765f.
[17] Bruce, *Secularization*, 24. There is an enormous literature on the secularization debate which we cannot enter here; in what follows I am dependent on Bruce.

beliefs, they are not beliefs; they are just how the world is.'[18] With economic growth and affluence came autonomy, which weakened ties to communities. With scientific knowledge of and technological mastery over areas previously mysterious, the recourse to religion gradually declined. 'A perfect example can be seen in the contrasting responses of the Church of England to the Black Death of 1348–50 and the HIV/AIDS "gay plague" of the 1980s. In the first, the Church called for weeks of fasting and special prayers. In the second, it called for more government investment in medical/scientific research.'[19] The secularization thesis claims not that science and technology have 'disproved' religion, but that they have brought about the subtle supplanting of religious attitudes of dependence and mystery by technology-induced 'can-do' attitudes of sufficiency and dominion. As a result of such profound and far-reaching changes in consciousness, many in the West no longer call themselves Christian, but probably for many more religion has simply receded to the periphery of their lives. They effectively operate on another register, although in many cases they remain quite ready to tick the box 'Christian' in a national census.

Statistics showing the decline of religion in Europe are clear. To take just one set: according to the Mannheim Eurobarometer, between 1970 and 1999 the percentage of people attending church once a week or more changed in France from 23 per cent to 5 per cent; in Belgium from 52 per cent to 10 per cent; in Holland from 41 per cent to 14 per cent; in Germany from 29 per cent to 15 per cent; in Italy from 56 per cent to 39 per cent, and in Ireland from 91 per cent to 65 per cent.[20] Roughly the same patterns are observable in the modern liberal democracies founded by European settlers (although some try to argue, unsuccessfully in my opinion, that the United States is a special case).[21] The pattern is more important than the actual numbers; in no cases has there been a reversal of decline. And along with attendance have also declined belonging, affiliation and belief. Moreover, the nature of Christianity has changed, from more dogmatically orthodox to more liberal, with churches reducing their exclusive claims, viewing themselves as one

---

[18] Ibid., 37.
[19] Ibid., 44.
[20] Cited in ibid., 10.
[21] For an attempt to argue a significant difference, see Peter Berger, Grace Davie and Effie Fokas, *Religious America, Secular Europe? A Theme and Variations*, Aldershot: Ashgate, 2008.

religious expression among others. Christianity has became more privatized, compartmentalized and individualized, focused more on this world than the next.

## A specifically Catholic crisis of authority

At the height of Catholicism's resistance to modernity, it was thought that Catholicism was immune to this secularization, but subsequently it has made up lost ground with a vengeance. Catholics, though, have another complication unique to them, from a resurgent Ultramontanism linked to *Humanae Vitae*, Pope Paul VI's 1968 encyclical banning artificial contraception. *Humanae Vitae* and its aftermath are worth a little explanation, because of their significance for modern Catholicism worldwide.

All religious traditions change over time as they of necessity adapt to new circumstances. The Catholic Church has adapted incessantly, in various ways. It simply and quietly dropped the Index of Forbidden Books in 1965. Doctrines have come to be presented in a different form. The Second Vatican Council Decree on Religious Liberty, in which the Catholic Church changed from the view that error had no rights to championing liberty of conscience, is a classic example—the document stresses continuities and ignores novelties to such an extent that an unwary reader might be unaware of the sea-change it represents.[22] Other pronouncements like the Syllabus of Errors, though never revoked or indeed revisited, have simply passed into oblivion. But *Humanae Vitae* is different.

The advent of the oral contraceptive pill in 1960 had raised the issue of artificial birth control in a new way: should the traditional Catholic prohibition on all forms of contraception be reexamined?[23] This issue

---

[22] In keeping with my contention that Vatican II was the Catholic Church's accommodating to the modern world, see O'Malley's admission that 'for Americans today, the declaration in the final form approved by the council reads almost like a statement of the obvious', for such principles 'have been operative in the United States since the ratification of the Constitution' (John W. O'Malley, *What Happened at Vatican II*, Cambridge, MA: Harvard University Press, 2008, 212).

[23] To put this in some historical context, until the 1930s every state in the USA had laws limiting or even prohibiting access to contraceptives; Leslie Woodcock Tentler, 'Souls and Bodies: the Birth Control Controversy and the Collapse of Confession', in Michael J. Lacey and Francis Oakley, *The Crisis of Authority in Catholic Modernity*, New York: Oxford University Press, 2011, 299.

was taken out of the hands of the Vatican Council and reserved for a Pontifical Commission, a rather secretive body of fluctuating composition. Even so, the overwhelming majority on this commission urged modifying Catholic teaching, with only a couple of individuals resisting (so this was not strictly speaking a question of any 'minority report'). However, Paul VI, not seeing how an infallible papacy could survive such a change on an issue on which it had pronounced so clearly and repeatedly, followed these individuals and issued his encyclical *Humanae Vitae*, declaring from 'natural law' (thus theoretically discernible by all) that all artificial means of birth control were sinful.

*Humanae Vitae* revealed the gulf that had developed between official Catholicism and modernity. Since the Enlightenment, and especially since the French and American revolutions, public affairs and other arenas had assumed some autonomy of their own. In this new world, creativity, originality, authenticity, independence and integrity became virtues. By the 1960s sensuality, sexuality and intimacy were often understood to be essential to identity and self-fulfilment. The place of women in society, the nature of the family, had changed. Marriage was ideally an equal partnership. Traditional class systems were breaking down, attitudes of deference undermined. With mass education and the flourishing of science and technology, a new intellectual climate evolved; the role of authority in searching for truth was rethought. By the 1960s, the Vietnam War was the focus of mass protests, widely seen as folly perpetrated by an out of touch military and political elite. 1968 itself saw the student protests in France and elsewhere, as also the Prague Spring crushed by Soviet tanks. *Humanae Vitae* was often seen as a similar abuse of authority by another elite, male and celibate and equally out of touch with new realities. (Thus Sir Kenneth Dover, classicist and former president of the British Academy with no obvious animus against Catholicism, could begin a chapter in his autobiography: 'What with *Humanae Vitae* and the Soviet invasion of Czechoslovakia, 1968 was not a good year for the world in general. [But] for me...').[24]

By proclaiming its infallibility, the Catholic Church had indubitably made change more difficult for itself, much more so than for Anglicans, for example, who without major problems adapted their teaching on contraception to modern *mores* at the Lambeth conference of 1930.

[24] Kenneth Dover, *Marginal Comment: a Memoir*, London: Duckworth, 1994, 144.

However, even the explicit ban promulgated in *Humanae Vitae* might have been negotiated, through notions like the 'hierarchy of truths' or primacy of conscience; indeed, in the aftermath of its publication, some national bishops conferences took that route, stating that although *Humanae Vitae* was indeed Catholic teaching, individual conscience remained the ultimate criterion. However, such escape routes were soon blocked, for subsequent popes insisted on the contraception ban as integral to Catholic teaching. Under John Paul II *Humanae Vitae* even became institutionalized; it seems that prospective bishops have been vetted on precisely this point, and unreliability on this matter has disqualified a candidate permanently.

There are undoubtedly those (not only among Roman officials) who champion *Humanae Vitae* as an integral part of divine revelation. But all indications are that the overwhelming majority of Western Catholics reject it—in the United States, polls consistently reveal up to 80 per cent.[25] Thus many Catholics give up Christianity, not as a result of the general secularizing forces already mentioned, but for a reason specifically Catholic. They see authority in the Catholic Church as plain wrong, immoral even, this not being an issue of morality at all but an attempt to protect authority.[26]

What is perhaps surprising, however, is that many have not turned their backs on Catholicism, but consider themselves true Catholics while blithely rejecting official teaching. Being a Catholic on one's own terms is not totally new, but the open and cheerful acknowledgement certainly is. This drew comment at the time of John Paul II's trip to Britain in 1982, when one survey of people attending his ceremonies revealed that less than a third of those identifying themselves as Catholic declared themselves bound to obey all the teachings of the pope.[27] It was even more commented on during his visits to the USA,

---

[25] William V. D'Antonio, James D. Davidson, Dean R. Hoge, and Mary L. Gautier, 'American Catholics and Church Authority', in Lacey *et al.*, *Crisis*, 279.

[26] The Catholic Church has experienced the greatest net loss by far of any religious group in the USA—one quarter of those raised as Catholics; Katarina Schuth, 'Assessing the Education of Priests and Lay Ministers', in Lacey *et al.*, *Crisis*, 345. I consider the authority crisis stemming from *Humanae Vitae* a far more important reason for this attrition than the scandal of clerical abuse and its cover-up.

[27] Michael P. Hornsby-Smith, *Roman Catholics in England: Studies in Social Structure since the Second World War*, Cambridge University Press, 1987. Michael P. Hornsby-Smith, *Roman Catholic Beliefs in England: Customary*

when enthusiastic crowds gathered to hear him highlight the deficiencies of capitalism and denounce abortion and the death penalty, large numbers of whom had not the slightest intention of following him on such points.

However, the phenomenon of Catholicism on one's own terms has a generational element. Many of those already Catholics can take the decision to remain Catholic despite papal teaching. It is less likely that someone convinced of the wrongheadedness, even immorality, of papal authority would commit to Catholicism.

*First citizen of human family*

From the 1970s particularly, the pope begins to play a new role. In Casanova's words, the Popes have become 'first citizens of an emerging global civil society'; the pope is 'the self-appointed spokesman of humanity, the *defensor hominis*'; 'the papacy has eagerly assumed the vacant role of spokesperson for humanity, for the sacred dignity of the human person, for world peace, and for a more fair division of labour and power in the world system'; 'the Pope has learned to play... the role of first citizen of a catholic (i.e., global and universal) human society'.[28] Casanova traces this shift to the documents of Vatican II, and especially the public role of John Paul II. Casanova claims this is a major triumph for Catholicism, showing the inadequacy of secularization theory. This shows, he argues, the breaking down of that 'liberal wall' which on the one hand restricted religion to the private sphere, and on the other, kept the private religious sphere from public intervention and public scrutiny.

The Catholic involvement that Casanova describes is not an unambiguous development, however. What he is essentially tracing is the

---

*Catholicism and Transformations of Religious Authority*, Cambridge University Press, 1991. Three surveys of 1,672 Catholics in Britain in mid-2013 found that '"faithful Catholics", according to official teaching, are now a rare and endangered species. If we measure such a person by the criteria of weekly churchgoing, certain belief in God, taking authority from religious sources, and opposition to abortion, same-sex marriage and euthanasia, only five percent of Catholics fit the mould, and only two percent of those under 30' (Linda Woodhead, 'Endangered Species', *Tablet*, 16 Nov. 2013, 7).

[28] José Casanova, 'Global Catholicism and the Politics of Civil Society', *Sociological Inquiry*, 66, 3 (1996), 356–73, quotations from 358, 362, 364, 365 respectively.

further 'internal secularization' of Catholicism, because Catholicism has now become a super-NGO, the supreme example of global civil society. Casanova admits that there are some 'tensions' involved. For example, he says that Rome will need to 'learn to live with social and cultural pluralism both outside and specially inside the church, (letting) the faithful participate in the constant elaboration and reformulation of its normative teachings'.[29] But that casual reference to 'normative teachings' both catches and obscures the full implications of the shift he is celebrating. The Catholic Church he is describing has entered the public sphere as one more body like UNICEF, Oxfam, Save the Children, Greenpeace or Amnesty International (albeit one with great 'competitive advantage',[30] through its enormous grassroots membership, international organizational structures, and moral authority). However, such is *not* the self-understanding of traditional Catholicism, and certainly not that of Ultramontane Catholicism, which sees itself as the continued presence of Christ on earth, the unique and infallible channel of revelation and grace, and the necessary door to eternal life. But how can an infallible and divinely-instituted magisterium see itself as just one other voice to be taken into consideration? While the popes have accepted the public role Casanova ascribes to them, they have resolutely refused to be reduced to that. Official Catholicism wants to embrace its new role, and to preserve its old.[31]

Casanova implies that 'participation in the transformation of the world' has become now 'a constitutive dimension of the church's divine mission'.[32] However, it has for many Catholics effectively become the extent of the divine mission. Many, including priests and nuns, selflessly dedicate themselves to justice and peace issues, without troubling themselves too much about earlier claims, which they may well regard as indefensible (even embarrassing). A generational element is operative here, too, and raises serious questions about the future of Catholicism. Many already in the church give meaning to their lives through the shift Casanova describes; it is less clear that any new generation will see the need to become Catholic rather than support Amnesty International or work for Médecins sans Frontières.

[29] Ibid., 367.
[30] Ibid., 364.
[31] At the time of writing, it is still too early to assess how Pope Francis (elected March 2013) may affect this.
[32] Casanova, 'Global Catholicism', 360.

## Cultural considerations

More significant than any of the above in shaping recent Western Catholicism has been its social and cultural context.

The centralizing and absolutizing trajectory of Ultramontanism was not the only or even the principal dynamic within Catholicism, despite appearances to the contrary. In old Europe, Catholics slowly but surely assimilated to those of other denominations and none, integrating themselves into the new nation states. The process is even more striking in the non-Catholic countries of the Anglo-Saxon new world, where the Catholics were immigrants—not only Irish, but in most places it was the Irish who determined the shape of things. As immigrants, they tended to be poorly educated, even illiterate, discriminated against, resented. Religion, in their case Ultramontane Catholicism, was a source of identity, pride, cohesion, support and empowerment. Their religion gave them meaning, order, values and goals. Its rituals gave colour, music and poetry. Their doctrines gave answers to deeper questions bearing on truth, afterlife and suffering. Their communities (especially the activity expended in building and maintaining them) provided opportunity for social interaction, business contacts, marriages, even sports (note the 'Celtic' clubs for so many different sports on different continents). They provided scope for responsibility and leadership. Their bishops, often of considerable ability and integrity, frequently became respected public figures. An enormous array of Catholic institutions, especially schools and even universities, were a means of improvement and economic advance.

But the lot of immigrants is not unchanging. The Second World War served to break down walls between previously segregated groups. The post-war economic boom benefited everyone. In America, Catholics had to 'try harder' to prove themselves true Americans, which they did with such enthusiasm that the Catholic John Kennedy could become president in 1961. If one word sums up the transformation of Catholicism it is education. In Chadwick's words: 'The nineteenth century turned vast illiterate Catholic populations into half-literate Catholic populations. The first half of the twentieth century turned half-literate Catholic populations into an almost entirely literate people.'[33] It was this transformation that was effectively complete by the 1960s.

---

[33] Chadwick, *A History of the Popes*, 520f.

In short, many elements of what were regarded as the essentials of Western Catholicism were the mechanisms defining and supporting migrant communities on their way to integration. With integration, education and affluence, the social and cultural scaffolding of Ultramontanism simply fell away. A student of social processes might say that the cultural and civic dynamics had been far more important throughout, even though these Catholics might have insisted if asked, especially by an outsider, on every detail of the Ultramontane system. According to this view, Catholic opposition to modernity would have collapsed anyway, and around that time it did, with or without the Vatican Council.

Two of the most prominent Catholic institutions in the USA illustrate this: Catholic universities and congregations of religious sisters. Catholic colleges and universities in the United States increased to about 230 through the twentieth century. Catholic higher education in the United States resisted modernity, peaking with the triumph of Thomism in the 1950s, only to see Thomism immediately collapse. American values triumphed in the 1960s, leading to an identity crisis in Catholic higher education that persists to this day. 'The crisis is not that Catholic educators do not want their institutions to remain Catholic, but that they are no longer sure what remaining Catholic means.'[34] However, the crisis for Catholic institutions of higher education now goes beyond the collapse of Thomism. It has been rendered acute in recent years, as Rome has required that 'in ways appropriate to the different academic disciplines, all Catholic teachers are to be faithful to, and all other teachers are to respect, Catholic doctrine and morals in their research and teaching'.[35] There are increasingly few academics, particularly philosophers, ethicists and social scientists, who find it easy to subscribe to the complete Vatican position on sex and gender issues.[36]

[34] Philip Gleason, *Contending with Modernity: Catholic Higher Education in the Twentieth Century*, New York: Oxford University Press, 1995, 320.
[35] Pope John Paul II, Apostolic Constitution *Ex Corde Ecclesiae*, 1990.
[36] For the extent of the continuing crisis, see Melanie M. Morey and John J. Piderit, *Catholic Higher Education: a Culture in Crisis*, New York: Oxford University Press, 2010. Morey and Piderit understand by Catholic Culture the entire official *magisterium*, and insist this is what Catholic institutions exist to promote; the fact that a large sector of American Catholics positively reject this gives rise to insuperable problems, evident throughout the book.

Consecrated or religious life is not unrelated to the issue of Catholic colleges and universities, because nearly all of these were founded by religious orders, many by women's congregations precisely to give their sisters the qualifications to teach in America's countless parochial schools—a move so successful that American nuns became the most highly educated group of women in the church. Throughout the twentieth century, these congregations were the cheap labour force of ultramontane Catholicism. (A 1952 study found that the average annual salary of a sister teaching in a US parochial school was $495—a mere $29 more than the average per capita cost of living for the same sister).[37] In the years 1948–52, 23,302 women entered religious life in the USA. In 1953–57 the number grew to 27,157. The high-water mark was reached in the period 1958–62, when 32,433 women entered religious life.[38] In the 1960s, again coinciding with the Vatican Council, these congregations transformed themselves out of all recognition.[39] These were the years of student protest, the Vietnam War, the feminist movement, the sexual revolution and rising awareness of justice, civil and individual rights. The traditional vows of poverty, chastity and obedience came to be rethought. Obedience as hitherto understood was now seen as infantilizing adult women; they were to be individuals, autonomous, choosing for themselves. Traditionally, poverty entailed renunciation of ownership, community ownership of most things, and limitation of personal possessions. Now nuns had spending money, drove cars and lived in apartments. Many came to understand their vow as resistance to consumerism and society's treatment of the poor, championing the marginalized. Traditionally, celibacy had been considered superior to marriage as a spiritual path and sign of God's redeeming love. The Vatican Council document *Lumen Gentium* had disavowed this spiritual elitism, and now nuns were left with a secular pragmatism: it enabled a sister to commit herself completely to Christ, the church and the poor. Daily schedules that kept women together for rest, recreation, meals and prayer all disappeared as sisters moved out of large convents and into smaller houses or apartments, with a few others, or

---

[37] Gleason, *Contending with Modernity*, 231.
[38] Cited in Morey and Piderit, *Catholic Higher Education*, 263.
[39] For a revealing case study of the Immaculate Heart of Mary Sisters, see Mark S. Massa SJ, *The American Catholic Revolution: How the '60s Changed the Church Forever*, New York: Oxford University Press, 2010, 75–102.

even to live by themselves. In 1965 there had been 181,421 religious sisters in the USA; by 2009 there were 55,944, most over seventy years of age.[40] What had been a totally defensible way of life in one set of socio-cultural circumstances had become much more problematic in others.

## Conclusion

This brief outline has raised points which will be significant for our discussion of African Catholicism. First, Western Christianity of all kinds has shed its enchanted elements. Second, over the last few centuries Western societies have been undergoing a process of secularization, not the least significant part of which is the internal secularization of mainline Christianity itself. Third, the modern papacy has attempted to preserve its authority by making issues of sex and gender a test of orthodoxy, appointing bishops to enforce it, to the despair of many on the front line, the disillusionment of many who leave the church either in sorrow or in anger, but also (perhaps surprisingly) to bemused indifference on the part of many others who insist they remain faithful Catholics despite disagreeing with popes and bishops. Fourth, Rome has become increasingly prominent in the fields of human rights and 'justice and peace', activities which have become a lifeline for many internally secularized, post-Ultramontane Catholics. Above all, the trajectory of Catholicism in the last two centuries has made it inescapably clear that any religion is crucially shaped by other factors than authoritative statements supposedly defining its essentials; religion is intimately influenced by, dependent on, and symbiotic with the social and cultural dynamics of its particular context.

[40] Mary Johnson and Patricia Wittberg, 'Reality Check', *America*, 13 Aug. 2012.

# 6

# CATHOLICISM AND DEVELOPMENT

The 2013 Catholic *Annuario* states that for 2011, the last year for which statistics were available, Africa's Catholic population was 176 million (up from 45 million in 1970). This represents only 16 per cent of the world's Catholics, far behind the Americas' 48.8 per cent, though the growth rate of 2.3 per cent was the highest of any region, as was the increase in priests (up 39 per cent), and in religious women (up 28 per cent). At 176 million the Catholic numbers are the highest for any denomination in Africa. However, I will not spend time on statistics, but address some issues behind them.

It is institutions that are African Catholicism's most salient feature, the most prominent of which is the school. Historically, churches were far more involved in education than colonial governments. Hastings notes that in 1945 in British tropical Africa, 96.4 per cent of pupils attending schools were in those of a mission.[1] This contribution is widely celebrated; thus Nelson Mandela, addressing the Eighth General Assembly of the WCC in Harare in 1998: 'My generation is the product of missionary education. Without (that) I would not be here today. I will never have sufficient words to thank the missionaries for what they did for us.'

---

[1] Adrian Hastings, *The Church in Africa, 1450–1950*, Oxford University Press, 1994, 542.

Although of all denominations the Catholic Church is now by far the most heavily committed, this was not always so. In fact, there was a time when the Catholic contribution to education was regarded as deficient. Monsignor Arthur Hinsley was appointed in 1927 as special Apostolic Visitor to the Catholic missions throughout British Africa, with the simple message of the necessity of cooperating with the British government's educational policies. In Dar es Salaam in August 1928, he told a conference of bishops and missionaries: 'Collaborate with all your power, and where it is impossible for you to carry on both the immediate task of evangelization and your educational work, neglect your churches in order to perfect your schools.'[2] Until then it was Protestants who had built the flagship education establishments; in the 1920s governments had followed suit, and now Catholics did the same. Now Catholics launched into secondary education, with (in British Africa) Irish and Canadians in the lead, and generous subsidies from the British administration. They built large educational empires, not least in Nigeria, where by the 1960s it was claimed that the bishops had more than thirty thousand Catholic teachers on their payroll.[3]

As Independence came to African countries, the status of these schools changed considerably. In most countries the newly independent state took greater control of schools; in Nigeria, after the Biafran War (1967–70), Catholic schools were taken over and the Holy Ghost Fathers who controlled them expelled for their alleged support of the Biafran cause. In Africa in 2009 there were claimed to be over 12,000 Catholic infant schools, 33,000 primary schools, and almost 10,000 secondary schools, plus about twenty universities. These figures, however, need some explanation because there is no uniform definition of what constitutes a Catholic school. In general, there are grant-aided schools (receiving government subsidy but Catholic to a degree which differs from country to country), and private schools (autonomous but subject to government regulation). The Catholic Church is prominent in both the grant-aided and the private sector, with the overwhelming majority grant-aided. In Kenya, for example, in 2013 the Catholic Church sponsored 5,766 public primary schools out of Kenya's total of 19,059. The Church sponsored 1,894 secondary schools out of

[2] Roland Oliver, *The Missionary Factor in East Africa*, London: Longmans, 1952, 275.
[3] J.P. Jordan, 'Catholic Educators and Catholicism in Nigeria', *AFER* 2 (1960), 61.

Kenya's total of 7,311.[4] However, Catholic private schools have dominated the private sector until Africa's very recent explosion of private education. Kenya is one of the countries that publishes annual league tables to show the academic ratings of schools, and Catholic schools have traditionally been very conspicuous at the top. Many of these schools of academic excellence have been junior seminaries or the secondary schools catering for prospective priests, where the investment in personnel and resources has often been considerable.[5]

As already noted, Catholic education varies from country to country, but consider Zambia which is not particularly exceptional. Zambia has three categories of school: government school, grant-aided and private. There are also different levels: primary (grades 1–7), basic (grades 1–9), and high school (grades 10–12). The Catholic Church in 2004 ran forty-three high schools, thirty-five grant-aided, and eight private. It ran thirty-two grant-aided basic schools, nine grant-aided special schools (mainly for the handicapped), and two grant-aided teachers colleges as well as two grant-aided technical and vocational institutes. It runs other educational institutions too, not in these categories: three nursing schools, forty home-craft centres, twenty-six community schools, and eighty-seven pre-schools. Since 2004, the Catholic Church has begun a Catholic university. In all, about 15 per cent of the total educational enterprise in Zambia is under the aegis of the Catholic Church. This does not capture the full contribution over the last century, for most of which other bodies did comparatively little.

Nor do these statistics convey the quality. In 1975, for instance, 68 per cent of all students at the University of Zambia had done part or all of their schooling in Catholic institutions, even though the overall number of students in Catholic schools would not have been above 30 per cent. In 2003 the average pass rate at Catholic schools was 90 per cent, while the national average was 64 per cent. In 2004, when Catholic schools had approximately 15 per cent of all students taking the grade XII examination (determining entrance to university), 37 per cent of the students at the University of Zambia had come from Catholic schools. Reasons given for the academic superiority include

---

[4] Fredrick Nzwili, 'Resisting the Takeover', *Tablet*, 20 July 2013, 6.
[5] Hastings noted that in the early 1960s, ten per cent of all priests in East Africa were engaged as minor seminary staff; Adrian Hastings, *In Filial Disobedience*, Great Wakering: Mayhew-McCrimmon, 1978, 71.

the discipline and organization, teacher and student morale, better-qualified staff, more adequate equipment, greater commitment of staff, and the fact that most have been single-sex schools.

After Zambia's independence, the Catholic Church entered into partnership with the government, and by the 1980s schools which had been very Catholic in personnel became much less so, with undoubted effect on Catholic ethos and practice. In 1969, religious priests, brothers and sisters constituted about 33 per cent of the staff; in 2004 it was less than 3 per cent.[6]

It is agreed that Catholic schools face enormous challenges today. The basic one is the Catholic identity of grant-aided schools, where government control differs from country to country, and in some cases can severely diminish any special Catholic character. The general deterioration of education in much of Africa affects Catholic as well as public schools. Also, Catholic private schools, often academically excellent, are increasingly classed with the burgeoning expensive private schools (in many countries one of Africa's growth industries, as middle-class parents seek an education that will get overseas opportunities for their children); it is increasingly asked what these schools are providing besides entry to the often corrupt elite. However, despite the problems, the church is increasing rather than reducing its involvement in education.

Detailed research on the dynamics within Africa's Catholic schools is in fact rather limited. One ethnographic study does shed a great deal of light on many of the points raised above, giving, with telling examples and great sympathy, an account of life in a Catholic mission school in Zambia. The author, Anthony Simpson, taught there in the 1970s and 1980s, and returned there in the early 1990s for the fieldwork that underpins his book.[7] The school he calls 'St Anthony's' but is known to

---

[6] See Brendan Carmody, 'Catholic Church and State Relations in Zambian Education: a Contemporary Analysis', in Gerald R. Grace and Joseph O'Keefe (eds), *International Handbook of Catholic Education: Challenges for School Systems in the 21st Century*, Dordrecht: Springer, 2007, 543–62. Also, Winston Jumba Akala, 'The Challenge of Curriculum in Kenya's Primary and Secondary Education: the Response of the Catholic Church', in Grace and O'Keefe, *International Handbook*, 619–35 (dealing with the battle over any form of sex education); Richard Omolade, 'Challenges for Catholic Schools in Nigeria', *International Studies in Catholic Education*, 1, 1 (2009), 30–41.

[7] Anthony Simpson, *'Half-London' in Zambia: Contested Identities in a Catholic Mission School*, Edinburgh University Press, 2003.

its five hundred students, nearly all male, as 'Half-London' because it was seen as a step to a better life, a means to put distance between themselves and their former, 'uncivilised', rural, village existence.

Simpson explains the original aim of Catholic education, in particular the philosophy of the Marist Brothers responsible for the school, French Canadians initially but more latterly Spaniards. Simpson explains the difficulties for a project centred on Mary, in an environment where the public attitude towards girls and women is 'extremely negative'. We meet the doubt and uncertainty characterizing the brothers. They were not sure, post-Vatican II, of their role. Certainly they did not proselytize in any direct way, and were reluctant even to speak at assemblies (which contrasts sharply with the religious certainties of some sectors of students theoretically in their charge). Many aspects of their way of life in fact separated them from the people they lived among. The celibate brothers, with their discipline and control, given to private reflection and quiet prayer, offered a very different ideal from the Zambian. Their stress on privacy appeared as selfishness. The timetable, for example, was an area central to the brothers' lives, yet was regarded as 'unnatural' by pupils. The Marist rule's stress on manual labour directly contradicted the sense of values of the students, for whom education was the sure escape route from any kind of physical work. As a result, the brothers, far from being at the centre or in control, were in many ways excluded from the life of the African communities all around them.

The school combined the vision of the Marist Brothers' founder with the English public school ethos, the latter most evident in the prefect and house system, effectively foisted on the brothers by colonial school inspectors. The disciplinary regime, so seemingly total, is revealed to have been in fact very fragile. Prefects were one sector of the school with power to subvert official Catholic discourse. Seventh Day Adventists (SDAs), largely as a result of their confidence in public speaking, came to dominate the prefects, managing to reject the Catholic vision of the school authorities and impose another instead. (At the time of Simpson's fieldwork, Catholics made up 31 per cent of the student numbers, SDAs 28 per cent.) The SDAs dominated preaching in the chapel, and also speaking in assemblies. They, and SDA members of staff, could be not just non Catholic but subtly anti-Catholic. The official Catholic and Marian discourse of the school was in many cases subverted by both the SDAs and Pentecostals in the school—up to directly denouncing the Pope as the Beast of Revelation, removing crucifixes (to which they took particular exception), denouncing Catholic 'worship' of Mary, questioning the notion of confessing to a priest, stressing the sinfulness of smoking and drinking (in direct reference to some of the brothers), and pointedly restricting the term 'brother' to each other, referring to the Marist Brothers as 'so-called brothers'.

The book admirably reveals the contribution of mission schooling to the processes of 'postcolonial identity formation' in Africa. It also reveals the complex religious dynamics in Africa. Simpson argues that the Catholic Church makes an enormous investment of resources and personnel, but the local recipients are primarily interested in becoming English (more accurately now, American) gentlemen, with all that that brings in postcolonial Africa. Specifically Catholic returns are much less evident.

Catholic education is a sector undergoing considerable change, especially with the diminishing role of religious sisters, brothers and priests, to whom the excellence of Catholic schooling has often been attributed. Their passing is widely regretted.

*Health care*

In Africa, in 2010, the Catholic Church operated 16,178 health centres, including 1,074 hospitals, 5,373 out-patient clinics, 186 leper colonies, 753 homes for the elderly and the physically and mentally disabled, 979 orphanages, and 2,947 educational and rehabilitation centres.[8] Again, the control varies from country to country, but no other single agency on the continent can rival this contribution. Often, the Catholic health institutions form part of a wider body incorporating all Christian health activity, for purposes of importing medicines in bulk and negotiating with governments; invariably the Catholic Church is the most significant member of these bodies. Zimbabwe is a good example. The Catholic Church is a member of the Zimbabwe Association of Church-Related Hospitals (ZACH). ZACH serves 126 church-related hospitals and clinics in Zimbabwe, of which fifty are Catholic. Of ZACH's sixty-eight full hospitals, forty-one are Catholic. In rural areas, mission hospitals and clinics may well be all that exist.

[8] www.indcatholicnews.com, posted 10 Feb. 2010, accessed 4 July 2013.

They are often recognized for the quality of their care, too, so many urban-dwellers return to their rural areas when needing attention. Again, this contribution is generally celebrated. In Zambia, in 2012, the Minister of Health gratefully acknowledged that 60 per cent of all the health services available in rural areas were provided by the Catholic Church.[9]

As with schools, the church led the way, long before governments. In southern Africa, by 1950, there were seventy-three Catholic hospitals in South Africa, Southern Rhodesia (now Zimbabwe), South West Africa (now Namibia), Swaziland and Basutoland (now Lesotho), which not only provided medical services but trained African personnel. Thus for a good part of the twentieth century, the vast majority of the population of southern Africa received health care not from colonial or independent governments, but from mission hospitals, of which the Catholic hospitals were the majority.[10]

Anecdotal evidence suggests that half of all AIDS-related services in Africa are provided by Catholic organizations; the proportion is even higher in rural areas.[11]

*Economics of development*

Protestant churches have long stressed the self-sufficiency of local churches. It is part of their 'three-self' mantra: local churches should be self-governing, self-propagating and self-funding. The Catholic Church is very different. It is funded almost entirely externally, recognition of which has given rise to the term 'the Catholic model'. Enwerem bluntly expresses the reality: 'Except for very few cases, every single diocese of the Nigerian Church is either partially or totally dependent on financial assistance from overseas.'[12]

[9] Agenziafides, posted 28 June 2012.
[10] Catholic Health Care Association of Southern Africa, *In the Service of Healing: a History of Catholic Health Care in Southern Africa*, Johannesburg: Cathca, 2011. Of the 41 Catholic hospitals in South Africa, most were in rural areas catering for blacks; the apartheid government confiscated all such mission hospitals between 1973 and 1976.
[11] Michael Czerny, 'The Second African Synod and AIDS in Africa', in Agbonkhianmeghe E. Orobator (ed.), *Reconciliation, Justice and Peace: the Second African Synod*, Nairobi: Acton, 2011, 194.
[12] Iheanyi M. Enwerem, *Crossing the Rubicon: a Socio-Political Analysis of*

Funds come in various ways. There is official Roman aid. Each diocese receives annually a substantial subsidy from the Vatican department of Propaganda Fide. Seminaries and religious novitiates are subsidized. Rome provides relatively little, however. Much larger sources are the agencies like Missio, Adveniat and Aid to the Church in Need. There are also semi-official channels like twinning (many Ugandan parishes have twinned with German parishes).[13]

Most important is funding from the religious congregations which accomplish so much Catholic activity on the continent. Most obviously, nearly all the costs of training are covered by the congregation; thus the majority of the personnel of the Catholic Church in Africa are trained at little cost to Africa. Equally obviously, the congregation pays for their high profile ministries: like, for example, publishing houses such as Paulines Publications in East Africa, or Mambo Press in Zimbabwe, or the Comboni Missionaries' magazine *New People*. A bishop wanting to start a new ministry or build a new facility may well entrust it to a religious congregation precisely to shift to them the burden of accessing resources. Religious congregations also have sources of funds beyond themselves. Some funds exist specially for them. Conrad Hilton, for example, the founder of the hotel chain, though not a Catholic, was cared for by Catholic nursing sisters at an important time of his life. As a result, one of the priority areas of the trust established by his will is that of Catholic Sisters. In 2009, of the $80 million distributed, $23.7 million (by far the biggest recipient) was the Conrad N. Hilton Fund for Sisters. Porticus, the trust of the richest

---

*Political Catholicism in Nigeria*, Ibadan: BookBuilders, 2010, 277. Wuthnow has well shown how much US funding contributes to Southern Christianity: US$3.7 billion a year to overseas missions alone. 'Figures reported in *Giving USA 2006* showed that Americans gave a total of $260.3 billion to various kinds of charities and voluntary organizations of which $93.2 billion went to religion. Thus, if churches set aside even 5 percent of that amount for international programs, the amount available would be in excess of US$4 billion' (Robert Wuthnow, *Boundless Faith: the Global Outreach of American Churches*, Berkeley: University of California Press, 2009, 24). But he implies that this funding is a helpful addition, a support, a supplement (ibid., 154). In the case of the Catholic Church this does not capture the reality: the Western resources are not an addition, they are the *sine qua non*.

[13] For twinning, see Janel Kragt Bakker, *Sister Churches: American Congregations and their Partners Abroad*, New York: Oxford University Press, 2014.

family in the Netherlands, is also a dedicated funder of Africa's religious orders.

There exist special Catholic agencies for development work, like England's Cafod, Holland's Cordaid, Ireland's Trocaire, Scotland's SCIAF. These are just a few cited at random. According to its 2008 report, the 165 Catholic aid bodies that make up Caritas International employ 440,000 paid staff and 625,000 volunteers, and have a combined estimated worth of US$5.5 billion.

There is an entire raft of smaller organizations like MIVA (Missionary Vehicle Association), a Catholic lay association founded in Liverpool in 1974 which by 2005 had financed 3,000 vehicles (ambulances, motorbikes, even boats) to help Catholic causes around the world. KAAD (the Catholic Academic Exchange Service) is the scholarship fund of the German Catholic bishops. There are numerous other agencies, not officially Catholic yet very receptive to funding Catholic activity, like Malteser International (the aid arm of the Knights of Malta), Ipsia (the development arm of the Italian Catholic Workers' Union), and the Konrad Adenauer Foundation (the aid arm of Germany's Christian Democrats).

It is unnecessary to list more. The list is virtually endless, and the extent of Western funding is virtually impossible to discover, because so much is invisible as it is personal. Many African bishops studied in Rome with classmates who have become bishops of Western dioceses, and who even if their dioceses are not particularly wealthy are often in a position to help. Some African dioceses take choirs and dance troupes on cultural tours essentially as fundraisers (as Archbishop Peter Kwesi Sarpong of Kumasi in Ghana did annually). Above all, individual Western missionaries have been able to access funds from personal contacts in their home countries. Consider Kenya, in Nairobi I met one European missionary who, with funds provided by 'family and friends at home' had been able to build a block of flats in a middle class suburb; on the security of those flats, he had been able to raise a bank loan of US$1 million to build twenty-two luxury apartments in an exclusive suburb. With the rent from those apartments, he has been able to embark on a whole range of development activity. That is by no means an isolated case. One American Maryknoll priest, a doctor before becoming a priest and with extensive personal contacts in North American medical circles, built St Mary's Hospital, Langata, from resources raised through his own networks. The Undugu Society of

Kenya, involved in rehabilitating street children, was the personal pro-ject of a Dutch White Father, Arnold Grol. Nyumbani, the home for and outreach to AIDS orphans, was the project of Fr Angelo D'Agostino, an American Jesuit. (He had such international recognition that the Vatican issued a stamp commemorating his work; that stamp alone brought him another US$620,000.) All missionaries seem able to tap into funds from contacts back home (as one Irish missionary put it: 'There is no Irishman without relatives in the US') or their native par-ish or diocese. Caritas Italiana, the aid arm of the Italian Catholic bish-ops, told me that the reason they are relatively uninvolved in Kenya is that Kenya has so many Italian missionaries (especially Consolata and Comboni priests and sisters) who can tap into personal channels, that official assistance from Italy's Catholic Church is better directed else-where. Personal links are actively sought: dioceses in Uganda have bought houses in the United States and rotate priests there each year precisely to make the personal contacts which will maintain their min-istries throughout their lives.

## The shifting evangelization/development balance

All lament that resources are not as easily accessed as hitherto. Yet this is not prompting a move to self-reliance. Quite the contrary. Although self-reliance is becoming a mantra for Catholics too, nobody means it for a moment. Many bishops simply don't pay their dues to regional Catholic structures, or to the continent-wide Symposium of Episcopal Conferences of Africa and Madagascar (SECAM), knowing that the necessary money will be found elsewhere. Diminishing resources just mean redoubling the effort to access them, not a rethinking of the model of church. The significant point is that the sources drying up have tended to be those that could be used for specifically religious purposes, or those accessed though personal contacts which could be used at the missionary's discretion, often for activity narrowly reli-gious; not surprisingly, the decrease in the numbers of Western mis-sionaries is affecting access to such resources. But as these funds were diminishing, secular agencies stepped up to fund religious groups' development activity. Agencies of official Western aid, reluctant to give to governments they considered corrupt, sought out more reliable local partners, often churches with their extensive networks, grassroots membership, and established structures. Thus church bodies have become recipients of massive development aid from the EU, the UN, DFID, USAID and other such agencies. Of course, the EU or the USAID will not provide aid for specifically religious purposes like evangelization; the aid is given for relief and development. Thus many church development agencies have two sources of funds, one Catholic and the other consisting of governments and international agencies. Jesuit Relief Services in 2009 spent 22 million euros (53 per cent of its budget) in Africa, nearly one half coming from governments and UN agencies, just over half from Jesuit sources, private donors, the Caritas network and other church sources. Catholic Relief Services' $55 million for Ethiopia came almost exclusively from USAID. There are all sorts of possible variations of the mix, but over the last decades as funding for specifically religious activity has diminished, church bodies have received enormous sums for development.

It is in health care, above all after the advent of the AIDS pandemic, that the shift is most evident. Enormous resources have been necessary, and considerable resources offered; church groups have been the most prominent recipients. Thus the Catholic Health Care Association of Southern Africa received $4.2 million for a three-year programme from the Global Fund (set up in 2000 by the United Nations to combat the three diseases of AIDS, TB and Malaria). Many Catholic health bodies have received funds from the President's Emergency Plan for AIDS Relief (PEPFAR). A perfect example of the new dynamics is the American Catholic Medical Mission Board (CMMB). In 1999 the CMMB formed a partnership with the pharmaceuticals giant Bristol-Myers Squibb. With such partners, in 2012 the CMMB distributed $1 billion of pharmaceuticals and medical supplies to the developing world. The CMMB provided $150 million for its 'Secure the Future' programme to find sustainable solutions to the HIV/AIDS crisis in Sub-Saharan Africa. Another CMMB 'Choose to Care' initiative for community based HIV/AIDS care sponsors 100 projects in five African countries. Their 'Born to Live' programme to reduce mother-to-child HIV infection is operative in Kenya, South Africa, Swaziland, Nigeria and Zambia.[14] 'Men taking Action' is a CMMB project in Zambia to involve men in the direct health care of their wives and families. The CMMB's ANISA ('together' in Zande) programme works for AIDS

[14] Tom Gallagher, 'Catholic Organization Exports US Health Care to the Poor around the World', *National Catholic Reporter*, 31 Jan. 2013.

prevention in South Sudan. The training, organization and management necessary to handle such grants to the level required by Western donors have necessitated a restructuring and professionalizing of the recipient Catholic institutions and a refocusing of their priorities; needless to say, the CMMB does not evangelize.

The Catholic Church, always a service provider and outstanding in fields of health and education, has now extended its service provision to cover almost everything imaginable, including rehabilitation of the justice system, strengthening food production, micro-finance, nutrition outreach programmes, water sanitation, HIV and AIDS education, conflict resolution and agricultural productivity. One finds dioceses effectively run by the bishop and his development officer. In Kenya, eight remote Catholic dioceses in undeveloped regions are invariably headed by European bishops who can bring the resources, not least of their particular religious congregations, not only for evangelization but also, and more obviously, for the extensive development work that characterizes all these dioceses. Nor do the local clergy, normally remarkably sensitive about missionary preferment, complain; it would be fruitless appointing a Kenyan, given the requirements of those areas. In 2005 a Kenyan was appointed to the remote diocese of Isiolo, but, as the national Catholic monthly disarmingly admitted, he was as good as a European because as a member of the Consolata Fathers, he could tap into the Italian resources of the Consolata missionary congregation.[15]

Development is not new to Catholicism. It never restricted itself to evangelization, preaching, sacraments. If, as is sometimes still claimed,[16] it used to be focused on the after-life, this has long ceased to be so; it is as rare to hear mention of the afterlife within Catholicism as it is in Pentecostalism. All this development has been justified as an integral and logical part of the Christian calling: genuinely Christian activity, motivated by Christianity, justified by Christian theology. However, as the church functions now, dependent on overseas funds which are increasingly for its development work, Catholicism is becoming identified with those works rather than anything particularly

---

[15] *National Mirror*, May 2006, 14.

[16] Emmanuel Katongole, *The Sacrifice of Africa: a Political Theology for Africa*, Grand Rapids: Eerdmans, 2011, 107f, 112f, 117; Ka Mana, *Christians and Churches of Africa: Salvation in Christ and Building a New African Society*, Maryknoll: Orbis, 2004, 93, 98, 103.

religious. From its development work comes its high visibility, its appeal, its status. These funds determine its priorities and internal organization, the way it is seen, and the expectations held of it.

## Tensions

The emphasis on development does not come without some tension. Tension arises on two scores. One exercised Pope Benedict particularly; his first encyclical made the point clearly: 'The church's charitable activity (must) not become just another form of social assistance'.[17] He was insisting: we are not a development agency, we are a religion. This concern motivated the removal of the Zimbabwean Lesley-Anne Knight as the head of Caritas International, because the organization under her direction was alleged to be not explicitly or not sufficiently Catholic. The Pope was making a very valid point: development is not religion, even if one believes that development is an essential element of religion. By removing her as head of Caritas, Benedict certainly made it easier for Vatican authorities to intervene when judged necessary, but uncertainty remains. It is not perfectly clear how one might distinguish a Catholic exercise of election monitoring from a non-Catholic monitoring exercise (especially if, as in Nigeria, it includes Muslims). Likewise, how does Catholic slum clearance differ from any other form? Or Catholic water purification?

But there is another issue besides the feared 'internal secularization' of Catholicism into an NGO. It may not be easy to distinguish Catholic election monitoring from the non-Catholic kind, but AIDS prevention, certainly, is a case where Benedict insisted there is an important difference. Most programmes to stop the spread of AIDS would allow some place for condoms. A truly Catholic programme, according to Benedict, would not. He issued a *motu proprio* on 'Charity in conformity with the demands of the Church's teaching'. Catholic charitable activity must 'follow Catholic principles'; 'In the activities and management of these agencies the norms of the Church's universal and particular law (must be) respected'; 'In particular, the diocesan Bishop is to ensure that charitable agencies dependent upon him do not receive financial support from groups or institutions that pursue ends contrary to the Church's teaching (and) that these charitable agencies do not accept

---

[17] *Deus Caritas Est*, 25 Dec. 2005, 31.

contributions for initiatives whose ends, or the means used to pursue them, are not in conformity with the Church's teaching.'[18] He subsequently warned against working with other charities that directly or indirectly support actions and projects contrary to 'Christian anthropology', or are inspired by 'dangerous ideologies' and 'deviations'.[19] As noted above, even if he failed to take the faithful with him, bishops were required to support him.

The Vatican's insistence on its procreative ethics agenda summed up in *Humanae Vitae* was evident in both Synods of Bishops for Africa. The first Synod in 1994 was in danger of being hijacked by the Pope's crusade against the United Nations International Conference on Population and Development to be held in Cairo later that year. The African bishops willingly leant him their support, which, it must be said, seemed to come as much from their Africanness as from papal teaching; they saw the UN Cairo agenda as the West's imposing itself on Africa as much as a religious issue.[20] At the second Synod in 2009, similarly, a constant refrain was the 'foreign agendas' being forced on Africa—code for any advocacy of population control. The question of condoms arose at the very beginning with the Pope's remarks to journalists on his way to Cameroon in March 2009 to launch the synod. In response to a question, the Pope said that condoms 'increase the problem' of AIDS, even though the Secretariat of State later doctored this slightly (but significantly) to 'risked increasing the problem'. His comment drew considerable fire from health officials, AIDS workers, government officials in several EU states, and even a Belgian parliamentary resolution calling on the Belgian government to lodge an official protest. Ghana's Cardinal Peter Turkson at the synod's opening press conference tied himself in knots responding to repeated questions on this. Above all, for me, this issue arose when Jacques Diouf, the head of the United Nations Food and Agriculture Organization, based in Rome, addressed the synod (the only outside 'expert' to do so). He spoke on the current situation in Africa, and one of the significant points he made was that Africa, having reached a population of one

[18] *Intima Ecclesiae Natura*, 11 Nov. 2012.

[19] *Tablet*, 29 Jan. 2013, 27.

[20] Interestingly, during the 1994 synod, *Adista* reported that 50 per cent of the Brazilian bishops supported their government's measure to promote birth control (*Adista*, No 33, 30 April 1994), a stance that would be impossible for Africa's bishops.

billion the previous month, would double its population in forty years, so that by 2050 Africa's population would be two billion, more than that of India and China. This population increase has enormous consequences for deforestation, overgrazing, depletion of water sources—and thus security, and peace and justice. Yet overpopulation is simply an issue that Catholicism cannot raise, much less grapple with.[21]

In July 2012 the Kenyan bishops reacted to a report of an international plan to make contraception available to 120 million women and girls in poor countries by 2020 by stating that the plan was 'unimaginable, dangerous and could lead to the destruction of human society and by extension the human race'. Nobody, they insisted, should be forced to abuse his/her dignity through contraceptives. The 'use of contraception, especially as radically proposed in the article, is both dehumanizing and goes against the teaching of the church… It already threatens the moral fabric of the society and is an insult to the dignity and integrity of the human person.' The bishops noted that if the money or a portion of it was used to develop the underdeveloped parts of Kenya, the so-called threatening population of 64 million people in 2040 would be too low.[22]

Similarly in Nigeria, with an estimated population of 170 million, a spokesman for the Catholic Bishops Conference of Nigeria called the mass distribution of condoms a trick. 'Nigeria is not overpopulated. What we lack are visionary leaders with the moral compass to equitably distribute the abundant resources for the well-being of every citizen.' He said that traditional methods of birth control and responsible parenthood should be properly explored and promoted by the authorities.[23]

In Malawi, ranked 170th out of 187 on the UNDP's 2012 Human Development Index, with the majority of the population living on less than $US1 daily, the government in 2014 sought the cooperation of

[21] Population seems a no-go area in development generally. For an exception, see the six-page 'Policy Brief: Population' of Save the Children (UK) released 15 March 2010, which draws attention to the correlation of unchecked population growth with poverty, political instability and climate change.

[22] CISA, 57, 20 July 2012. Cardinal Njue, the chair of the Kenya Episcopal Conference, stated on 11 August 2012 that some people in Europe had already destroyed their families and wanted to do the same in Africa: 'A lot of money is today being dished out in the name of family planning while in actual fact, the idea is to destroy it, the family' (CISA, 65, 14 Aug. 2012).

[23] CISA, 100, 18 Dec. 2012.

religious leaders in an initiative to control growth of the population— then 15 million and projected to grow to about 40 million by 2035. Some, like the Anglicans, could see the need to curb population growth, but Muslims and Catholics opposed the initiative. 'As Catholics, we are deeply rooted in faith. We follow to the letter what the Bible says,' Fr George Buleya, Secretary General of the Episcopal Conference of Malawi, said on 29 March 2014. 'The Holy Book is very clear on population growth. We cannot therefore, support any measures which are in conflict with the Bible… By encouraging people to use contraceptives, what it is saying is that government is failing to provide for the people. But no matter how many people could be there, God will always provide for his people.'[24]

In schools, curricula aiming at 'sex education' are strictly monitored for any signs that they might fall short of the full Roman agenda. In early 2013 the Kenyan bishops called for the banning of the Maori Witi Ihimaera's *Whale Rider* from Kenya's secondary school examination syllabus because of hints of homosexuality: in order, the General Secretary of the Bishops' Conference explained, 'to guard the society now and in future, since gay practices are against human dignity and human life'.[25]

Some episcopal conferences make Rome's procreative preoccupations almost their principal crusade. At times they do this in terms that do them little credit. On 19 August 1993 the Family Life Counselling Association of Kenya published a newspaper supplement celebrating the twenty-fifth anniversary of *Humanae Vitae*. This drew a response from a prominent surgeon and respected social commentator, and I will draw on his response here, because I suspect it expresses the sentiments of many, even committed Catholics, including priests and nuns. He praised some of the contributions in the supplement, especially the call to become a person and be open to others. But he called other sections untruths and propaganda.

I have resorted to write yet another letter on this issue not because I am obsessed with hate and spite against the Catholic Church, neither because I have ulterior motives. I am writing because I think it would be irresponsible not to point out yet again where these representatives of the Church overstate their case and where their eagerness merges into recklessness. There are a number of

[24] CISA, 26, 1 April 2014.
[25] *Tablet*, 19 Jan. 2013, 29.

points in these writings which I wish to address, but before I do so I wish to say with great emphasis and clarity that not only am I pro-life, against vice, immorality, abuse and exploitation, but I also greatly admire the coherence and erudition of the Catholic Church. I further recognize the pastoral experience and grave concern of the episcopate. Yet... I maintain that this attitude of the bishops in Africa over the last 25 years has contributed to the increasing misery of our people, that it is reckless, irresponsible and uncharitable.

After pointing out the problems with 'natural family planning' in Africa's conditions, he continues:

The Family Life Counseling Association in its publication stoops to dishonesty. It does not quote figures on the reliability of this method at all, although figures are available not least from huge WHO studies. It does not say either 'Sorry, this method is not foolproof, it is not even as good as others, but we Catholics cannot resort to other methods because God forbade them etc etc'. No, we are told the pet Catholic story about condoms, namely that they have a failure rate of 30 percent and above... The rest of the piece celebrating the twenty-fifth anniversary of *Humanae Vitae* suggests that there really is no population growth problem. It insinuates that contraception is advocated because it is big business. It repeats the usual nonsense about the pill. It even asserts that the HIV virus can penetrate the condom and so on... It is scandalous disservice to the Third World to continue to propagate these ideas, particularly as they are, even within the Church, disputed opinions... Our bishops should stop making untruthful statements about the efficacy and the dangers of proved methods of contraception.[26]

Few Catholics challenge such episcopal statements. Some theologians and ethicists, particularly those involved in health care, turn somersaults arguing 'the Catholic Church has no officially articulated position on condom use in relation to HIV/AIDS'.[27] However, most Catholic professionals simply 'follow their own consciences or simple common sense', up to and including distributing condoms.[28]

---

[26] Imre Loefler, *Nation*, 18 Sept. 1993, reprinted in Rupert Watson (ed.), *Pills, Planes and Politics: the Wisdom of Imre Loefler*, Nairobi: Salmia Trust, 2008, 98–101. Calderisi, also, can deplore the 'havoc created' by official Catholic 'extremism'; see Robert Calderisi, *Earthly Mission: the Catholic Church and World Development*, London: Yale University Press, 2013, 196, 203; see all 179–204.

[27] Paterne-Auxence Mombe, 'Moving beyond the Condom Debate', in Orobator (ed.), *Reconciliation*, 204.

[28] Calderisi, *Earthly Mission*, 189. He notes Italian and French nuns distributing, even demonstrating the use of, condoms in West Africa (ibid., 194–96). So too, the founding executive director of UNAIDS notes nuns giving out condoms in

In Kenya, if public political involvement in the early 1990s focused on issues of human rights and multi-party democracy, enhancing enormously the prestige of the Catholic Church, the Catholic authorities' stance on the 2010 referendum on the new constitution was just as revealing. The constitution tried to address several of the issues that had made Kenya so dysfunctional. It attempted to restrict the overweening powers of the president, replace the corrupt judicial apparatus, and address the issue of distribution of land. However, at the same time, it allowed for abortion in limited cases, and allowed the Muslims to keep their *kadhi* courts (strictly for matters of Islamic law). The churches in general, with the Catholic Church at the forefront, the Catholic bishops most articulate, led the campaign against approving the proposed constitution, on those two grounds. It was not that they were insensitive to the need to reduce the power of the presidency, reform the judiciary, tackle the land question, but those issues were completely secondary to the issues of abortion and *kadhi* courts. It was not adequate that the constitution pass, and these two issues be taken up later; these two were so central that the constitution must be rejected. The constitution was passed on 4 July 2010 by an overwhelming majority of Kenyans, Catholics included, which did little to enhance the authority of the Catholic bishops.

*Conclusion*

Across the continent, the effects on Catholicism itself of its enormous commitment to relief and development are profound. I first heard the term 'the NGO-ization of the churches' at the All Africa Conference of Churches in the early 1990s. The term was intended to draw attention to the changing nature and function of Africa's mainline churches,

---

Namibia and Ivory Coast: Peter Piot, *No Time to Lose: a Life in Pursuit of Deadly Viruses*, New York: W.W. Norton and Company, 2012. In Madagascar in July 2013 the (Catholic founded) Population Research Institute alleged that some local CRS workers were engaged in family planning programmes and distribution of contraceptives and abortifacients, which drew a speedy denial from the US Conference of Catholic Bishops, insisting that the CRS acts only in accord with Catholic teaching, as Archbishop Tsarahazana of Toamasina, president of the Bishops' Conference of Madagascar, hastened to reassure his CRS donors (CISA, 69, 6 Aug. 2013).

none more so than the Catholic. We noted in chapter five that the supernatural has been rendered peripheral in the rational and bureaucratic West, a process that is effecting the 'internal secularization' of Western Christianity. This thoroughly Western phenomenon is not without relevance for Africa. An enormous amount of Christian involvement is not obviously about relating to the divine; it is most obviously about access to Western resources and the whole range of things this brings: education, health, employment, global opportunities. This Christianity brings not so much redemption as development. It is associated less with grace than with science and technology. It operates with a vocabulary not so much of atonement, sacraments, conversion, as one of micro-finance, capacity building, and women's empowerment. The virtues it promotes are accountability, transparency, and good governance as much as faith, hope and charity. It operates as much from human rights reports and poverty-reduction strategies as from scriptures and creeds. Its sacramentals are as much computer software and SUVs as bread, wine, and oil. Its register is not so much theology as social science. Its level of engagement is as much the natural and the human as the supernatural or the spiritual. These aid flows and what they involve have become increasingly significant for, even constitutive of, the Catholic Church. None of this means that Catholic devotions, even or especially Ultramontane ones like those to the Sacred Heart or Our Lady of Lourdes, do not flourish on the continent. They do; 'Our Lady has become precisely the sign of Catholicism in Benin' announced a priest in July 2013.[29] But the balance has palpably shifted.

In her study of a particular rural area of Uganda, Christensen noted that the Anglican priest received as monthly wage the equivalent of US$6, or of two hens or four kilograms of wheat. As a result, within the Anglican church there was a lack of financial accountability, corruption, impoverishment and little social capital. By contrast, the Catholic priest had spent time overseas, and found patrons prepared to support him after his return. Christiansen notes that as he acquired more funds his priorities shifted; running his AIDS orphanage and operating his secondary school became a full time job. AIDS and the school were what attracted the money; that was where his priorities lay.[30] The trend was

[29] CISA, 62, 12 July 2013.
[30] Catrine Christiansen, 'Development *by* Churches, Development *of* Churches:

driven by availability of resources. There, in microcosm, is the continent-wide shift.

Stan Chu Ilo's *The Church and Development in Africa: Aid and Development from the Perspective of Catholic Social Ethics* illustrates many of the issues touched on above. The book is almost a handbook for Catholic involvement in human rights, ecology, development, aid, business ethics, social justice, reconciliation, poverty eradication and countless other causes. Ilo insists that 'changing the face of Africa… is the vocation of all Christians'.[31] Papal reproduction concerns are plainly evident throughout: 'Openness to life is at the centre of all authentic development',[32] and Catholics must have nothing to do with 'anti-population ideologies… and anti-life messages';[33] indeed, the book is essentially a commentary on Benedict XVI's encyclical *Charity in Truth* (2009): 'A theological theistic anthropology is the only authentic way of understanding development',[34] and 'a non-theistic anthropology always diminishes the full truth about the human person'.[35]

For our purposes here, however, the most important point to note is that he attacks almost everyone involved in development for not taking Africa seriously or for not listening to Africans. He insists that that is what must be done, and sees himself as contributing this dimension. He demands for any true development 'an immersion in (Africans') story, and a direct and immediate identification with their condition'.[36] We must have 'the fullness of truth of the reality of Africans'.[37] We need 'their inherent traditional cultural and economic creativity',[38] 'the moral and spiritual forces (moulding) the inner soul of their citizens',[39] 'African cultural realities or African worldviews',[40] 'their cultural and

---

Institutional Trajectories in Rural Uganda', PhD, University of Copenhagen, 2010, 132–40.

[31] Stan Chu Ilo, *The Church and Development in Africa: Aid and Development from the Perspective of Catholic Social Ethics*, Nairobi: Paulines, 2013, 17.

[32] Ibid., 59.

[33] Ibid., 220.

[34] Ibid., 85.

[35] Ibid., 48.

[36] Ibid., 27.

[37] Ibid., 32.

[38] Ibid., 88.

[39] Ibid., 119.

[40] Ibid., 128.

spiritual roots',[41] 'their locally based science and technology',[42] 'their own proper genius',[43] their 'self-understanding'.[44] One might think then that his own approach might lead him to address the enchanted imagination that we outlined in earlier chapters of this book, but only in a couple of instances does he even allude to it. He mentions in passing the traditional worldview that 'all created things, in African cosmology, have life because they give vital force'.[45] He makes one passing reference to the appeal to curses which he suspects is rather defeatist.[46] He deplores 'unscientific' if religiously satisfying explanations for death.[47] In a few sentences he raises the question whether Catholics might learn from Pentecostal healing practices,[48] and in one sentence whether (to avoid the financial dependency seemingly pervasive in Catholicism) something might be learned from Pentecostals' ways of raising funds.[49] He laments that Africa's 'new churches' are 'pioneering and promoting the idea of "big men of the big God"',[50] and calls it a scandal that many church leaders claim to cure AIDS 'as a testimony to their supernatural power and healing gifts'.[51] Yet he ignores the tens of millions of Nigerians, many of them Catholics, who flock to those making such claims, and support them handsomely. It is unthinkable that a Nigerian like Ilo is unaware of the issues raised here. He has deliberately chosen not to address them. He teaches in the West, and is writing for the West, where witches, demons, curses and spells have ceased to have much traction. He notes that Africa's burgeoning Christianity 'offers one of the most exciting narratives for interpreting and understanding Africa's social context'.[52] It is an offer he does not take up. He deplores 'the pervasive influence of Western theological categories and frameworks',[53] but does not consider why

[41] Ibid., 140.
[42] Ibid., 151.
[43] Ibid., 189.
[44] Ibid., 193.
[45] Ibid., 110.
[46] Ibid., 236.
[47] Ibid., 249.
[48] Ibid., 252.
[49] Ibid., 240.
[50] Ibid., 233.
[51] Ibid., 170.
[52] Ibid., 196.
[53] Ibid., 228.

categories such as those raised by Olukoya and Oyedepo might have such appeal. In joining those who choose to ignore this enchanted dimension, he gives a most inadequate picture both of development in Africa and of African Christianity.

It will be obvious that the religious imagination underpinning the Catholic involvement in development is far from the enchanted religious imagination underpinning a Pentecostalism like Olukoya's. This does not mean that many loyal Catholics don't operate from the enchanted imagination; we will address the phenomenon of enchanted Catholicism in the next chapter.

7

# ENCHANTED CATHOLICISM

We have noted that African Catholicism is primarily characterized by development. Countless African Catholics, though, live in an enchanted world. I will briefly outline some examples of enchanted Catholicism, not least to see the official Catholic response. The most famous example is that of Archbishop Emmanuel Milingo. Milingo was named Archbishop of Lusaka, Zambia, in 1969. In 1973 he became aware that he possessed healing powers, and conducted healing and exorcism sessions which drew great crowds. Controversy surrounded these public services, and in 1981 Rome sent two Kenyan bishops to conduct an investigation, with the result that in 1982 Milingo was summoned to Rome where the following year he was forced to offer his resignation as archbishop. Rome has never made public the reason for its intervention, and all sorts of personal, administrative and even political reasons have been suggested, but the overriding one was almost certainly his enchanted understanding of healing. The following cases are less well known.

*Cameroon*

Fr Meinrad Hebga, born in 1928, a Bassa of southern Cameroon, a diocesan priest turned Jesuit, in 1976 founded his movement Ephphata, which in 2005 claimed 200 groups in Cameroon and beyond, and could draw up to 2,000 for its weekly gathering in Yaounde.[1]

[1] Ludovic Lado, *Catholic Pentecostalism and the Paradoxes of Africanization:*

For these weekly meetings, clients wrote beforehand to Fr Hebga, spelling out their problems and what measures had already been taken to counter them. These letters covered every imaginable kind of misfortune: cancer, car accidents, HIV and AIDS, night rapes (*couches de nuit*) and having meals in dreams (*repas de nuit* which many think witches use to damage reproductive systems), untypical behaviour, fertility problems, multiple deaths in the family, problems resulting from (conscious or unconscious) contact with religious groups (especially Rosicrucians and Freemasons), problems in obtaining a visa for the West, misfortunes attributed to undergoing abortion, failure in school, general poverty. In nearly all of these cases (95 per cent) the reason was presumed, sometimes explicitly stated, to be witchcraft.

The letters often explained that the patient had sought help from diviners, and often from Western medicine. In most cases the witchcraft was thought to stem from someone known to the patient, with whom the patient already had strained relations; problems of fertility especially were thought to be caused by evil forces unleashed by jealous relatives. Many patients gave importance to dreams as sources of revelation. Hebga distinguished four categories of possessing spirits; spirits of the dead; genii (usually spirits of rivers, forests, mountains and the like); living witches or sorcerers (by far the most common kind of possession); and demons (Hebga detected this specifically satanic possession far less frequently). The prayer sessions took place every Wednesday afternoon from about half past three to half past six, and attracted up to 2,000, of all social classes, mainly active members of Ephphata, often dressed in the distinctive red of the movement. The prayer session was supplemented with a 'reception of patients'. This latter was contingent on Hebga's presence; indeed, his non-appearance could mean considerable falling off in numbers of patients. Patients were led to Hebga in groups of ten or fifteen, sorted according to the initial diagnosis, introduced by aides, and Hebga imposed his crucifix on them, and recited a biblical text. An aide would anoint a patient's forehead, chest and sometimes neck (the part of the body where witches usually store their evil substances). After this, the group would return to the main prayer session, and a new group was brought in.

---

*Processes of Localization in a Catholic Charismatic Movement in Cameroon*, Leiden: Brill, 2009, based on field work conducted in 2004–06.

This part of the service lasted about an hour. The prayer session included testimonies (often attributing much to Hebga) and preaching, not always by Hebga himself, but virtually no speaking in tongues.

The group's prayer camp, situated about 60 kms from Yaounde, consisted only of dormitories and a chapel (the proposed infirmary, orphanage and library were never built). The camp dealt with severe cases, and suspected possession requiring follow-up. Patients could choose to stay there until cured (at any one time there were between thirty-five and fifty in residence) and every second weekend brought several hundred patients, of whom at least fifty were suspected cases of possession. The deliverance sessions were on Friday evening and Saturday morning. Most of the deliverance activity took place in workrooms where two or three intercessors handled up to fifteen patients. Their tools included holy water, blessed salt, crucifixes, incense, a Bible, prayer books, and a bucket in which patients expectorated as they usually did during deliverance. The process also involved short dialogues with the patient about problems, prayer over the patient with a crucifix, use of biblical texts and advice on how to deal with the problem after the ritual. Hebga himself came to handle only cases of simple misfortune—not least because the physical demands of exorcism became too taxing; in a majority of these cases, the patient would go into a trance requiring physical energy to handle her.

The movement formed cells in Paris and London, which required Hebga's time too. As well, he would travel to villages when asked to deal with tensions arising from witchcraft accusations. Hebga died in France in 2008. His movement still exists, but the group essentially revolved around Hebga's authority over witchcraft spirits, and without Hebga is experiencing considerable problems.

*Zaire*

Mary Douglas had done fieldwork among the Lele in the 1940s and 1950s, and returned in 1987 where she learned of events that occurred not long before. The devout Catholic that she was, she was reluctant to publish an account of them, but eventually did.

Belief in sorcery was part of the ancient tradition of the Lele, but before they were Christianized they had established ways of controlling their fear and of limiting accusations, not least by the poison ordeal which, however drastic, required the accuser to undergo the same ritual himself. However, under Belgian colonial rule the poison ordeal was made illegal, so unless the Lele could be persuaded to give up their belief in sorcery, 'they were stranded in a sorcery-ridden environment in which they could do nothing to protect themselves'.[2] And it was difficult to disbelieve in sorcery, because it was embedded in the central social institutions. 'Sorcery pumped material wealth through the economy. Sorcery beliefs maintained a kind of precarious gerontocracy; they upheld a venerable system of marriage exchanges, they explained illness and death and justified compensation being paid out to grieving relatives.'[3] Everyone had an interest in the system. In the 1950s, however, missionaries denounced such thinking as a foolish delusion, telling converted Christians to trust instead divine grace and the sacraments. The missionaries did not understand the unravelling of the social structure which they were advocating. Moreover, the older beliefs did not go away. Instead, 'the god of the Lele had become the Satan of Christian traditions'.[4]

Whereas before they had believed in one God, the universe now was governed by two deities, one good, one bad. And the bad one often seemed to be the most powerful, so by a perverse paradox they remained as strongly as ever convinced of the power of the old religion. The new Christian teaching was not saying, as it had [in the 1950s] that the pagan religion was foolish delusion. It now trashed the old religion as sorcery, its priests as sorcerers, and sorcery as Satan's weapon, a grim menace. Sorcerers were Satan's servants and the people lived in continual fear of attack. And at the same time, everyone, old and young, lived in fear of being accused of sorcery.[5]

The mission priests were worried by the lack of trust and the mutual hate that characterized the lives of their congregation. A mission priest in 1974 started a movement to end this hatred; to the Lele this could only mean that he was going to put an end to sorcery. The missionaries were not issuing threats against sorcerers; their avowed aim was to stop the officiants of the old religion from intimidating villagers by threats. As they had always done, the missionaries rebuked evildoing,

[2] Mary Douglas, 'Sorcery Accusations Unleashed: the Lele Revisited 1987', *Africa*, 69 (1999), 181; the article is reprinted in Richard Fardon (ed.), *Mary Douglas: a Very Personal Method: Anthropological Writings Drawn from Life*, London: Sage, 2013, 79–94.

[3] Ibid., 182.

[4] Ibid., 178.

[5] Ibid., 179.

intimidation and disturbing of the peace. But to the Lele this could only mean that they were issuing counter-threats against sorcerers. Diviners began spontaneously to hand in their oracles, medicine horns and other ritual objects. The mission thought it was making progress, but actually the movement for Christian love was being assimilated in people's thought to the pattern of the old anti-sorcery movements, with the priest as the cult leader. A young priest, a Lele himself and very charismatic, launched a direct attack on sorcerers. He found he had great power for identifying sorcerers and healing by the laying on of hands. The demand for his services was immense. The priest went from one village to another, escorted by his choir, 'a sinister gang of thugs',[6] commanding everyone who possessed the paraphernalia of the old religion to bring it out to be publicly destroyed. Those who were suspected of sorcery were beaten until they confessed.

The priest would come for a few days to a village that had invited him to purge its sorcerers. He made discreet enquiries. When he was ready, everyone passed before him in file, spitting the traditional blessing on chalk. He took these to his house to examine. The next morning, the villagers filed past him again so he could separate the guilty, who were then fenced off in the village square to be beaten and burned till they confessed. Once they had confessed and handed over their instruments of divination, he would exorcise them and undo the harm of their spells. The people rejoiced that Satan was rebuked, God's rule was upheld, and health and prosperity were assured. The priest and choir would then move to another village to repeat the exercise. 'No one said they were paid for their services, but it would be in the anti-sorcery tradition for them to receive a hefty fee.'[7] Douglas experienced great reluctance on the part of villagers, even relatives of those killed, to talk about these events.

When the anti-sorcery activities of the clergy came to the attention of the apostolic nuncio or Vatican representative in Kinshasa, he arranged for the two priests who led the cult to be sent abroad for two years. Officially the incident was closed. But some years later Douglas found that the issue was very much alive. Douglas does not explain this witch-hunting from theories of socio-economic breakdown (though villagers at the time were near destitution), but from rivalry

[6] Ibid., 184.
[7] Ibid., 185.

between a dominant imported religion and the local one it had suppressed. In an aside very relevant for our purposes, she notes that the Catholic Church was in competition with other Christian denominations 'which have clearly defined their doctrines concerning demons in a way that accommodates local sorcery beliefs'.[8]

## Uganda

Heike Behrend has studied the Batooro in Western Uganda. The kingdom of Tooro has experienced several catastrophes since the 1990s: earthquake, the death of the king, guerrilla war, acute economic depression, instability of all sorts, and the AIDS pandemic. Order broke down, with police so corrupt that no justice could be expected from them. The death rates from AIDS brought 'internal terror', and the Hobbesian nightmare of a war of everybody against everybody.[9] In Western Uganda, it is the witch or cannibal who is used to explain the inexplicable.[10] Neither the king, who in pre-colonial times had the duty to cleanse the country from evil, nor the government took effective measure to fight the epidemic of witches and cannibals; it was a lay Catholic movement, the Uganda Martyrs Guild (UMG), that stepped up to deal with this situation of internal terror, using witch hunts to negotiate and restore the moral order.[11] The UMG went beyond the Catholic charismatic movement to concentrate on fighting the demonic powers which they saw as their enemies and as responsible for disease, poverty and death. Many such attempts, right up to the 1980s, were

---

[8] Ibid., 189.

[9] Heike Behrend, *Resurrecting Cannibals: the Catholic Church, Witch-Hunts and the Production of Pagans in Western Uganda*, Woodbridge, Suffolk: James Currey, 2011, 79. Among her other publications on this topic, see Heike Behrend, 'The Rise of Occult Powers, AIDS and the Roman Catholic Church in Western Uganda', *Journal of Religion in Africa*, 37 (2007), 41–58; idem, '"Satan gekreuzigt": Interner Terror und Katharsis in Tororo, Westuganda', *Historische Anthropologie*, 12, 2 (2004), 211–27.

[10] The connection between witches and cannibals is so close (*Resurrecting Cannibals*, 58) that for our purposes here we needn't distinguish them. Behrend's wider argument is that the figure of the 'resurrecting cannibal' draws on both pre-Christian ideas and Catholic doctrines of bodily resurrection and sacramental communion.

[11] Ibid., 81.

not accepted by the Catholic Church, which strongly opposed any fight against witches.

In Tooro, however, against the background of increasing competition between established and independent churches, the Catholic Church changed its attitude towards witchcraft. After having lost several thousands of 'souls' to [independent churches] and to Pentecostal movements, the UMG entered the political arena from the 1990s and started to fight witches and cannibals. By doing so, the UMG enhanced the authority of the Catholic Church, undermined that of her opponents and regained some of the lost believers.[12]

The UMG claimed 10,000 members by 2002.[13] Thus any distinction between the charismatic movement and the UMG became blurred; both demonized the traditional religion. In this they were helped by American Holy Cross priests and sisters, particularly one of the priests who was a principal protagonist of the witch hunts (and later a student of an Indian priest, one of the best known exorcists of the Catholic deliverance world); he fully entered 'a world filled with satanic forces, cannibals, witches and fetishes, a rather paranoid system, and accused even frogs and lizards of being satanic agents'.[14]

The UMG emphasized a new moral order, forbidding drink, cigarettes, discos, corruption, visiting witch doctors, 'satanic practices' and womanizing. They were encouraged to monitor each other, formed self-help groups, collected money so couples could afford church weddings, visited members in prison, assisted each other in building houses and keeping gardens. They attempted to turn the guild into an endogamous group in which men would exchange their daughters and sisters without bride price. Also, they radically transformed the funeral rites, something significant in this time of AIDS-related deaths, abolishing time-consuming and ostentatious ceremonies. Behrend notes that although they avoided the term 'spirit possession' because of its 'pagan' connotations, they effectively transformed their movement according to local spirit possession cults.

The UMG called their witch hunts 'crusades'. Initially these were violent. Behrend was told of one woman identified as a notorious cannibal; when caught by the UMG, it was said, she turned into a cat, was

[12] Ibid., 95.
[13] To give some idea of numbers, in 2006 the diocese of Fort Portal claimed 696,000 Catholics, out of population of 1,486,000; ibid., 130.
[14] Ibid., 104.

beaten and burned, but when turned back into the woman, she was so seriously injured she had to be taken to hospital. Because of this violence, Catholic authorities forbade further crusades. After a lull of two years, they recommenced, but now relying on faith, prayers and healing. Crusades would be prepared by a vigil of prayer. The next morning, members assembled en masse at the village they hoped to cleanse. There they formed teams, made up of people with different gifts: of discernment, deliverance, physical strength (for countering violence), singing, knowledge and revealing. Those with discernment, when approaching a witch or satanic instruments or object, would tremble, fall to the ground, and disclose the satanic object. Children particularly were said to be gifted in this way and became fervent witch hunters. One priest told Behrend of children who on one crusade found fetishes that filled seven pickups (small trucks). Following this event, children started accusing their parents of being witches and cannibals. The priest had to give accommodation in the church to about 100 children, either because they did not want to go home, or because their parents did not wish to have them in the house. (Thus a generational conflict entered into the crusades.) Once the cannibals and witches had been identified, and all their objects and instruments (like cooking pots) collected, they were publicly displayed in front of the church, often photographed and put into albums to show visitors the UMG's power and success. After being displayed and photographed, these objects were burned.

In place of the violence of the first couple of years, now the witches were led to confession and healing. They narrated whom they had eaten, and how and when. Virtually all confessed, to save their lives and return home; Behrend met only one woman who had insisted on her innocence, and had paid for it with ostracism. The revelations extended and reinforced the picture of the occult world. Healing often involved vomiting, or trembling when touched with UMG weapons (like rosaries, crucifixes or holy water). Spirits might refuse to leave their victims, which would require more intense treatment, often leaving the victims exhausted. At the end, the formerly possessed, if allowed by the priest, would attend mass and receive communion.

*Tanzania*

Comoro and Sivalon studied the Marian Faith Healing Ministry (MFHM) of Tanzania, founded by Fr Felician Nkwera, a priest and school inspector who in the early 1970s developed his own prayer services for healing. After some years of uneasy coexistence, in 1980 the Tanzanian Episcopal Conference ordered him to stop these healing services, and in 1990 his own bishop suspended him and ordered him back to his own diocese; Nkwera, however, remained in Dar es Salaam. MFHM members, reputedly about 14,000 in the mid-1990s at the time of their study, have a deep belief in Nkwera, who they believe receives direct revelations from Mary, through whom he has the power to heal. She has revealed to him her requirements of repentance, prayer and holy life. Members provide all sorts of supports to one another. MFHM is also almost unique in that it does not charge fees for its services, something of some importance to the marginalized for whom the movement caters.

Their central ritual is the all-night vigil on the first Saturday of each month in Dar es Salaam. The vigil opens with prayers from the Catholic liturgy of the hours. The second part consists of biblical readings, a lengthy homily, prayers and adoration of the blessed sacrament (since Nkwera's suspension they cannot celebrate the eucharist). During his sermon, he often dialogues with demonic spirits challenging him from the congregation. The third part consists of prayers of exorcism and healing, some taken from the Latin ritual, and a special healing rite for those possessed. People line up to be washed in holy water and have hands laid on them. Assistants control the lines, and cover the women thrashing around on the floor struggling with the demons within; meanwhile, the congregation continues the rosary, singing, and the traditional Catholic devotion of adoration of the blessed sacrament. The final session is a time of testimony when a few witness to the healing they have experienced in the service, often after long and fruitless search elsewhere. There are other shorter services during the week, and followers have various other characteristic items and objects, including a holy oil (a mixture of Christ's blood and tears of Mary), and holy water which serves as protection against the devil and medicine for the sick.

Comoro and Sivalon state that followers stress that theirs is true Catholicism 'and in no way is it a Catholicism that has made an accommodation with African culture'.[15] For them, it revives 'tradi-

---

[15] Christopher Comoro and John Sivalon, 'Marian Faith Healing Ministry', in Thomas Bamat and F. Wiest (eds), *Popular Catholicism in a World Church: Seven Case Studies in Inculturation*, Maryknoll, NY: Orbis, 1998, 169.

tional practices and beliefs of Roman Catholicism against the dominant secularized explanations of Roman Catholicism presented by foreign missioners'.[16] Followers' problems, like sickness, injury, unemployment and marital strife, are 'connected to how one lives one's life, to evil spirits and people's control of these spirits, or to the behavior of ones relatives and friends. This is very similar to a general African understanding of sickness and death as opposed to biomedical theory';[17] indeed, it is 'the same explanation that Roman Catholicism offered before it abandoned that function to science'.[18] Problems of all sorts are seen as ultimately stemming from spiritual forces, and only solvable by conquering them. Nkwera is strong in denouncing the evils of Tanzanian society, even if his remedies are restricted to praying God to conquer the demonic forces responsible. The war with spirits is carried out even within the church, many of whose officials, according to Nkwera's followers, are used by Satan (and indeed, not long after this study was completed the movement was excommunicated).

## Kenya

In the early 1990s, demands grew for an inquiry into satanic activity in Kenya. When the 'Presidential Commission of Inquiry into the Cult of Devil Worship in Kenya' was officially set up, it was broadly welcomed, by Anglican bishops, Catholic bishops and the media.[19] The commission invited both oral and written submissions from interested parties (they eventually gathered 274 such submissions), and travelled round the country holding hearings both in public and in private. They submitted their report in 1995 to President Moi, and although (like so many other Kenyan official reports) it has never been publicly released, in August 1999 it was released to religious leaders, from whom parts of it quickly found their way into Kenya's newspapers.

In the bulk of the report, the commissioners survey the evidence submitted to them, which they arrange into three categories. First there are allegations or hearsay, in which the commission detected recurring motifs: signs and symbols, initiation rites, riches, nakedness, human

---

[16] Ibid., 163.
[17] Ibid., 174.
[18] Ibid., 170.
[19] *Nation*, 23 Oct. 1994, 1; *Nation*, 31 Oct. 1994, 7; *Nation*, 22 Oct. 1994; editorial 'Here is a Most Welcome Probe', *Nation*, 21 Oct. 1994, 6.

sacrifice, eating of human flesh, drinking of human blood, astral travel (often to India), the ability to transform oneself into cats or snakes, and to cause natural disasters like ferry and train accidents. The commissioners found the consistency indicative of some substratum of reality. Then follows what the commission calls 'secondary evidence': three case studies of people who tell of their activities during years spent serving Satan but which could not be independently verified. Then follows 'primary evidence', case studies very similar to those immediately preceding, but this time 'confirmed to be true by independent sources such as Heads of Institutions and pastors who were instrumental in (the former satanists') deliverance and rehabilitation'.[20]

The first of these 'confirmed to be true' cases gives the flavour. A Nyeri schoolgirl was recruited into devil worship when spirits and ghosts took her to their home. The demons made demands on her: that she sacrifice a member of her family, especially the last born (when she refused, the child fell sick); that she have sex with demons (she succumbed to this demand). They also cut her body before rubbing in some substance which gave her mystical powers. These enabled her 'to transform herself into anything' and to cause accidents, in some of which fellow students and staff were injured. She was able to turn herself into a man and enter Masonic temples where she took part in activities. She could also 'communicate with other creatures such as birds, travel to distant places in spirit form and appear/disappear mysteriously'. During seven years of devil worship, she ate human flesh, drank human blood and possessed 'satanic paraphernalia which included blood in powder form, bangles, rings and a knife'. The girl was rescued from the cult when she was 'saved' in 1994, whereupon she entered a Bible school.[21] From copious evidence of this kind, the commission concluded 'that the cult of Devil Worship exists in Kenya both in the learning institutions and the society in general'. The interest for us is that this commission was chaired by a Catholic Archbishop, Nicodemus Kirima of Nyeri.[22]

---

[20] Government of Kenya, *Report of the Presidential Commission of Inquiry into the Cult of Devil Worship in Kenya*, n.d., 41. A pirated version, [John Omino], *Satanism: How the Devil is Trapping God's People*, Nairobi: Pawak Computer Services, 2000, contains much of the *Report*.

[21] Ibid., 56.

[22] And comprised an Anglican bishop, the Moderator of the Presbyterian Church,

It is to be noted that the religious imagination developed in this Kenyan report is much less like that of our previous examples from other African countries, which was the religious imagination traditionally associated with African religious sensibilities, formulated in terms of witchcraft, sorcery, spirit possession, witch-finding.[23] This Kenyan report seems to conflate two worlds, that of the enchanted religious imagination and a form of Christian dualism, and also throws in Western cultism (exemplified in the Church of Satan set up in California in 1967, which the report makes much of). Some key ideas in this report—doorways of satanic entry, intrinsically satanic symbols, rock music as satanic—seem to come from sections (even quite marginal sections) of US Pentecostalism.[24]

## The Catholic Charismatic Movement

Mention should be made here of the Catholic Charismatic Movement. Theoretically, there is a form of Catholic charismaticism that is 'merely' Catholicism with tongues, handclapping, exuberant participation. In some countries such as Ghana and Senegal the charismatic movement seems more or less integrated into church structures. But beneath the surface the fully-fledged enchanted imagination is often lurking. Sometimes we get a glimpse of this—for example, the Nigerian priest and seminary lecturer who, after acknowledging his debt to his bishop, goes on to express his debt to Derek Prince and his wife: 'Their video tape recording on "Release from the Curse" provided the initial

---

the pastor of a large Nairobi church, a professor of religious studies at one of Kenya's universities, a chaplain of a national school, a prominent lawyer and a senior police officer.

[23] Revealingly, some comment on the Kenyan report in neighbouring Uganda argued that in Uganda, by contrast, child sacrifice (of which over 20 cases were reported in the first eight months of 1999 alone) is still linked to witchcraft, not organized Satanism (*Sunday Vision*, 22 Aug. 1999, 13).

[24] The sources cursorily cited in this report would support this impression. The bibliography is a mixture of new age, Freemasonry, the Bhagavadgita, the occult, Time-Life books, the *Book of Mormon* and Shirley Maclaine. Archbishop Milingo, too, had become firmly linked to the Western charismatic movement before he began formulating his accounts of possession and deliverance; see e.g., Emmanuel Milingo, *Face to Face with the Devil*, Broadford, Victoria: Scripture Keyes Ministries, 1991.

ENCHANTED CATHOLICISM

tonic I needed to write this book. Their format helped me to put together more clearly what I had been doing in an unclear manner.'[25] Derek Prince, although a controversial and even marginal figure in North American Pentecostalism, has been extremely influential in African Pentecostalism.[26] In 1996 the Catholic Bishops Conference of Ghana issued guidelines for deliverance ministries. The bishops admitted that deliverance was part of Christ's ministry, but noted that 'both wise pastoral guidance and discernment of spirits are absolute requirements'. They distinguished prayers of deliverance (for 'something more than ordinary temptation and less than the total control found in full possession') from exorcism. 'Silent prayers of deliverance can be offered by every Christian'; vocal prayer for deliverance was to be done by a team recognized by the bishop: 'Exorcism is the power received through ordination'. The bishops continued: 'Excessive preoccupation with the demonic and indiscriminate exercise of deliverance ministries are based upon a distortion of biblical evidence and are pastorally harmful'. Prayer for deliverance is one aspect of a total healing ministry ('medical, psychological, social, spiritual'). 'Various approaches to the deliverance ministries are still evolving and publications are available representing the [various] perspectives.'[27]

Subsequently, Ghana's Catholic Charismatic Renewal produced its own manual. The manual itself lists its sources: canon law, the Catholic ritual and sacramental, 'Pope Paul IV's encyclical on the devil' (probably Paul VI's address 'Confronting the Devil's Power' of 15 November 1972), and Cardinal Ratzinger's 1975 'Report on the Situation of the World'. It also notes the need not to trespass on the preserve of the ordained clergy, and to use priests wherever available. But the manual reveals the full enchanted imagination. Traditional practices are dangerous: libations invite spirits, water gods, fetishes, stools (powers) and demons into one's life; rites to protect children constitute blood covenants; cultural dances bring people under the

[25] Stephen Uche Njoku, *Curses: Effects and Release*, Enugu: Christian Living Publications, 1993, iv.

[26] Paul Gifford, *African Christianity: its Public Role*, London: Hurst, 1998, 101–08.

[27] Cited in Catholic Charismatic Renewal, *Healing and Deliverance Training Manual*, Kumasi: CCR, 1996.

119

influence of the spirits, gods, and deities they invoke. Questionnaires (about incisions, frequenting spiritual churches, dreams, gifts received, inheritances and the like) are used to identify the spirits responsible for problems. Ancestors are the source of curses and covenants. Witchcraft can be inherited, or acquired through dreams, food, accepting jewellery from unknown people and the like. So this manual has sharpened the restraint of the bishops' original guidelines into the complete enchanted worldview of Olukoya. And this worldview seems difficult to constrain within Catholic structures; indeed Ghana has several fully-blown Pentecostal churches which developed out of the Catholic charismatic sector.

A *Novena of Spiritual Protection and Liberation: Prayers against Occult Attacks and the Evils of Witchcraft and Esoterism*, from the director of the Catholic Charismatic Renewal in Benin, marshals all the usual sources of evils, even adding some more: satanic rituals, fetishes, masks, amulets, talismans, witches, hypnosis, divination, clairvoyance, witches and people invoking spirits and pagan divinities of the sea, land, air or fire, spirits of the dead, new age sects or esoteric orders (Freemasons, Rosicrucians), Eastern religions, Scientology, Zen meditation, or *marabouts*, astrologers and gurus. Against them it marshals the entire Catholic apparatus, including rosaries and litanies. Devotions from Francophone West Africa like this novena have gone the furthest in Catholicizing the enchanted worldview. Another *Novena and Prayers to St Michael and the Assembled Nine Choirs of Angels* gives the flavour perfectly. Again, we have the panoply of Catholic sources: Leo XIII (an exorcism of Satan and the rebellious angels), Mary Queen of Angels, the Archangels Raphael, Michael and Gabriel, St Gerard Magella, traditional Catholic prayers, litanies of the angels. Indulgences attached to the prayers and litanies are listed. This particular novena seems to be attributed to a Boudouin, Archdeacon of Evreux. All the heavenly forces are invoked: Seraphim, Cherubim, Thrones, Dominations, Powers, Virtues, Principalities. Other devotions are of the same kind: *A Novena to the Archangel Raphael for Spiritual Protection* includes a rosary of the angels (said to have been approved by Pope Pius IX in 1877). *Praying with St Michael, St Benedict and St Gerard, the Holy Spirit and the Virgin Mary for Spiritual Warfare* has the same litanies and prayers invoking all the heavenly hosts to combat the myriad forces of darkness. French and Canadian influences are sometimes detectable beneath the surface, with prayers of Père Emilien Tardif,

Père Louis-Edouard Cestac and Chanoine Guerinel included. These practices represent a genuine attempt to cater for the enchanted imagination from a traditional Catholic perspective, but they seem promoted by individual priests (often mavericks) with little support from the hierarchy.[28]

In Kenya in 2007, soon after becoming Archbishop of Nairobi, Cardinal Njue banned the Catholic Charismatic Movement. His dilemma was that the Catholic Charismatic Movement normally seems a stage on the way to fully-fledged Pentecostalism of Olukoya's kind rather than a way of situating this enchanted vision within Catholicism. Indeed, the official Catholic Church sees no place for this vision; the Catholic explanation of evil is of another order altogether. The official rejection of the enchanted understanding of evil reached a climax in September 2000 when the Vatican issued an instruction regularizing healing services in the Catholic Church.[29] This instruction was widely seen as prompted by the activities of Archbishop Milingo.

## Conclusion

Pentecostal denunciations of Catholicism are nowhere near as frequent as twenty years ago—probably because Pentecostals realize that in most countries the Catholics are simply too strong to antagonize gratuitously—but Catholic antagonism to Pentecostalism is still widespread. The Catholic Church in Angola is not alone in agitating to curb the proliferation of Pentecostal churches—in Angola on the grounds that they are 'taking advantage of the poverty and ignorance of citizens by preaching a supposed salvation by "miracles"'.[30] I was an accredited press correspondent at both Synods of Bishops for Africa, in 1994 and

---

[28] *Neuvaine de protection spirituelle et de libération: prières contre les attaques occultes et les maléfices de la sorcellerie et de l'ésoterisme, présentées par Jean Pliya*, Cotonou: no date, but 7th *version définitive* was on sale in Popenguine, Senegal, in June 2012; *Neuvaine et prières à Saint Michel et aux neuf choeurs des anges réunies*, npd; *Neuvaine à l'archange Raphael pour la protection spirituelle*, npd; *Prier avec Saint Michel, Saint Benoît, Saint Gérard, l'Esprit Saint et la Vierge Marie pour le combat spirituel*, npd; the last three on sale at cathedral book depot, Ouagadougou, Burkina Faso, March 2013.

[29] Congregation for Divine Worship, *Instruction on Prayer for Healing*, dated 14 Sept. 2000.

[30] CISA, 35, 17 June 2011.

2009. It seemed to me that at both events many bishops' interventions on Pentecostalism did little but denounce 'the sects', even seeing them as part of a concerted attack on Catholicism. The fact that these Pentecostal churches are addressing deeply felt needs that Catholicism fails to address seemed entirely missed. Some of this ignorance of Pentecostalism seemed disingenuous; many of these bishops have family members who have left Catholicism to join Pentecostal churches. The bishops simply seemed unwilling—in Rome—to admit the existence of the enchanted religious imagination.

The two forms of Christianity function with little formal contact. Africa has had one well-known case of cooperation between the two: the Christian Association of Nigeria (CAN), founded in 1976 and representing all Nigeria's Christian groupings—the Catholic Secretariat, the Christian Council, the Pentecostal Fellowship of Nigeria, the Evangelical Fellowship of West Africa, and the Organisation of African Instituted Churches. But in 2010 the Pentecostal Ayo Oritsejafor won a contested election for CAN president. The Catholic bishops became increasingly uncomfortable with him, accusing him of politicizing the CAN, and were uneasy about his personal opulence (his Christianity is not very different from Oyedepo's), especially when in November 2012 Oritsejafor received a multi-million dollar private jet 'from unnamed members of his church'. The Catholic bishops even hinted that behind the gift was President Goodluck Jonathan, from the same ethnic group as Oritsejafor, and building up much-needed support for a reelection bid in 2015. The bishops also favoured dialogue with the militant Islamists Boko Haram, while Oritsejafor (with President Jonathan) favoured a military solution. In early 2013 the Catholic bishops made public the indefinite suspension of their membership of CAN. Oritsejafor's defenders claim the Catholics are simply unable to operate under any leadership but their own.

Official Catholicism is very wary of enchanted Christianity wherever it is found. As mentioned above, Archbishop Milingo was removed to Rome. Even there his activity was circumscribed; Cardinal Carlo Martini, Archbishop of Milan, banned him from holding services in the Milan archdiocese, precisely because of fears that he might encourage a 'credulity which explains all psycho-physical ills as due to the influence of the devil, and lead people to expect exorcism, healings and miracles'.[31]

---

[31] *Tablet*, 20 April 1996, 525.

The priests performing witch-hunts in Zaire were transferred to Rome. Tanzania's Marian Faith Healing Ministry was eventually excommunicated. In their study of this Marian Ministry, Comoro and Sivalon reinforce the point made above in presenting contemporary Catholicism: whereas it is sometimes claimed that Vatican II was opening up to all cultures, in fact Vatican II was bringing Catholicism into line with the modern, Western world.

The worldview and cosmology of pre-Vatican II Roman Catholicism were in fact an inculturated understanding based on a culture and consciousness very similar to traditional African culture. Vatican II, while marking an opening up to the world, was in fact opening up to a world, worldview and culture of modernity that are quite different from African culture. As the church accommodated itself to scientific and secularised culture it moved dramatically away from the cultures of indigenous people around the world.[32]

Similarly, in his widely acclaimed study of the Second Vatican Council, O'Malley makes every effort to find a global significance for the council. But his claim that at the council the Catholic Church showed itself 'ready to appropriate non-superstitious aspects of different cultural traditions' reveals just how Western the council's agenda was. For those operating from an enchanted religious imagination, there is nothing 'superstitious' about pervasive spiritual forces; they are reality.

It may be thought that Hebga's case constitutes something of an exception. He was permitted to operate relatively unchecked. But special factors worked in his favour. Unlike Milingo, Hebga was not the official leader of the church in the country. Above all, he possessed a considerably high profile, being one of the original African priests contributing to *Des Prêtres noirs s'interrogent*, which is often hailed as the first assertion by African Catholics of the right to express an African Christianity.[33] He was a Jesuit, with the protection of a powerful order. He had a doctorate from the Sorbonne, and was a professor at the University of Yaounde until he retired in 1999, and furthermore was revered as one of the pioneers of Cameroonian philosophy. He had written scholarly articles in progressive theological journals like *Concilium*, and since his whole agenda was to validate African ways before the world, muzzling him would have caused enormous prob-

---

[32] Comoro and Sivalon, 'Tanzania: Marian Faith Healing Ministry', 170.

[33] Meinrad Hebga, 'Christianisme et négritude', in A. Abble *et al, Des Prêtres noirs s'interrogent*, Paris: Editions de Clef, 2nd ed, 1957, 202–23.

lems. He had sizeable support, not least from clergy and religious (even if their support was mainly by night). Although operating totally from an enchanted viewpoint, he went out of his way to distance himself from Pentecostalism and claim a middle way: he discounted speaking in tongues, and insisted that not everything could be attributed to witchcraft. He made enormous efforts to Catholicize his movement: his emphasis was on the crucifix in diagnosing witches, and on the use of sacramentals (holy water, salt, oil) in cures. He used traditional Catholic prayers, and promoted devotion to Mary. Yet he identified demons by name, broke ancestral curses, reversed curses and healed AIDS. Therein lies the problem. His movement represents exactly what official Catholicism does not want.

Mary Douglas, having reluctantly publicized the witch-hunting among the Lele, spelt out her considered position on Christian conceptions of evil. Let this introduce our next chapter, for what Douglas advocated is *exactly what has not happened*:

For the Catholic Church, with its coordinated and centralized doctrines, there is a problem. Doctrines about sin and evil are not minor, peripheral matters. On such a central issue the church in the industrial West is isolated. It does not believe in the devil. Should it, can it impose its historically unique view, peculiar to certain intellectual circles in the West, upon the rest of the Church? Trying to talk to African philosophers and theologians about the place of sorcery beliefs in Christianity, I received the strong impression that the subject was delicate. They are very aware of the disbelief of their fellow Christians from the West. They do not want to quarrel or expose themselves to ridicule, so their ways of dealing with the devil are driven underground. A frank discussion of sorcery and satanism is only just beginning to emerge.

My personal view is that the Third World theologians should take up these problems without regard to the contemporary bias of Western theology... The teaching on evil will come from Africa, and that is what Africanisation will mean.[34]

---

[34] Mary Douglas, 'The Devil Vanishes', *Tablet*, 28 April 1990, 514; reprinted in Fardon (ed.), *Mary Douglas*, 95–9.

# 8

# AFRICAN CATHOLIC THEOLOGY

The most incisive overview of African theology is that by Paul Bowers whose analysis will provide the structure for this chapter. According to Bowers, the most traumatic event in African history was its encounter with the West, which led not only to a loss of political control, but also to a damaged self-understanding. Thus Independent Africa's preoccupations have been to resist continued Western economic domination and assert African identity vis-à-vis the West, especially by affirming its identity with Africa's traditional heritage and resisting Western intellectual hegemony. In the last half of the twentieth century this issue of African authenticity and self-reliance, coupled with a comprehensive critique of the West and its role in Africa, has been the principal dynamic of Africa's intellectual life in all fields—theology included.[1]

## Inculturation

Here lies the rationale for the emphasis on inculturation. The original thrust was mainly pastoral, and related to externals—particularly liturgy. There have been many successes. The Bethlehem mission of Serima in Zimbabwe pioneered carvings depicting biblical and religious themes in African forms. The abbey of Keur Moussa in Senegal

[1] Paul Bowers, 'African Theology: its History, Dynamics, Scope and Future', *Africa Journal of Evangelical Theology*, 21, 2 (2002), 109–25.

is renowned for its wedding of Gregorian chant to the *kora*, the local string instrument. The Swahili hymnbook in East Africa is a similar attempt to indigenize church music. The most famous case of all is the Zairean rite of the Mass, approved by Rome in 1988; in this rite, African rituals, symbols and dance were thoroughly incorporated.

However, there is a programme of inculturation in a hard sense that African theologians have made their own. Inculturation theology starts from the premise that Africans have been despised and exploited from the time of the slave trade and then colonialism. Through greed the West plundered the continent, but cultural annihilation was even worse; for Western contempt damaged the African soul. Kanyandago expresses it thus: 'The African has been hurt and humiliated in what constitutes his/her world and system of values, especially his/her symbolic structure... This has led to psychological and social alienation expressed in all forms of self-denial by Africans as they express and live hatred for what is African because this is perceived as primitive and backward. This is the worst form of poverty because it attacks the African in what makes him/her African; this is anthropological poverty'.[2] And Tarimo says:

For centuries, African cultures have been systematically regarded as primitive and inferior by Western civilisation. It was assumed that Africans had no culture, religion, thinking capacity, or civilization. Others went as far as saying Africans had no soul. This attitude was basically motivated by ignorance, prejudice and the desire to dominate others for economic gain. Under the influence of this experience, an inferiority complex has been internalised and made a part of African identity. On the international scene, Africa has become synonymous with diseases, political chaos and socio-cultural backwardness. In order to change this image, we have to develop a critical understanding of African cultures beyond racist prejudices, colonial contempt, and fatalism.[3]

Africans now must reverse their situation by rediscovering their culture and standing tall as Africans.

Particularly to be repudiated is the claim that missionaries 'brought God to Africa'. God was present in African cultures before missionar-

---

[2] Peter Kanyandago, 'Rich but Rendered Poor: a Christian Response to the Paradox of Poverty in Africa', in Peter Kanyandago (ed.), *The Cries of the Poor in Africa: Questions and Responses for African Christianity*, Kisubi: Marianum Publishing, 2002, 50.

[3] Aquiline Tarimo, *Applied Ethics and Africa's Social Reconstruction*, Nairobi: Acton, 2005, 7.

ies came. Thus Mutabazi: 'Inculturation requires the acceptance of the fact that God has been at work in the history of all peoples and that their history is sacred. Culture is the sacred space of people. Hence any agent of inculturation has to discern the presence of God within these traditions and cultures.'[4] Kanyandago expresses this even more forcefully: 'God manifests him/herself in each human being, society and culture... The negation of the unique mission of Africa, as one can appreciate, has very serious theological implications. Tampering with Africa means tampering with humanity and therefore tampering with God.'[5]

However, this theological project of inculturation raises enormous questions. First, making culture the beginning and end, the fulcrum on which the theology turns, seems to leave much unexamined. For example, what exactly is African culture? In cases of disagreement, who would decide? Does it solve the problem by reserving the decision to 'only those with a genuine African outlook'?[6] Who would decide that? And where do we look for this African culture? In many of Africa's huge informal settlements, what would most naturally be regarded as culture (even language) seems fast disappearing.

Above all, this determination to celebrate African culture can lead to some very idealized presentations. Theuri provides a good example:

African development was holistic and inclusive, it was always guided by fundamental values of generosity, solidarity and hospitality to all... Everyone was 'equal' to each other; resources were well and equally distributed among all. The sick, the orphaned, the widows, the Africans lived in the model that is only reflective of the Early Church... African communities practised more or less what the early church practised (Acts 4, 1–3). Bearing this argument in mind, one can say with certainty that Africa was developed in all aspects of life... Everyone did what was best for the community regardless of their personal gains... The African traditional system thus seems in many ways to be the ideal one.[7]

Often the contrast is made explicitly: Western culture is bad, African culture is good. Juvenalis Baitu, Professor of Moral Theology and

---

[4] Emmanuel Mutabazi, 'Process and Method in the Theology of Inculturation', in Patrick Ryan (ed.), *Theology of Inculturation in Africa Today: Methods, Praxis and Mission*, Nairobi: CUEA, 2004, 63; 'Every authentic culture is, in fact, in its own way a bearer of the universal values established by God', ibid., 64.

[5] Kanyandago, 'Rich but Rendered Poor', 47–9.

[6] Mutabazi, 'Process and Method', 74.

[7] Matthew M. Theuri, 'Religion and Culture', in Mary N. Getui and Matthew M. Theuri (eds), *Quests for Abundant Life in Africa*, Nairobi: Acton, 2002, 193f.

Director, Centre for the Social Teaching of the Church at the Catholic University of Eastern Africa, laments that Africa's media now 'mostly reflect the interests, problems, values and ideals of Euro-American societies with its (their?) sexual mores, organised crime, violence, drug addiction, alcoholism, romance, immoral attitudes, practices and behavioural patterns'. These Western influences 'have distorted *the right understanding* of moral demands in the areas of human sexuality, the family, social, political, economic, cultural and religious life as conceived by traditional African societies'.[8] Any deficiencies in Africa must arise from Western influence:

Most of the manifestations of this violence cannot be traced in African traditional societies. With all proper proportions guarded, one can say that the following are not 'African' problems: modern forms of torture; imperialism and colonialism; slave trade, exploitative economic systems; exploitation of workers; abuse of addictive substances; racism and apartheid; urbanisation and its tandems including slums, crime, anonymity. One can include prostitution, beggary, discriminative, irrelevant and expensive education, and inappropriate political systems which produce corruption and oppression.[9]

Magesa sees Western involvement as the cause of Africa's problems, as a result of which 'conflict—*once unknown in Africa*—has now become perhaps one of the greatest sources of Africa's suffering'.[10]

In fact, many admit the necessity of change, and many admit that some aspects of African culture (like the inheritance of his widow by the dead husband's brother in a time of AIDS) are dysfunctional.[11] Yet they give few criteria for distinguishing valid aspects of African culture from dysfunctional ones—normally it is 'African culture' itself that is privileged.[12] Nor has Tarimo avoided these difficulties by talking of

---

[8] Juvenalis Baitu, 'The Moral Crisis in Contemporary Africa', *AFER*, 45, 3 (2003), 248–62, citations from 256, 260, italics added.

[9] Peter Kanyandago, 'Violence in Africa: a Search for Causes and Remedies', in Mary N. Getui and Peter Kanyandago (eds), *From Violence to Peace: a Challenge for African Christianity*, Nairobi: Acton, 2003, 10.

[10] Laurenti Magesa, 'African Renaissance: the Jubilee and Africa's Position in the International Context', in Peter Kanyandago (ed.), *Marginalised Africa: an International Perspective*, Nairobi: Paulines, 2002, 15, italics added.

[11] e.g. Laurenti Magesa, *Anatomy of Inculturation: Transforming the Church in Africa*, Maryknoll, NY: Orbis, 2004, 197, 256.

[12] Tarimo deals at length with both tribalism and the extended family (*Applied Ethics*, 65–76 and 162–86 respectively); in both he finds things to praise and to

'reformulated', 're-appropriated' or 'reformed' cultural traditions.[13] Again, what constitutes a reformulated culture, and who decides?

The one thing this inculturation theology does not address is the enchanted worldview of spiritual forces and spiritual causality, which on the face of it might be thought the first requirement of inculturation. This is the very issue Mary Douglas urged African theologians to address, as we noted at the end of the last chapter. Her remarks suggest why they don't. African theologians, with their priority of asserting African culture, are determined not to draw attention to witches and spells that the West dismisses as superstition. One of the few to address this issue is Malawi's Patrick Kalilombe.[14] He insists that this primal imagination is precisely the area inculturation must address. It is because this world-view is ignored that ordinary people have little interest in the writings of the theologians.

According to Kalilombe, the people are not caught up in this celebration of Africanness on the part of the intellectuals: 'In the total culture change in which they are engaged, [many expressions of traditional culture] are areas which they would very gladly do away with. They would make other choices, like the more "Europeanised" forms, because for them this represents their wish for "development" and change. In those areas they are opting for modernity. The way we [namely, theologians] are promoting "traditional" forms is such as to valorize regressive values; return to a past that demonstrated our incapacity to move forward with the times.'[15]

It is the insistence on the equality of cultures that is the problem. In many respects such an insistence obscures what is really happening in Africa. Gellner argues that to talk about equality of cultures not only

---

fault; on what score is never made clear. Ngona reminds us that Vatican II (*Ad Gentes*, 19) speaks of '*healthy* customs of the locality'. But who decides what a healthy custom is? (Dieudonné Ngona, 'Theology of Inculturation in Africa Today', in Ryan, *Theology*, 19).

[13] Tarimo, *Applied Ethics*, 27, 179.

[14] Kalilombe, 'Praxis and Methods of Inculturation in Africa', in Ryan (ed.), *Theology*, 38–48.

[15] Ibid., 44. 'Cultural change... results from choices that people themselves make when confronted with new options. They are the ones who should decide what to retain from the past and what to adopt from among the new options, taking into account what they want the configuration of their new way of life to be like' (ibid., 48).

fails to address the problem; it is simple unwillingness to face the central fact of our time. In his words, the 'hermeneutically formulated doctrine of symmetry (of cultures)... makes any realistic thought impossible'.[16] In a similar way, I argue here that this stress on cultural equivalence makes thinking about global Catholicism and particularly its African involvement impossible. The Catholic Church, despite its missiological theory and theological stress on inculturation, is thoroughly involved in modifying Africa's cultures. The Catholic Church is best known in Africa for its involvement in education, including teaching physics and chemistry. Then for its health involvement, in introducing antibiotics, primary health schemes, maternal care, preventive medicine, modern sanitation. It is widely involved in development schemes of all kinds, from introducing insecticides and fertilizers to promoting food security, water harvesting, crop rotation, separation of powers, human rights and freedoms, and rule of law. If this is not cultural modification, what is? 'Cultural modification' describes this activity better than talk of imposing one culture on another, because the realities which are the aim of this activity are not essential to 'Western culture' as though they are part of the DNA of Europeans, for they have been associated with the West for only a relatively short time and are still clearly a work-in-progress. They arose as a result of the scientific revolution of very recent centuries. Rather than being Western impositions, they are characteristics of the modern world, and necessary for any nation wishing to join it. So, given the Catholic Church's involvement in development, any simple appeal to the equality of all cultures is rather misleading. Foregrounding African culture and its untouchability, as so much contemporary African Catholic theology does, prevents us both from admitting what is actually happening, and recognizing the issues to be considered.

Christopher Clapham has well observed: 'It is not only the Western mindset on Africa that needs to be decolonized, but also the African one: the grand project of Africa's intellectual elite has overwhelmingly been to avoid responsibility for the problems of African development, rather than devise means (other than a jejune revolutionary socialism) through which they might be overcome. The lesson both of Asia and

---

[16] Ernest Gellner, *Postmodernism, Reason and Religion*, London: Routledge, 1992, 62.

Latin America is that the path to change begins in the minds of its indigenous thinkers.'[17]

*Political involvement*

Bowers captures the dynamics here perfectly:

From the mid-1970s onward, African theology increasingly included a political theology of liberation as part of its agenda. Unlike Black theology in South Africa, for the most part this has not attended to forces of oppression within Africa, but has rather addressed the Western political and economic exploitation of Africa. While African church leadership, especially in eastern and southern Africa and not least within Roman Catholic circles has often found it necessary to speak against the injustice and repression practised by various African governments since independence, little of this has been reflected in theological discussion.[18]

Bishops have denounced abuses on the part of African leaders, but to the extent that theology has addressed liberation, the liberation envisaged is from Western oppression. African theologians tend to focus on external causes of Africa's situation. They denounce institutions like the World Bank and the IMF for crippling Africa with 'their neo-classical death-dealing economic theories'.[19] Globalization too: 'a continuation of Western imperialism that goes back to the slave trade'.[20] The intellectuals—including the theologians, philosophers and ethicists—denounce the external forces deemed responsible for Africa's ills.

In passing, we can mention one much celebrated aspect of Latin America's liberation theology, its 'conscientizing' of ordinary people. From Sierra Leone to Kenya, Nigeria to Zimbabwe, one can find DELTA (Development, Education, and Leadership teams in Action) grassroots programmes of empowerment. The standard programme, with a social analysis component, consisting of workshops spread over two years, integrates several major streams: Paulo Freire's work on critical awareness, human relations training in group work, organizational development, social analysis, and the Christian concept of transformation with application to literacy, agriculture, health, manage-

[17] Christopher Clapham reviewing Stephen Ellis, *Season of Rains: Africa in the World*, London: Hurst, 2011, in *International Affairs* 87, 6 (2011), 1548.

[18] Bowers, 'African Theology', 119f.

[19] Ilo, *Church and Development*, 189.

[20] Ibid., 184.

ment, family and social spheres, and small Christian groups.[21] At one stage in Kenya, this involved 50,000 participants, but it is again revealing that in the repressive atmosphere after Kenya's attempted coup in 1982, the Catholic bishops phased out the programme in what can only be called a great failure of nerve. Such programmes do exist in Africa, but they are hardly representative of Africa's Catholic Church.

As already noted, injustice and oppression have been denounced by church leaders. In discussing the political intervention of the hierarchy, it is helpful to distinguish time periods and the mode of involvement. In the period leading up to the independence of most African countries, the early 1960s, no mission churches were distinguished for their support for nationalist movements. If anything, they were rather supportive of the colonial enterprise and apprehensive of nationalist aims. Complicating this was the fear of communism, even in the diluted form of African socialism which was espoused by some nationalists. This, of course, was before liberation theology as a conscious activity emerged in Latin America.

In those countries that came to a delayed independence (namely the Portuguese colonies, Zimbabwe and South Africa), the picture was more mixed. Independence came after armed struggles which required the church to take sides, and after the word 'liberation' had entered the church lexicon as a legitimate topic for religious debate.[22]

In the Portuguese cases, the Catholic Church was heavily compromised on the side of Portugal, through Concordats which gave the church enormous privileges (not least the salary of a state governor for each bishop) in return for support for Portuguese colonial aims. By contrast, it was the Protestant churches which were associated with the anti-colonial struggle. This did not forestall some Catholic sympathy for those fighting for independence; the White Fathers chose to leave Mozambique altogether rather than be co-opted on the side of Portugal, publicly denouncing the official Catholic stance as they departed.

In Zimbabwe, by the time of independence in 1980, the Catholic Church was identified with the liberation struggle. The official support

---

[21] Anne Hope and Sally Timmel, *Training for Transformation; a Handbook for Community Workers*, Gweru: Mambo Press, 1984.

[22] The word liberation appeared for the first time in a papal document in Paul VI's *Evangelii Nuntiandi* in 1975; Tristan Anne Borer, *Challenging the State: Churches as Political Actors in South Africa 1980–1994*, Notre Dame, IN: University of Notre Dame Press, 1998, 86.

was gradual, even reluctant. Bishop Donal Lamont of Umtali who was tried, convicted and deported for refusing to report rebel activity to the authorities was as anti-communist as the white regime; it was precisely because he felt that the white government was driving the Blacks into the communist camp that he opposed it. Again, mirroring the non-monolithic nature of the church, the Catholic Commission for Justice and Peace was heroically committed to the struggle for African rights, which enabled the official church both to keep its distance and (rather opportunistically) to take credit when the struggle was won. After independence, the Catholic Church attempted to maintain a critical voice, but its efforts in 1984 to publicize the repression in Matabeleland drew the full ire of Mugabe and his government. Ever since, the Church has had difficulty relating to power, even after Mugabe's descent after 2000 into full wrecking mode. The church was compromised by its officiating at the lavish celebration of Mugabe's second marriage, and, despite the much-publicized opposition of Pius Ncube, at the time Archbishop of Bulawayo, there were others, like the Jesuit provincial superior, who were identified as very close to Mugabe.[23] The most that can be said is that the official Catholic witness in Zimbabwe's post-2000 collapse has been very mixed.

In apartheid South Africa, the Catholic Church was very expatriate, comparatively small, and hindered by its very marginalized relations with the government, quintessentially of Dutch Reformed faith. The Catholic bishops were, by the end, identified with the fight against apartheid, with Archbishop Denis Hurley of Durban the symbol of this involvement. Their support was hardly radical—especially by comparison with the South African Council of Churches (SACC), the umbrella body of the mainline Protestants. However, as Borer has shown, a support which is less radical but promoted more consistently is not unimportant.[24] Again, subsidiary Catholic bodies came to be far more involved, not least the Institute of Contextual Theology associated with the Dominican priest Albert Nolan, which was the dominant force behind the Kairos Document, produced by grassroots pastors in Soweto, which came to be the classic text of African liberation

---

[23] Heidi Holland, *Dinner With Mugabe: the Untold Story of a Freedom Fighter who became a Tyrant*, London: Penguin, 2008, 126–44, in a chapter entitled 'The Faithful Priest'.

[24] Borer, *Challenging the State*.

theology.[25] Since the end of apartheid, the Catholic Church has attempted to give prophetic guidance, but (as in Zimbabwe) has been forced to the margins by a triumphant liberation movement enjoying overwhelming support.[26]

In general, after Independence, Africa's Catholic Church, which had been so identified with colonization and often reminded of its 'lack of legitimacy' by new governments, quietly turned its attention to indigenizing its personnel and institutions, and was not prominent in the public sphere. However, by the fall of the Berlin Wall in 1989, most African governments, often dysfunctional one-party despotisms, had run their countries into chaos and penury. It surprised everyone that, at this hour of need, so many Francophone countries turned to Catholic bishops to chair the national conferences called to chart a way forward: Gabon, Congo, Benin, Togo and Zaire all had Catholic prelates presiding over these assemblies, and Cameroon would have had one also if President Paul Biya had not managed to forestall any such conference. It should be noted that the Catholic bishops, almost *faute de mieux*, were asked because of their moral authority, not because they were associated with any liberation theology.

At the same time, in Anglophone countries too, the Catholic Church was intervening publicly, most spectacularly in Malawi. On 8 March 1992, the Catholic bishops of Malawi issued a Lenten pastoral letter, 'Living our Faith', which though praising the government for several achievements drew attention to Malawi's public corruption, growing social inequalities and abuses of human rights. In the fiercely repressive Malawi, ruled since independence in 1964 by the despotic

---

[25] Kairos Document: *Challenge to the Church: a Theological Comment on the Political Crisis in South Africa*, Braamfontein: the Kairos Theologians, 1985.

[26] Cochrane, comparing the SACC and the Southern African Catholic Bishops Conference (SACBC), notes that the SACBC is much better equipped to contribute to government consultations. On a consultation on euthanasia, for example, 'The SACBC representative was intimately acquainted with both the law, the technologies of euthanasia, and the nuances of his own tradition in this regard'. 'This signals a larger reality, namely the ability of the Roman Catholic Church to draw into the public sphere a powerful apparatus of international reach and great sophistication, compared to the relative weakness of the ecumenical movement, at least in South Africa' (James R. Cochrane, 'Reframing the Political Economy of the Sacred: Readings of Post Apartheid Christianity', in Klaus Koschorke (ed.), *Falling Walls: the Year 1989 as a Turning Point in the History of World Christianity*, Wiesbaden: Harrassowitz Verlag, 2009, 100f).

Hastings Banda, this was the first public criticism of authority for decades. As the letter was read, it was reported that congregations broke into applause. The culture of fear was broken. Within days students were demonstrating, and unions had called strikes. Before long, pressure built up forcing a referendum on a one-party state; Banda lost that referendum, and in the election in 1994 was voted out of office.

Almost simultaneously, on 23 March 1992, the Catholic bishops of Kenya issued a pastoral letter called 'A Call to Justice, Love and Peace'. The immediate context was an outbreak of looting, killing and arson in western Kenya which in the space of five months had left sixty-five dead. The government called these 'ethnic clashes', but the bishops denied that the clashes were ethnic, accused the government of complicity (to 'prove' that Kenya could not handle a multi-party system), accused the security services of bias, and called for the arrest of the politicians responsible for fomenting the unrest. President Moi had succeeded Kenyatta in 1978; since 1983 his Kenya African National Union (KANU) had been the only legal party. Government had been inept, oppressive, and corrupt. For some years there had been calls for reform, mainly from lawyers and outspoken individual Protestant clerics, but these were easily silenced. The Catholic Church, united, could not be dismissed so easily. I stood in the huge crowd that day as the bishops took turns to read out their letter on the steps of the Holy Family Basilica, almost directly facing the huge KANU headquarters only a few hundred yards away. I could not help thinking that this could be seen as something of a confrontation between the political Big Men and the religious Big Men, the former largely discredited, the latter enjoying considerable moral authority. In this regard, it was significant that when at the end of the pastoral letter, the names of the eighteen bishops were read out, each was greeted with a spontaneous round of applause. The church increased its demands over the next months. Moi was forced to allow multi-party elections, although a skilful manipulation of the opposition kept him in power until 2002.

Such interventions in matters of public concern do not all belong to the past. Burkina Faso in 2013 was split by a proposal to introduce a legislative upper chamber or senate. Since the members of this senate were to be nominated by the president, this was widely seen as a way for President Blaise Compaore to engineer a constitutional change permitting him yet another term in 2015. The bishops entered the fray in a letter which rehearsed the plight of the nation: ranked 183rd of 187 countries on the UNDP's index of human development; with 32 per cent literacy in 2012; with two fifths of the country living on less than 50 US cents a day. The bishops decried the social effects resulting from a situation in which youth became marginalized and disillusioned while the elite became ostentatiously wealthier. In the light of this, the bishops failed to see the value of the proposed and enormously costly new senate.[27] This remarkably unconfrontational document was rightly understood as a strong stand against an ongoing Compaore presidency.

There is no need for further examples; these are sufficient to show that Catholic leaders have spoken out against oppressive regimes, often with courage and tenacity.[28] However, before claims are made that the Catholic Church has been 'the conscience of the nation', some caveats are in order. Pastoral letters usually remain at a level of considerable generality; more recently in Kenya, for example: 'Let us once and for all remove all semblance of corruption from Kenya', or 'Selfishness and greed must stop... The rule of law and order must be upheld.'[29] General exhortations to avoid corruption and promote justice have come to be seen as rather hollow, almost evasions. No names are mentioned, and specifics avoided. Some statements are remarkable in what they manage to ignore. The Southern African bishops issued a letter in October 2013 on corruption. 'It has been reported that almost half of the citizens in our countries of Southern Africa admit to having paid a bribe, mostly to police officers and government officials. This means that the challenge to work for the eradication of this illness is addressed to all of us.' Therefore 'corruption is not the government's problem alone, it is our problem. We need ... to resist the temptation to participate in corrupt actions', and to commit 'to greater transparency in the home, parish, and the work place'.[30] This focus on petty corruption, avoiding any reference to the mega-corruption on the part of ANC cadres which threatens the future of the entire country, is an evasion, and one which must have been deliberate.

[27] Burkina Faso Bishops, *Lettre Pastorale des évêques aux fils et filles de l'église famille de Dieu qui est au Burkina Faso et aux hommes et femmes de bonne volonté*, dated 15 July 2013.

[28] Mention should perhaps be made of Archbishop Michael Francis, in Liberia under Doe, almost the sole voice speaking out against corruption and abuse; see Gifford, *Christianity and Politics*, 71–83.

[29] Statements released 28 April 2006 and 15 Aug. 2007.

[30] Bishops of Southern Africa, *A Call to Examine Ourselves in the Widespread Practice of Corruption*, released 16 Oct. 2013.

In many cases statements lack follow-up, to such an extent that one wonders how serious they were. A perfect illustration of their limitations is Kenya's anti-debt campaign. The Catholic bishops in May 2005 issued a pastoral letter entitled 'On the Burden of International Debt', in which they called for transparency and accountability in the nation's finances. The Catholic Economic Justice Group (which had in fact drafted the bishops' letter) shortly afterwards fronted a campaign on this issue. By the end of 2006 Kenya had a debt of about US$10 billion, and paid US$1.6 billion (22 per cent of the national budget) on debt servicing—compared to US$1.4 billion on education, $0.4 billion on health and another $0.4 billion on roads. However, much of that debt (according to some campaign literature possibly 80 per cent) was incurred by corrupt officials enriching themselves rather than in developing the country. The CEJ group fronted a campaign (funded by the German Catholic agency Misereor and the British agency Cafod) so that Kenyans could see just where this borrowed money went, and corrupt officials be forced to repay it. Politicians, however, refused to open the debt register, even though it is legally a public document, and simply spurned the CEJ group. The bishops showed that they had no intention of owning the follow-up campaign. Had they made it their own, giving it the priority they give, say, to resisting any form of 'family life' education in schools, they might well have achieved something. But their priorities are elsewhere—as we have seen, in their development activity.

And that point is significant. To be as involved in development as is Africa's Catholic Church requires enormous resources, which creates dependence on foreign donors, as we have seen, but also on the local political elites who are often very willing to place the churches in their debt, effectively buying their silence.[31] Their dependence is part of the reason why Catholic bishops so frequently treat patrimonialism, political violence and tribalism as aberrations rather than as essential planks of a political system. That is why they maintain the image of a president and ministers as advocates of good governance, justice and national unity, rather than denouncing their complicity in violence, corruption and obstruction of justice. As in Rwanda before the 1994 genocide, Catholic spheres of development from which the church derives so much influence and status might be threatened if bishops

---

[31] Gifford, *Christianity*, 216–23, for the abuse of fund-raising *harambees* in Kenya.

descended to specifics about the political system, to the extent that they threatened the elite. Thus issuing pastoral letters often becomes a ritual that is performed, a game that is played.

Constraints on critical commentary are particularly evident when the elite profess to be Catholic. In June 2012 Kenya's Internal Security Minister George Saitoti was killed with five others in a helicopter crash, travelling to a fundraiser at a Catholic church. Saitoti had been a long-serving Vice-President under President Daniel arap Moi, and also Minister of Finance in the early 1990s at the time of the 'Goldenberg Scam', an 'export incentive' fraud so massive—of perhaps 160 billion shillings, one tenth of Kenya's GDP—that it almost wrecked the economy. The government had to devalue the currency by 25 per cent in February 1993 and by another 23.5 per cent in April, a devaluation of almost 50 per cent in two months, leading to price rises of between 50 and 100 per cent; interest rates went from around 20 per cent to 120 per cent.[32]

At the death of Saitoti and his companions, according to CISA, 'Kenya Episcopal Conference deeply mourned the loss of these political leaders, who were staunch patriots and God-fearing Kenyan Citizens', the statement mentioning 'their unwavering support for the rule of law'. Speaking at the Holy Family Basilica in Nairobi while presiding at Saitoti's requiem mass, in the presence of President Kibaki, the vice president and several ministers, Cardinal Njue said, 'Our brother the late Minister Saitoti will be remembered for the great work that he did for this nation in his various capacities as minister of finance, as vice-president, in education and in security. There is no doubt that he will be deeply missed in this country... Let us thank God for whom [what?] Saitoti had been to his family, constituency and the world. It is our duty and responsibility to make use of the legacy he has left behind'.[33]

Yet at the same time, media were covering his death in articles like 'Where is Saitoti's Goldenberg loot?' That particular article mourns those who died in the accident, Saitoti included, 'but not as a hero, because a hero he was not'. He was named as one of the dozen involved in the Goldenberg scam; he went to court and obtained an

---

[32] In October 1992 the US$ was worth about 33 Kenyan shillings; by February 1993 US$1 was worth 66 ksh.
[33] CISA, 46, 12 June 2012; CISA, 47, 15 June 2012.

injunction expunging his name from the inquiry report. (Kenyans have an aphorism: 'Why hire a lawyer when you can buy a judge?') The Attorney General immediately appealed, but the appeal was quietly dismissed on a technicality years later, as the political elite turned a blind eye. That article concludes by lamenting Kenya's 'disease called impunity': 'We must not glorify those who steal Kenyan funds'.[34]

In 2013 Cardinal Njue, with the Apostolic Delegate and three other bishops, conducted a requiem mass for Kenya's Minister of the Environment, John Njoroge Michuke, who died on 21 February. CISA reports that Cardinal Njue 'urged those present to emulate the virtues that were shown by Mr Michuki in his service to the nation for five decades'. The Cardinal praised Michuki's commitment in all the ministries in which he served: 'In all these areas, the late minister has exercised a total commitment to serve his fellow human beings'. According to CISA, 'During the Mass, President Mwai Kibaki eulogized the late Environment Minister as a man who was committed to the principles and values of honesty, consistency and discipline.' Three other bishops concelebrated at the interment in Michuki's home in Kangema.[35] In his long life Michuki had filled various posts in the treasury and later as executive chairman of the Kenya Commercial Bank, positions he used to acquire enormous wealth, land and property (including the major stake in the Windsor Golf and Country Club Resort). As Kibaki's Internal Security Minister he ordered a raid on the *Standard* newspaper, led by a duo of Armenian mercenaries (probably to prevent publication of a story about Kibaki's family). He also allegedly gave 'shoot to kill' orders against the Mungiki sect whom he viewed as terrorists; hundreds of young Kikuyu men 'disappeared' and were killed in 2007–09. Allegations of his role in these events were never investigated.[36]

It is hard for the church to project itself as champion of justice, good governance and rule of law, with such public praise for examples of so much that holds Africa back.

Enwerem gives a revealing first-hand account of the functioning of the Catholic Bishops' Conference of Nigeria (CBCN).[37] Election mon-

---

[34] Mwalimu Mati, 'Where is Saitoti's Goldenberg Loot?' *Star*, 18 June 2012, 1.
[35] CISA, 16, 28 February 2012.
[36] *Africa Confidential*, vol. 53, no. 5, 2 March 2012, 5.
[37] Enwerem is by his own admission not a disinterested observer; he was the director of the Department of Church and Society of the Catholic Secretariat, heading

itoring (training observers to monitor proceedings at voting booths during elections) came late to the CBCN (the Zambian Episcopal Conference had cooperated with ecumenical partners to pioneer this activity very successfully in 1991), but the Catholic Secretariat through its Justice, Development and Peace Committee (JDPC) decided to mount a comprehensive coverage for Nigeria's 2003 elections, in which President Obasanjo attempted to win a second term. With considerable international funding, they drew up a plan to cover the whole country. The CBCN endorsed this plan in early 2001, and for two years the JDPC trained up to 30,000 monitors (even distributing mobile phones for the day itself). Coordination was thorough, lines of communication clear. Individual parishes reported to the forty-nine diocesan offices, diocesan offices to the offices of the nine ecclesiastical provinces, and the ecclesiastical provinces to the 'control room' in the national secretariat.

A key requirement was to pronounce a judgment within forty-eight hours of the elections, before the government and its agencies had time to doctor results. To this end it was decided that the president of the CBCN, at that time Archbishop John Onaiyekan, would give a press conference at 1pm on 21 April. Election day came, and the monitoring, despite the occasional glitch, went essentially according to plan. The monitoring revealed widespread fraud, irregularity and intimidation. Reports were swiftly collated into a statement, but Onaiyekan did not hold the press conference; he was inexplicably unavailable. Instead, in the early hours of the following day he sent his own official statement to the secretariat, at the same time as to the national newspapers in time for their editions the following day. In his report he claimed that 'on the whole' the presidential election was 'generally free and fair'—to the consternation and despair of the enormous number of grassroots monitors. The point to be made here is that in a society distinguished for its 'Big Man' leadership (and Enwerem's theme is that the Catholic bishops are religious 'Big Men' whose mode of operation differs little from their political counterparts), it is far easier to pronounce as one feels, or in one's own interests, than to operate as the representative of a team or a spokesman constrained by data painstak-

---

up the 2003 monitoring exercise he describes: Enwerem, *Crossing the Rubicon*, esp. 153–99.

ingly gathered by colleagues. Enwerem allows himself fleetingly to raise the question of Onaiyekan's motivation in making his statement, not least because within three years Onaiyekan had changed his mind and denounced the elections, and (in keeping with a point made earlier this chapter) blamed the West for accepting the legitimacy of the elections in the first place: 'If the EU or the United States had insisted that we can't accept (the results), we probably would have gotten something better. But the outside powers calculated that they were doing good business with these people... The major corporations, such as the oil companies, play a big role.'[38]

Enwerem notes that for Nigeria's 2007 elections, the JDPC mounted a similar plan (though less ambitious, not least because of the 2003 fiasco). After these elections, even more fraudulent, the then CBCN chairman acted in accordance with the agreed plan: a summary within forty-eight hours, faithfully and accurately reflecting the monitors' findings. This may indicate that the trend is towards collegial, consensual leadership.

## The need for a new agenda

Bowers, in the article used to structure this chapter, noted that the end of the Cold War and the end of apartheid changed the reality in Africa, and Africa's theological agenda needed to reflect that. Negotiating a future in a globalized world has identified new needs: 'For these needs African theology for the most part has had little to say'.[39]

The sheer novelty of the modern world is left unaddressed in the preoccupation with African culture. If the goal is to participate equally on the world stage (and that surely lies behind laments about marginalization), a preoccupation with 'the way we have always operated' may be less than helpful. Is something that is 'traditionally African' calculated to bring Africa into the socio-economic and political systems obtaining in the modern world? Ka Mana goes so far as to argue that 'there is no doubt that the central drive of our cultural, human and vital strength emanates from pharaonic Egypt, the place which gave rise to the spirit and intellect of black civilizations'.[40] These pharaonic myths

---

[38] 'Nigeria: Western Greed to blame for Corruption in Africa, says Archbishop', CISA, 67, 16 June 2006; Enwerem, *Crossing the Rubicon*, 197.

[39] Bowers, 'African Theology', 122.

[40] Ka Mana, *Christians and Churches of Africa; Salvation in Christ and Building a*

are 'permanent forces that structure the consciousness that God wants to give to humanity', and Africans should acknowledge 'the original founding myths of African culture as the true path of humankind'.[41] Would anyone urge modern Scandinavians to organize their societies from the myths of Wodin and Thor? Why should Africa be different?

The awareness that theology must address Africa's new realities may already be changing emphases. The first Synod of Bishops for Africa took place in 1994 almost at the high tide of this stress on culture. The synod made much of a new theological insight, specially African, of the church as 'family of God', and soon afterwards SECAM produced a document celebrating this.[42] However, it was noteworthy at the 2009 second Synod for Africa that when African culture was mentioned, it was just as likely to be discussed negatively as positively. In Pope Benedict's post-synodal exhortation *Africae Munus* this is evident. There is praise for traditional culture, including reverence for life and for the aged, but the missionaries are said to have freed 'numerous traditional cultures' from 'ancestral fears and from unclean spirits',[43] and the document deplores 'the intolerable treatment to which so many children in Africa are subjected'.[44] A footnote immediately adds that 'the synod fathers referred to different situations, including those involving children killed before birth, unwanted children, orphans, albinos, street children, abandoned children, child soldiers, child prisoners, children forced into labour, children ill-treated on account of physical or mental handicap, children said to be witches or warlocks, children said to be serpents, children sold as sex slaves, traumatized children without any future prospects etc.' Such a list would have been less likely in the past.

---

*New African Society*, Maryknoll, NY: Orbis, 2004, 25. Ka Mana is not now a Catholic, but studied his theology as a Catholic (in the 1990s this led some at the All Africa Conference of Churches, displaying a certain inferiority complex vis-à-vis Catholics, to joke that to find a significant Protestant theologian in Africa one had to turn to a Catholic).

[41] Ibid., 69, 76.

[42] The notion is not without problems; see Frans Wijsen, *Seeds of Conflict in a Haven of Peace: from Religious Studies to Interreligious Studies in Africa*, Amsterdam: Rodopi, 2007, 205–10.

[43] Benedict XVI, *Africa's Commitment*, Nairobi: Paulines, 2011, par. 113.

[44] Ibid., par. 67.

A volume of essays by African theologians devoted to develop the themes of the synod and entitled *Reconciliation, Justice and Peace: the Second African Synod*, mirrors some of this. The older themes are there. Magesa denounces the missionaries' 'demonizing (Africans') cultural identity (and, by implication), their humanity'.[45] Kanyandago denounces foreign economic control of Africa's resources, though he admits some African responsibility for Africa's situation: 'The root causes of Africa's poverty can be traced to historical and present practices and ideologies perpetuated by Africans themselves as well as outsiders, albeit the latter have historically played a preponderant role.'[46] But the editor admits in the introduction both the wide variety of contributors' views that 'read Africa and the church differently', and that 'the West will not serve as perpetual scapegoat'.[47] Pope Benedict's homily opening the synod in which he had implied that the West had 'imported poison' into Africa is critiqued at various places, notably, by Nathanael Yaovi Soede: 'The viruses that provoke the sickness of Africa come more from Africa than the West'.[48]

A similar volume, also edited by Orobator, *Practising Reconciliation, Doing Justice, Building Peace*, is totally concerned with addressing the situation in Africa, even containing case studies by senior churchmen of the Catholic Church's involvement in the problems of Northern Uganda, Southern Sudan and Nigeria.[49] In his introduction to another volume of such essays, *Africa is not Destined to Die: Signs of Hope*

---

[45] Laurenti Magesa, 'On Speaking Terms: African Religion and Christianity in Dialogue', in Orobator, *Reconciliation*, 33.

[46] Peter Kanyandago, '"Let us First Feed the Children" (Mark 7,27): the Church's Response to the Inequitable Extraction of Resources and Related Violence', in Orobator, *Reconciliation*, 179. Katongole's *Sacrifice of Africa* apportions blame similarly, arguing that the problems of Africa stem from its brutal colonization, and the nation state which perpetuates this colonial violence (something he realized fully only on reading Adam Hochschild's *King Leopold's Ghost: a Story of Greed, Terror and Heroism in Colonial Africa*, Boston: Houghton Mifflin, 1998).

[47] Agbonkhianmeghe E. Orobator, 'The Synod as Ecclesial Conversation', in Orobator, *Reconciliation*, 5, 10.

[48] Nathanael Yaovi Soede, 'The Enduring Scourge of Poverty and Evangelization in Africa', in Orobator, *Reconciliation*, 185.

[49] Agbonkhianmeghe E. Orobator (ed.), *Practising Reconciliation, Doing Justice, Building Peace: Conversations on Catholic Theological Ethics in Africa*, Nairobi: Paulines, 2013.

*and Renewal*, Kampala's Cardinal Emmanuel Wamala expresses the hope that the contributors will 'be concerned with articulating those factors that make African people unique and different, providing them with a special contribution to make to the evolution of civilisation';[50] however, in large measure the volume addresses issues like food and water security, managing oil reserves, and improving education. If works such as these illustrate a newer direction for African Catholic theology, they also support the picture I have presented here of the ongoing 'internal secularization' of Catholicism.

African Catholic theologians have historically given their main attention to culture. Although bishops, too, have often mouthed the word 'culture', their main focus is on precisely the opposite, bringing Africa into the modern world through development. The rank and file of African Catholics have remained largely unmoved by theological debate, not least because it entirely ignores the religious imagination of so many of them.

---

[50] Ambrose John Bwangatto (ed.), *Africa is not Destined to Die: Signs of Hope and Renewal*, Nairobi: Paulines, 2012, 15. The essays here are from a conference in Uganda in 2012, devoted to presenting a more positive picture of Africa than that of a conference ten years before, whose proceedings are found in Kanyandago (ed.), *Marginalized Africa*.

9

## CONCLUSION

### AFRICAN CHRISTIANITY AND MODERNITY

In seventeenth and eighteenth century Europe a new kind of society began to take shape. This new society was relatively secularized. Faith had retreated more to the private area, at least to the extent that it had ceased to sacralize the social order. The social order was coming to be characterized by functional pragmatic compromise. There was nothing that could not be questioned. At the same time, the division of labour was growing more refined and extensive. Economic and social activities began to be distinguished from centralized order-maintaining activities. Some were engaging in business, and simply leaving the protective or security arrangements to others. The new society was marked by individualism. People no longer identified so closely with their position in village or lineage; they belonged to a much more mobile society. There arose a whole cluster of institutions and associations, and they could be entered and left freely: belonging to any one was not imposed by birth or sustained by ritual. 'Modular man' had been born.[1]

The novelty of this new form of society was particularly evident in the matter of authority. Many areas began to have real autonomy, not subject to central autocratic control. In many areas, it was no longer

[1] Ernest Gellner, 'The Importance of Being Modular', in John A Hall (ed.), *Civil Society: Theory, History, Comparison*, Cambridge: Polity Press, 1995, 32–55.

quite clear exactly who was boss. Other institutions could check the state. Power was reduced to an instrument, to be judged by its effectiveness and service, and was no longer a master. This taming of power was, in Gellner's phrase, 'perhaps mankind's greatest triumph'.[2] Previously, since the state provided a source of power and wealth entirely disproportionate to that available from any other organized force within society, political power had been fought for with some ferocity. But now leaders were no longer paid out of all proportion to all others; on the contrary, their rewards became relatively feeble. Positions of power came to be rotated like all others. Those who amassed wealth did not use it for the acquisition of power, and thus they broke through the vicious circle which in the past obliged power-holders to suppress successful accumulators of wealth as an imminent political menace. The emerging bourgeoisie could be tolerated, as they themselves no longer sought power, at least as individuals. Indeed, these developments should be seen as the emerging middle class seeking a form of collective power in the name of the whole, increasingly understood as the modern nation state. Henceforth, in these commercial and industrial societies, using power as the way to personal wealth was not altogether unknown, but this route has been incomparably less important: in Gellner's words, in these societies, 'the best way to make money is to make money'.[3]

The roots of this new order lay in the social and intellectual upheavals associated with the Reformation, and its development was intimately linked to the Industrial Revolution. This new order depended on economic expansion. Expectation of improvement replaced coercion as the ultimate basis of the social order. Only in conditions of overall growth can a majority have an interest in conforming, even without intimidation. Increasing wealth functioned effectively as a 'social bribery fund'; the new order could buy its way out of any external or internal threat.[4] Economic growth for its part required cognitive growth. It was the unending innovation of the scientific revolution that brought about an apparently unending exponential increase in productive

[2] Ernest Gellner, *Conditions of Liberty: Civil Society and its Rivals*, London: Hamish Hamilton, 1994, 206. My debt here to Gellner is gratefully acknowledged.
[3] Ibid., 74.
[4] Ibid., 73.

power, until human skills rather than raw materials became the key element in wealth production. If such growth was to be maintained, ideological monopoly was impossible, and reason came to be applied not just to raw materials and productive processes but to society itself. Rational procedures were demanded by an informed public opinion; the rising bourgeoisie could not tolerate arbitrariness on the part of rulers. In this way productive values came to triumph over all others. This new social order is almost defined by its strong civil society, the myriad groups which force the state to cater for their interests.

To outline the features of this new social order is not necessarily to celebrate it, certainly not every aspect of it. Nor is it implied that this order is a finished product or perfect in any way (a claim that would be hard to sustain after the financial crash of 2008), or even sustainable in its present form (not least because of the levels of inequality and debt incurred). It is merely to state that this is the way the modern world operates. In this book I have sought to ask: what role are different forms of Christianity playing in helping Africa join that world?

We first considered Pentecostalism. African Pentecostalism is not monolithic. In outlining Olukoya's belief system, I noted considerable confusion, even contradictions, in different diagnoses of spiritual causality. Pype gives a reason: 'Pentecostal ideology at large is something that is still being fashioned; it is a belief system in the making, under construction and certainly not (yet) fine-tuned… This ambiguity produces space for creativity and improvisation and consequently leads to variety within the Pentecostal scene.'[5] I used Olukoya as my example, but I have argued that the enchanted imagination is pervasive in African Pentecostalism. One of the strengths of Pype's study of Pentecostal media in Kinshasa is the open admission of this. She well portrays the imagination (which she calls apocalyptic, but I have called enchanted) through the concept of 'key scenarios', which in any culture sort out 'complex and undifferentiated feelings and ideas and make them comprehensible to the individual, communicable to others, and translatable into orderly action'. One might thus formulate

---

[5] Katrien Pype, *The Making of the Pentecostal Melodrama: Religion, Media and Gender in Kinshasa*, New York: Berghahn Books, 2012, 58. Witchcraft, so closely related to Pentecostalism, is no more fixed: 'The polyvalent and elusive nature of witchcraft renders it difficult, maybe even impossible, to give a complete overview of witchcraft beliefs in the city' (ibid., 45).

the 'key scenario' of the USA, better known as 'the American dream', in this way: 'a boy of low status, but with total faith in the American system, works very hard and ultimately becomes rich and powerful'. This key scenario offers a clear-cut mode of action appropriate to correct and successful living in America. More abstractly, key scenarios formulate local definitions of good life and social success, as well as key cultural strategies to attain these. Pype briefly presents Kinshasa's Christian 'key scenario': 'Life in Kinshasa is hazardous because of the workings of the Devil and his demons. They invade the domestic sphere with the help of witches, who threaten collective and individual health (in a physical and social sense). Christians, however, can arm themselves against evil through prayer and by listening closely to the advice of pastors.'[6] This imaginary, she claims, is pervasive. For all *kinois*, 'the "Real" is located within the invisible'.[7] 'Kinshasa's Christians sometimes disagree on the "right type" of Christianity, but the Christian God and the spiritual battle between God and Devil are never questioned.'[8] The enchanted imagination is evident everywhere: currently there is a 'hegemony of Pentecostal-Charismatic Christianity in Kinshasa's public culture'.[9] An anthropologist's admission of the pervasiveness of this imagination stands in sharp contrast to the stance of so many Christian theologians, who affect to see no trace of it.

Let me turn to another relevant anthropological study. Isak Niehaus has movingly described the death of his research assistant from AIDS. The assistant had two university degrees, and he and his relatives (a younger brother with an MA in computer science) sought the explanation of a series of misfortunes afflicting them. Scientific explanations would not do; they were convinced that their problems were caused by witchcraft. Convinced that their father was a witch and the cause of their ills, four sons tried to kill him—mystically, because it is less dangerous than a physical attack which might lead to arrest. They by and large accepted what the spiritual specialists told them, did what was

[6] Ibid., 10. For the concept of 'key scenario', Pype acknowledges Sherry Ortner, 'On Key Symbols', in M. Lambek (ed.), *A Reader in the Anthropology of Religion*, London: Blackwell, 2002 [1973], 158–67.

[7] Pype, *The Making of the Pentecostal Medodrama*, 102.

[8] Ibid., 39.

[9] Ibid., 115.

required, and, even in the light of continual failure, persisted in that mindset. The point I want to highlight is that they indiscriminately turned for advice to 'diviners and Christian prophets', passing from diviner to prophet, and back again, in the understanding that the traditional diviner and the Christian prophet were essentially the same thing—and indeed the solutions urged were not very different.[10] Niehaus talks of Zionist and Apostolic prophets, so these were the 'spiritual experts' of the classical African Independent Churches (AICs). In my opinion, the main difference between the AICs and African Pentecostalism is Pentecostalism's modern accoutrements or incidentals: the sound systems, the power-point presentations, the DVDs, the conventions, the Mercedes, the use of English, the hymns sung to modern instruments and rhythms. In terms of religious imagination, however, African Pentecostalism largely perpetuates that of so many AICs.

According to Niehaus' account, some of the diviners/prophets admitted the insufficiency of their powers. In fact, some diviners/prophets admitted they lacked the power to kill a really powerful witch. However, I have never heard a Pentecostal pastor admit a case in which he was deficient.[11] Within Pentecostalism, we have noted the readiness to kill by reversing curses (Oyedepo, a prosperity preacher, no less than the more flamboyantly enchanted Olukoya). Yes, Pentecostalism, or some forms of it, also teaches entrepreneurship and management skills and good life-practice, but this must be kept in perspective. In my experience, it is the underlying religious imagination that is more important. Pentecostal adherents too want to have their

---

[10] Niehaus, *Witchcraft*. Niehaus mentions, on the part of diviners, throwing bones, sniffing out an offending spirit, drinking or applying potions (often at a distance), incisions into which potions are rubbed, ointments, reeds, examination of faeces, charcoal, oil, inhaled herbs. The prophets prescribe special tea, coffee, Vicks, Vaseline and Coca Cola (the coke bottle to be taken outside and smashed against a stone at midnight, ibid., 170), multicoloured cords, wool, inorganic medicines (in contrast to the normally organic potions of diviners). Almost a prototype of Niehaus' work is Adam Ashforth, *Madumo: a Man Bewitched*, University of Chicago Press, 2000, which also describes a friend convinced by his family's accusations that he used witchcraft to kill his mother, and the gruelling regimen he undergoes to remove the curse. Again, the Christian professional is functionally identified with the *inyanga* (144–50).

[11] Oyedepo boasts: 'It won't take me too much effort to destroy a witch' (*Releasing the Supernatural*, 33).

misfortunes explained, to know the reason for 'blocked progress in life',[12] through a rationality very different from that of modernity. A comparison of the economics is revealing, too. Niehaus shows that the costs are considerable. However, many of the diviners/prophets will take money only after delivery. Many of them are in fact individuals to whom one goes for consultation, as to a doctor. Although this is also the case within Pentecostalism to a degree far greater than is usually acknowledged, most Pentecostal pastors also claim to be leaders of a faith community, where money is required up front (tithes and offerings beforehand, often as the *sine qua non* of one's victory).

What is also significant for us is Niehaus' reaction to the harrowing case he described. It led him to combat 'the long history of exceedingly "generous" or "charitable" anthropological treatment of witchcraft and divination'.[13] Many anthropologists have been keen to challenge the ethnocentric, often racist, use of Western values and thinking as a yardstick. Some have even rejected the claim that witchcraft and divination are based on erroneous ontological assumptions. Others argue that such practices are popular, accessible, psychologically soothing, culturally appropriate and shift blame from the victim. Niehaus, on the contrary, claims that witchcraft is dysfunctional; witchcraft enhances fears, and insecurities, and can lead to brutal killings. For him, as for me, 'Critical empathy seems to be a more appropriate intellectual and ethical stance'.[14]

The prosperity of Oyedepo is of course narrowly linked to his mystical power over spiritual forces. His wealth is testament to his unlimited and all-encompassing spiritual power. Pype writes of Kinshasa:

The pastor and the pastor's wife have nowadays become the ideal types of masculinity and femininity in the city, for they combine several aspects of social success; others depend on them, and they enjoy material and financial wealth and occupy a privileged position with regard to the spiritual world. The pastor is the ultimate 'strong man' in contemporary Kinshasa. *Pasteurs* acquire

---

[12] Niehaus, *Witchcraft*, 205.

[13] Ibid., 211.

[14] Ibid., 214; see the whole discussion on relativist anthropology, 210–15. Pype too, although far more relativist than Niehaus, agrees that the enchanted worldview causes widespread 'spiritual confusion'. No one, not even a pastor, need be what he seems, which engenders widespread fear and doubt (*Melodrama*, 42). The pastor associated with Pype's TV film crew was rumoured to have killed three people by cursing them (ibid., 83).

material goods such as cell phones, luxurious cars and designer clothes from their followers and show off their opulence in public, and semipublic spaces. The wealthier the pastor, the more he is believed to be in touch with God since his life of luxury is due to gifts of appreciation from satisfied followers.[15]

The prosperity pastor replicates the role of the healer diviner. They are thought to control two contrasting domains of the invisible, the divine and the demonic respectively.[16]

Catholicism, in contrast to Pentecostalism, is very reluctant to countenance any form of enchanted Christianity. I have argued that it is the biggest single development agency on the continent. No other single body can rival its involvement in health and education. Inevitably African Catholicism mirrors all the tensions of global Catholicism. The bishops are very Roman, as is evident from their public statements. There is nothing surprising in that; they were made bishops precisely because of their readiness to promote Rome's agenda. The lower professional ranks, those of priests and nuns, although not publicly opposing or even necessarily signifying dissatisfaction with Roman positions, are in fact engaged in something else. Their main preoccupations are development—historically schools and clinics, but now development in the widest possible sense, often human rights, justice and peace. In fact, development is increasingly what the bishops are involved in too, not least because this is the concern of the major donors, whose resources are having considerable effect on the nature of African Catholicism through a process of 'NGO-ization' (leading to 'Oxfam with Incense', perhaps). Theologians have until now been rather peripheral to this engagement in development, concerned as they have been with the issue of Africanness—in their own way, of course, because they studiously ignore the issues of African culture so obtrusive in Pentecostalism.

These then are two distinct religious visions on the continent. One is the enchanted religious imagination of so many Africans (often Catholics themselves). The other is the increasingly 'internally secularized' Christianity of the Catholic professionals. The more Catholicism

[15] Ibid., 80f.

[16] Pype elaborates on the similarities: both attempt to restore the 'life flow'; both transmit life-bearing forces between spirits and their followers; both have the same enemy, the witch; both bring what is hidden into the open (ibid., 115–18).

has opted for development, the more it has ceased to cater for or appeal to Africans with an enchanted religious imagination. Although many such people stay with Catholicism and have these 'religious' needs met quietly elsewhere, many have left the Catholic Church. Enchanted religious concerns, not addressed by official Catholicism, are catered for by Pentecostals.

## Multiple modernities

The assumption behind the whole notion of 'development' in the latter part of the twentieth century was that the former colonized lands would 'modernize' and take their place alongside the nations earlier industrialized in the process outlined at the beginning of this chapter. It is fashionable now in some circles to challenge this assumption, in the name of 'postmodernism' and 'multiple modernities'. Postmodernism in this context seems to mean precisely the rejection of a single overarching narrative like 'modernization'; all knowledge, it is insinuated, is valid in its own context, and no viewpoint should be privileged over another. The expression 'multiple modernities' is invoked to indicate that different people can take their place in the twenty-first century without becoming 'occidentalized'; they have their own way of being modern. A clear expression of this view is given by Moore and Sanders. Writing about the perceived increase of witchcraft in contemporary Africa (not its eclipse, as development theorists had predicted), they state:

We can only think such 'enchantments' should wither and die if we think in narrow teleological terms of progress, development, and modernization. However, once we admit to 'multiple modernities', to the idea that 'progress', 'development' and 'modernity' are multiplex, undecidable and contextually specific, there is no reason to suppose that the occult *should* vanish... Are western teleological beliefs about progress, development, rationality and modernity... really so different from the idea that occult forces move the world?[17]

According to this view, some people think in terms of rationality or development, other people think in terms of witchcraft and curses; all are abstract nouns of the same order, and the latter two are just as good as the former two.

[17] Henrietta L. Moore and Todd Sanders, 'Magical Interpretations and Material Realities: an Introduction', in Moore and Sanders (eds), *Magical Interpretations, Material Realities: Modernity, Witchcraft and the Occult in Postcolonial Africa*, Abingdon: Routledge, 2001, 19.

Ernest Gellner attacks this relativist position, with fervour:

You cannot understand the human condition if you ignore or deny its total transformation by the success of the scientific revolution... (This) has totally transformed the terms of reference in which human societies operate. To pretend that the scientific revolution of the seventeenth century, and its eventual application in the later stage of the industrial revolution, have not transformed the world but are merely changes from one culture to another, is simply an irresponsible affectation.[18]

The significant thing about scientific/technological knowledge is that it is *not* restricted to particular peoples, but is transcultural; this 'cognitive strategy' would be 'the correct strategy in *any* world'.[19] It is not 'Western' in any hard sense, like 'in Western genes', for it has come to the West only recently and fitfully. Other forms of knowing cannot compete: 'Pre-enlightenment cultures (have) their own forms of cognition... but this is precisely why they were so feeble technically, and why they are being swept aside so brutally once (scientific/technological knowledge) has seen the light of day or of history.'[20] All societies have had to make their peace with it and adopt it. 'The shocking inequalities of power of diverse cognitive styles' constitute harsh reality, and reality is getting harsher by the day.[21] This position 'has nothing to do with a racist or any other glorification of one segment of humanity over another.'[22] This approach to the world had to emerge somewhere, but the country where it sprang up (at least in some measure fortuitously) is not currently doing spectacularly well with it; other nations where it could probably not have sprung up spontaneously are arguably doing better. Nor has the rise of science and technology solved personal or social problems. It hasn't helped Westerners to avoid alienation, depression, divorce and suicide. And the two grand revolutionary attempts to create a new society on such a basis have ended in tears—floods of them. Gellner admits that the consequences of this new form of knowing are 'a pretty mixed lot, some exciting, but many of them terrifying'.[23]

[18] Ernest Gellner, 'Anything Goes', *TLS*, 16 June 1995, 8.
[19] Ernest Gellner, *Postmodernism, Reason and Religion*, London: Routledge, 1992 82.
[20] Ibid.
[21] Ibid., 69.
[22] Ibid., 61.
[23] Ibid., 78.

I have never considered the concept of 'multiple modernities' very helpful in Africa. To be clear, by 'modern' I mean more than just existing in the twenty-first century. Modernization means something like 'that combination of changes—in the mode of production and government, in the social and institutional order, in the corpus of knowledge, and in attitudes and values—that makes it possible for a society to hold its own in the twenty-first century; that is, to compete on even terms in the generation of material and cultural wealth, to sustain its independence, and to promote and accommodate to further change.'[24] Japan may be a case which is 'alternatively modern'. But the Soviet Union was not 'modern'—that's why it no longer exists. India and China may yet show alternative modernities, but surely again there is a case to be made that they are 'joining the modern world' precisely to the extent that they are now adopting the very planks of the modernity pioneered in the West: education, science, technology, meritocracy, democratic reform, rule of law, free-ish markets and trade.

For me, far more fruitful in Africa is the idea of 'Getting to Denmark'. For people in many developing countries, 'Denmark' is an almost mythical place that is known to have good political and economic institutions; it is relatively stable, democratic, peaceful, prosperous, inclusive; it has extremely low levels of political corruption. The challenge is surely for Nigeria, Congo, Zimbabwe etc. to move themselves 'towards Denmark'.[25] Their route will not be the same route that Denmark took, but the destination is the same.

Encouraging movement 'towards Denmark' opens one to the same criticisms directed at nineteenth century missionaries for attempting to 'civilize Africa', and the same accusations of 'destroying African cultures'—the very criticisms constantly repeated by contemporary African theologians. Gellner refuses to be cowed by such charges (which could be made against anyone teaching physics in a secondary school): 'One particular style of knowledge has proved so overwhelmingly powerful, economically, militarily, administratively, that all societies have had to make their peace with it and adopt it. Some have

---

[24] David S. Landes, *The Unbound Prometheus*, Cambridge University Press, 1969, 6; Landes wrote 'twentieth century'.

[25] For the 'Getting to Denmark' motif, see Francis Fukuyama, *The Origins of Political Order: from Prehuman Times to the French Revolution*, New York: Farrar, Straus and Giroux, 2011, 14, 431.

done it more successfully than others, and some more willingly or more quickly than others; but all of them have had to do it, or perish. Some have retained more, and some less, of their previous cultures.'[26] Africa's Catholic Church is in fact fully engaged in Africa's move towards Denmark. Not perfectly, of course; the bishops have their Roman agenda to pursue, and bishops' relations with the political elite curtail a fully-fledged commitment to essential components of modernity like rule of law, good governance, accountability. But Denmark is the destination to which the Africa's Catholic Church in general is nudging Africa. By contrast, as repeatedly asserted above, I am not convinced by the evidence adduced so far that the enchanted worldview (so often accompanied by the faith gospel or the 'anointing' of prophets) moves Africa along this road, or creates some specially African alternative to Denmark.

## Combining the two?

Could the two worldviews, that of functional rationality and that of enchanted forces, be combined? After all, one might argue, the enchanted religious imagination does not rigidly exclude causality on the natural level; rather, its *primary and immediate* focus is on the spiritual realm, and a 'why' question is added to the 'how'. One thinking from an enchanted viewpoint is perfectly aware that falling from a great height causes death, but wants further to enquire why this person fell on this particular occasion when she had negotiated this cliff path countless times before. Might the enchanted Christianity of Olukoya be combined with the functional rationality that Weber described? I mentioned above that Olukoya claims to be a scientist, with seventy scientific papers published. However, I argued that Olukoya has not reconciled two forms of rationality, nor does he embody a special 'Afromodernity'; he has rather turned his back on the particular rationality which underpins modern science.

In some recent writing, Berger seems to lean towards the possibility of combining the two. 'A pilot of a modern aircraft cannot operate it on the metaphysical assumptions and the incantations of shamanic magic—as long as he or she sits in the cockpit. But when the pilot goes home—say, to an ancestral village—he or she can engage in any num-

[26] Gellner, *Postmodernism*, 61.

ber of magical ideas and practices.'[27] I think Berger was far closer to reality in an earlier work, *The Homeless Mind*: 'Social change invariably entails change in plausibility structures. Thus, as modernization proceeds, it is very likely that communication with dead grandfathers becomes progressively less plausible.'[28]

*The Homeless Mind* explains why this is so, analyzing modernity in terms of a cognitive style resulting from characteristics like technology and bureaucracy. Technology inevitably entails mechanisticity, reproducibility, measurability. These qualities inseparable from technology bring with them mental habits which constitute a 'cognitive style' including componentiality, separability of means and ends, implicit abstraction, problem-solving inventiveness, assumption of maximalization, and also inevitably introduces segregation of work from private life, anonymous social relations, multi-relationality. Likewise, bureaucracy functions through competence, referral, coverage, proper procedure, anonymity, and access to redress. The 'cognitive style' that necessarily flows from such bureaucratic functioning comprises orderliness, general and autonomous organizability, predictability, a general expectation of justice, moralized anonymity and explicit abstraction. Thus a society structured through technology and bureaucracy carries with it an entire way of experiencing reality. An individual socialized into such a society absorbs this cognitive style and operates in terms of a 'modern' worldview, where explanations in terms of witches and curses simply have no place.[29]

That is why I think the two imaginations cannot be combined. The two mindsets are not just different, but alternative. Not just diverse, but incompatible.[30] This constitutes the dilemma for the mainline

---

[27] Peter Berger, Grace Davie and Effie Fokas, *Religious America, Secular Europe? A Theme and Variations*, Aldershot: Ashgate, 2008, 142; see also Peter L. Berger, *Adventures of an Accidental Sociologist: How to Explain the World without Becoming a Bore*, Amherst: Prometheus, 2011, 122–4.

[28] Peter L. Berger, Brigitte Berger and Hansfried Kellner, *The Homeless Mind: Modernization and Consciousness*, London: Penguin, 1974, 22.

[29] Another quality of modernity discussed in *Homeless Mind* is the pluralization of social life worlds, but the above is sufficient to make the point relevant here.

[30] Matthew Schoffeleers, comparing political and ritual healing churches in southern Africa, argued that the latter are strongly inclined to political acquiescence, not just as a matter of contingent fact but from an underlying logic: 'healing ... individualizes and therefore depoliticizes the causes of sickness'. Matthew Schoffeleers, 'Ritual Healing and Political Acquiescence: the Case of the Zionist

churches. Williamson, writing of Akan religion, grasped this: 'The (mainline) church has not provided a creative answer to the Akan's problems. It may well be that, at least by the church as historically implanted, no such answer was possible.'[31] The two worldviews or imaginations operate on different planes. They are simply incommensurable.[32] The official Catholic Church has taken the easy way out, and simply refuses to admit the existence of the enchanted religious imagination, but the pastoral inadequacy of this position is obvious.

*Wider issues*

In this book I have been presenting two very different forms of Christianity: an enchanted Christianity that operates from a belief in pervasive spiritual forces, and a disenchanted and internally secularized Christianity that operates on a totally different plane, that of human development. But we have touched on other issues too.

First, most observers of global Christianity are not interested in the different religious imaginations behind the different Christianities described in this book. Christian theologians seem not aware of them, or more probably simply don't want to know. It is almost exclusively anthropologists whom we have used in discussing these issues. Christians who admit the phenomenon seem not greatly exercised by it. Consider this quotation from a World Council of Churches publication which seems fairly representative of Africa's mainline Christians:

The issue of witchcraft goes to the heart of the African psyche. African societies, like the biblical-Semitic world, have a religious and spiritual understanding of reality. We are surrounded by hosts of spirit beings—some good, some bad—which are considered able to influence the course of human lives. For that reason calamities are attributed to personal forces of evil. In such a setting

---

Churches in Southern Africa', *Africa*, 61 (1991), 1–25. I am grateful to J.D.Y. Peel for this reference.

[31] Sidney George Williamson, *Akan Religion and the Christian Faith: a Comparative Study of the Impact of Two Religions*, Accra: Ghana Universities Press, 1965, 156f.

[32] 'Western rational thinking does not accept the coexistence of magic and science… But for Kinshasa's born-again Christians, the two are commensurable' (Pype, *Melodrama*, 146). So television is appropriated through a local cultural logic of witchcraft and magic; television thus mediates spiritual influence (ibid., 163–5).

it is an important role of religion to help free humanity from the tyranny of those forces of evil. *It is useless to debate the reality of such spirit beings.*[33]

That publication is a laudable celebration of African Christian initiatives, and a welcome admission that to have appeal an African religion must combat those forces of evil. However, it is not useless to debate the reality of such spirit beings. It is true that in the West the existence of witches was not strictly disproved, but Western societies moved to operate on a totally different plane, where such postulates simply did not arise. We have already cited Keith Thomas: the 'animistic conception of the universe which had constituted the basic rationale for magical thinking' simply fell away, to be replaced by a conception of an orderly and rational universe in which effect follows cause in a predictable manner.[34] Accusations of witchcraft 'were thus rejected not because they had been closely scrutinized and found defective in some particular respect, but because they implied a conception of nature which now appeared inherently absurd.'[35] It was the 'intellectual and social structure' which underpinned belief in witches that needed to be broken. Hugh Trevor-Roper concludes his *The European Witch Craze of the Sixteenth and Seventeenth Centuries* by noting that, 'In the mid-seventeenth century this was done. Then the medieval synthesis, which Reformation and Counter-Reformation had artificially prolonged, was at last broken... Thereafter society might persecute its dissidents as Huguenots or as Jews. It might discover a new stereotype, the 'Jacobin', the 'Red'. But the stereotype of witch had gone.'[36]

Second, I have used the term 'internally secularized' to describe the Catholicism exemplified by so many rank and file Catholic professionals, particularly in religious orders. Our study has little direct bearing on the secularization debate more broadly. It is often said that the upsurge of religion globally in the last twenty or thirty years has definitively disproved the secularization thesis that 'with modernity comes

[33] John S. Pobee and Gabriel Ositelu II, *African Initiatives in Christianity: the Growth, Gifts and Diversities of Indigenous African Churches: a Challenge to the Ecumenical Movement*, Geneva: WCC Publications, 1998, 29, emphasis added.
[34] Thomas, *Religion and the Decline*, 771, 786.
[35] Ibid., 690.
[36] Hugh Trevor-Roper, *The European Witch Craze of the Sixteenth and Seventeenth Centuries*, London: Penguin, 1969, 122.

secularization'. However, whatever may be the case in other parts of the world, I doubt if the salience of religion in Africa can be used to swing the secularization debate one way or the other, for the reason that I have given earlier: their education, health, legal, transport and communication systems, their technological, scientific and industrial base, their socio-political institutions, mean that African countries rarely provide data for a debate about modernity. It seems that the jury is still out on the wider question of the effect of modernity on religion, but Africa gives little reason to contradict Bruce's rather restrained suggestion: 'If we want to extend the secularization paradigm outside its European base, the key prediction is not that all societies will modernize with the results for religion seen in Europe. It is that, *if other places modernize in ways similar to the European experience, then we can expect the nature and status of religion also to change in similar ways.*'[37]

It is worth drawing attention to the seemingly cheerful acquiescence in 'internal secularization' or 'NGO-ization' that characterizes an increasing number of books on Catholicism. Linden's *Global Catholicism*, for example, despite its genuine strengths, is essentially an examination of the justice and peace involvement of Catholicism in selected countries. Justice and peace are exactly what countless NGOs are promoting in Africa, an activity for many Africans not religious at all.[38] Even more striking, John Allen's *The Future Church* purports to offer, as the title suggests, a picture of what global Catholicism is becoming.[39] He presents Catholicism, not as a tradition and an institution for conceptualizing and relating to supernatural realities, but as a pressure group or lobby with a vision for improving this world. His book outlines possible Catholic contributions to living in harmony

---

[37] Bruce, *Secularization*, 201; emphasis in original.

[38] Ian Linden, *Global Catholicism: Diversity and Change since Vatican II*, London: Hurst, 2009.

[39] John L. Allen, *The Future Church: How Ten Trends are Revolutionizing the Catholic Church*, New York: Doubleday, 2009. In a book on Catholicism's future, it is remarkable how little it contains about Africa. It also exemplifies the essentialism mentioned above; Allen discusses Brazil's, China's, Russia's and India's Catholics without even raising the question whether, say, India's Catholics in their mythologizing, ritualized polytheistic setting have much in common with Chinese Catholics in their pervasive shamanistic ethos—much, that is, except the self-identification of 'Catholic'. The presumption that they are all the one reality is just that, a presumption; it calls for analysis, not uncritical acceptance.

with Muslims, coping with ageing populations, living more equitably. There are chapters on biotechnology, globalization and ecology, with detailed expositions on water wars, protecting the Amazon, preserving the traditions and cultures of indigenous peoples, a pro-Dalit crusade. In short, Catholicism is concerned with almost everything that Oxfam and the United Nations are concerned with. There is virtually nothing about how in the twenty-first century Catholics might conceptualize a supra-mundane realm, how they might relate to it, what living in such a relationship might require. His suggested Catholic involvement seems religious only in the sense of 'performed by an institution historically considered religious'. Revealingly, it is in a comparison with Pentecostalism that he casually notes that different streams in Catholicism will have different 'attitudes towards the supernatural'.[40] That is one of the few hints in the book that Catholicism is anything more than a more cohesive United Nations.

Robert Calderisi, in his *Earthly Mission: the Catholic Church and World Development*, is, as the title makes plain, expressly concerned with the church's development efforts. Yet nowhere does he even hint that the Catholic Church might be anything more than a development agency. He cites several people, many of them priests and nuns, who discount specifically religious motivation. A priest in Bangladesh whom Calderisi obviously admires becomes impatient when asked if he regarded himself as a Catholic or a humanitarian: 'I don't use those categories. I'm just a person who is here and can help.'[41] A Breton woman in the Philippines, asked the same question, replies: 'Both, I suppose. Although I think I would do this even if I had no faith.'[42] Calderisi hopes the church can keep 'issues of identity under control and sharpen its social message'[43]—for the opportunities to transform lives are numerous, 'if only the church can overcome its current preoccupations with identity.'[44]

Of course, Catholics involved in development today can justify their involvement as a theological imperative, and can articulate their personal Christian motivation. However, even for them, their involvement

[40] Ibid., 410; see also 434f.
[41] Calderisi, *Earthly Mission*, 136.
[42] Ibid., 206.
[43] Ibid., 236.
[44] Ibid., 246.

itself seems little different from that performed by other NGOs. For such activity, Christian motivation is not necessary. More importantly for the future of the institution, it seems difficult to transfer that motivation to another generation. Calderisi captures some of the dynamics in his description of Lacor hospital in northern Uganda, one of the largest referral hospitals in East Africa, founded by a husband and wife team as a Catholic hospital, heavily funded by Catholic bodies, and with a board of governors still headed by the local bishop. 'Its greatest success is that two imaginative and dedicated individuals devoted their lives to creating it for their own humanitarian reasons, inspired by their faith but eager to pass it on intact to a new generation that would not be interested in religious labels.'[45]

Third, we have raised the difficulty of labelling religion. In chapter one I observed that so much writing on global Christianity is vitiated by a kind of essentialism. 'Baptist' as a label can be misleading, since it suggests a Baptist in Ghana is the same thing as a Baptist in Denmark. In reality, a Baptist in Ghana may, despite proudly-asserted denominational identification, have more in common with a Ghanaian Presbyterian than a Baptist in Denmark; as the Baptist in Denmark may have more in common with a Danish Lutheran than a Baptist in Ghana. However, one can go further. Essentialism encourages the presumption that a Christian is a Christian, and we all know what this is. Equally, a Muslim is something different, and we all know what that is. In fact, speaking from a purely study of religions viewpoint, at grass roots in many African countries there is probably very little difference in religious vision between Muslim, Christian, and traditionalist. Their religion, whatever it is called, must deal with the spirits impinging on them at every turn, counter the spirits' evil effects, and ensure their benevolence. We have seen above Niehaus' research assistant and his family, convinced they were bewitched, and turning indiscriminately to healer-diviners and Christian prophets as if they were exactly the same thing.[46] In Pype's Kinshasa, the traditional and the Christian form an amalgam, which Pype calls both 'indigenous beliefs interpreted within an apocalyptic Christian grid' and 'a particular form of

---

[45] Ibid., 222.

[46] Niehaus, *Witchcraft*, passim. Pype too notes: 'The mere fact that *Kinois* consult both types of experts (Christians and diviners) indicates that, at least among ordinary *Kinois*, there is still some puzzlement about the localization of the Real' (*Melodrama*, 128, n 9).

appropriation of the "foreign" religion into autochthonous structures of causality'.[47] So what might be a convenient shorthand label for identifying African Pentecostalism?

The pervasiveness of the success or victory motif makes it difficult to equate African Pentecostalism with evangelicalism, for even basic ideas of British/American evangelicalism (if we take the accepted four: biblicentrism, the cross, personal conversion, mission) have been transformed out of all recognition, even when the words are preserved. The cross is not frequently mentioned, but when it is, it is more in the following vein: Jesus 'hung on the cross so you can experience sweet things in your own life'.[48] The blood of Jesus is frequently invoked in the mantra 'By the blood of Jesus', but even this is reduced to a means of possessing. For Oyedepo, *The Blood Triumph* won for us our 'original inheritance' lost in Adam, namely power, riches, wisdom, strength, honour, glory and 'blessings which maketh rich and addeth no sorrow to it'.[49]

'Conversion' is problematic too. Pype's study of Kinshasa queries that African Pentecostalism must inevitably be 'conversionist'. Although 'it is commonly assumed that becoming a Christian entails a thorough transformation of one's identity',[50] reality 'compels us to take a very flexible approach to the notion of "Christian"'.[51] Such is the almost paradigmatic status of Paul's experience on the road to Damascus that the word 'conversion' normally implies some significant change in attitudes or worldview. Yet it is attitudes and worldview that often persist. In 2012 countless Muslims, by far outnumbering Christians, attended a crusade in Senegal conducted by the Ghanaian Pentecostal Dag Heward-Mills, not from any desire to turn from Islam to Christianity, but because Heward-Mills' publicity indicated he had more power over spiritual realities than local *marabouts* (Heward-Mills insists he has raised the dead). Similarly, in 2011 mobs were incited by *marabouts* to sack five Pentecostal churches in Senegal in

---

[47] Pype, *Melodrama*, 41, 116.

[48] David O. Oyedepo, *The Miracle Meal*, Lagos: Dominion, 2002, 79.

[49] David O. Oyedepo, *The Blood Triumph*, Lagos: Dominion, 1995, 38–47. The testimonies to the power of the blood concern giving life to a stillborn baby, a miraculous exam pass, and selling chemicals that had previously been unsellable (ibid., 71–74).

[50] Pype, *Melodrama*, 78.

[51] Ibid., 96; see also 275–7, 287.

two weeks, not from any narrowly anti-Christian animus but because the Nigerian Pentecostal pastors were thought to be surpassing the *marabouts'* spiritual powers, with corresponding loss of revenue for the latter.

Sharing what is in essence the one religious vision is quite compatible with fierce identification with either Islam or Christianity. These different allegiances can even serve as markers of identity in armed conflict, though only in a very loose sense could such conflict be called religious.

Fourth, the diversity of religious visions (enchanted and disenchanted) is crucial to understanding the nature and role of religion in the world today. Yet this difference is often missed. This is an opportunity to refer to a significant contribution to the question of religion and modernity, Norris and Inglehart's *Sacred and Secular: Religion and Politics Worldwide*, in which they formulate a revised 'secularization thesis' based on 'existential security'. Their novelty is to go beyond individual case studies, or the usual comparison between Europe and the United States, to a global comparison. The World Values Survey (WVS) carried out national surveys of beliefs and values in four waves between 1981 and 2001. The first surveyed twenty-two European countries, and later waves encompassed fifty-six nations. For their theory, Norris and Inglehart construct a variety of measures of 'religiosity'. They then classify the 'predominant religious culture' (like Muslim, Protestant) of various societies. Also, using principally the UNDP Human Development Index (which combines per capita GDP income, educational achievement and life expectancy), they divide societies into three kinds: agrarian, industrial and post-industrial (the last characterized by services rather than manufacturing). They demonstrate an unambiguous link between the type of society and religiosity. All indications of religiosity decrease as a society of any religious tradition moves from agrarian to industrial to post-industrial. They explain the decline of religion through their theory of 'existential security'; as a society (and an individual) becomes more comfortable and secure and moves from fear of disaster and death to feelings of relative well-being, the demand for religion diminishes.[52]

---

[52] Pippa Norris and Ronald Inglehart, *Sacred and Secular: Religion and Politics Worldwide*, second edition, Cambridge University Press, 2011. The second edition enables them to add data from the 2007 Gallup World Poll, which they

My purpose in introducing Norris and Inglehart is not to quibble with their results, which seem broadly defensible. My purpose is to draw attention to the fact that the specifics of African Christianity are not well served by such a study, so obviously based on Western realities. The standard markers of 'religiosity' (frequency of religious participation, frequency of prayer, stated importance of religion, and claimed belief in heaven, hell, life after death, and souls) reveal little and miss everything important about much African religion. Important for Norris and Inglehart's theory are 'predominant religious cultures', understood 'as path-dependent, adapting and devolving in response to developments in the contemporary world, and yet also strongly reflecting the legacy of the past centuries'.[53] However, no attempt is made to elevate Africa's religious traditions to their own category along with the standard religious categories of Muslim, Orthodox, Protestant, Catholic or 'Eastern'. On the contrary, to take just West Africa, Nigeria is classified as Muslim, Ghana as traditional, and Liberia as Christian, which seems questionable for societies with so much in common.[54] The stimulating discussion of religion and social capital, with the data provided by answers to the standard WVS question: 'Generally speaking, would you say that most people can be trusted or that you can't be too careful in dealing with people?' completely misses the particular dynamics introduced by witchcraft fears, as we saw in discussing Olukoya's Christianity.[55] The authors are concerned with the 'growing religiosity gap worldwide' which they claim increasingly divides traditional agrarian societies from post-industrial ones. Yet they have missed the bigger religious divide: the religion that two thirds of those living in poorer societies regard as 'very important' is often a totally different animal from the religion that four fifths of those living in post-industrial societies regard as 'not important'.[56]

Norris and Inglehart are not alone. When the Pew Forum compared the importance of religion in selected African countries and the West,

---

claim support the findings of the first edition. Bruce provides a stimulating reworking of their theory in terms of plausibility rather than prosperity and peace, *Secularization*, 194–9.

[53] Norris and Inglehart, *Sacred*, 20.

[54] Ibid., 45–7.

[55] Ibid., 181–9.

[56] Ibid., 58.

they simply presumed that the term 'religion' is one and univocal.[57] Similarly, from answers to the question: 'Irrespective of whether you attend a place of worship or not, would you say you are a religious person, not a religious person or a convinced atheist?' WIN-Gallup International drew up a 'Religion and Atheism Index' of fifty-seven countries, with Ghana top of the poll with 96 per cent of respondents considering themselves religious, followed closely by Nigeria at 93 per cent.[58] The presumption that religion is simply religion, whether one is talking about Ghana or Sweden, is the claim that I have challenged in this book.

---

[57] Report *Tolerance and Tension: Islam and Christianity in Sub-Saharan Africa*, 15 April 2010.

[58] http://www.huffingtonpost.com/2013/07/23/most-religious-countries-least-religious_n_3640033.html accessed 8 Aug. 2013.

# BIBLIOGRAPHY

(1) *Books by Daniel Olukoya used here* (all published by MFM or Battle Cry Ministries, both imprints of his church)

*100 Facts about Idolatry*, 2009.
*Abraham's Children in Bondage*, 2010.
*Battle against the Masters*, 2012.
*Be Prepared*, 1999.
*Born Great but Tied Down*, 2005.
*Born to Overcome*, 2012.
*Brokenness*, 1997.
*Candidates of Bewitchment*, 2012.
*Captured by the Slave Masters*, 2011.
*Contending for the Kingdom*, 2005.
*Criminals in the House of God*, 2002.
*Dancers at the Gate of Death*, 2009.
*Dealing with Local Satanic Technology*, 2001.
*Dealing with the Evil Powers of Your Father's House*, 2002.
*Dealing with the Powers of the Night*, 2012.
*Dealing with the Satanic Exchange*, 2005.
*Dealing with the Secret Poison in Your Life*, 2012.
*Dealing with Unprofitable Roots*, 1999.
*Dealing with Witchcraft Barbers*, 2001.
*Deep Secrets, Deep Deliverance*, 2012.
*Deliverance by Fire*, 2000.
*Deliverance from Evil Load*, 2009.
*Deliverance from Limiting Powers*, 2005.
*Deliverance from Spirit Husband and Spirit Wife: Incubi and Succubi*, 1999.
*Deliverance from Triangular Powers*, 2012.
*Deliverance through the Watches for Protection*, 2011.
*Deliverance through the Watches from Sexual Perversion*, 2011.

*Deliverance: God's Medicine Bottle*, 2002.
*Destiny Clinic*, 2005.
*Destroying Satanic Mask*, 2009.
*Destroying the Evil Umbrella*, 2005.
*Disgracing Soul Hunters*, 2005.
*Disgracing Water Spirits: Deliverance Manual for Indigenes of Riverine Areas*, 2012.
*Divine Military Training*, 2009.
*Divine Protection*, n.d.
*Divine Repositioning*, 2013.
*Divine Yellow Card*, 2007.
*Dominion Prosperity*, 2003.
*Drawers of Power from the Heavenlies*, 2nd ed., 2010.
*Dreaming Divine Dreams*, 2009.
*Facing Both Ways*, 2004.
*Financial Deliverance*, 2012.
*Freedom from the Grip of Witchcraft*, 2005.
*Holy Madness or Horrible Disgrace*, 2009.
*How to Obtain Personal Deliverance*, 1995.
*I Plug Myself into Your Resurrection Power*, 2009.
*Idols of the Heart*, 2005.
*Kill your Goliath by Fire*, 2011.
*Lord, Behold their Threatening*, 2010.
*Meat for Champions*, 2000.
*O God, Terminate the Joy of my Enemy*, 2012.
*Open Heavens through Holy Disturbance*, 2005.
*Overpowering Witchcraft*, 1999.
*Paralysing the Rider and the Horse*, 2005.
*Passing through the Valley of the Shadow of Death*, 2010.
*Paying Evil Tithes*, 2005.
*Power against Business Bewitchment*, 2012.
*Power against Dream Criminals*, 2001.
*Power against Marine Spirits*, 1999.
*Power against the Enemy Opposed to your Shining*, 2012.
*Power against Unclean Spirits*, 2011.
*Power of Brokenness*, 2011.
*Power to Achieve Success*, 2012.
*Power to Disgrace the Oppressor*, 2011.
*Power to Magnetise Money and Reject Poverty*, 2012.
*Power to Put the Enemy to Shame*, 2012.
*Power to Recover Your Birthright*, 2011.
*Power to Shut Satanic Doors*, 2011.
*Prayer Strategies for Spinsters and Bachelors* (with Shade Olukoya), 1999.
*Praying against the Spirit of the Valley*, 2005.
*Praying to Destroy Satanic Roadblocks*, 2005.

*Provocation at the Corridor of Breakthroughs*, 2005.
*Pulling Down Foundational Jericho*, 2012.
*Raiding the House of the Strongman*, 2011.
*Satanic Diversion of the Black Race*, 1998.
*Slaves who Love their Chains shall Remain in their Bondage*, 1999.
*Smite the Enemy and He will Flee*, 2000.
*Snake in the Power House*, 2003.
*Speaking Destruction unto Dark Rivers*, 2009.
*Spiritual Warfare and the Home: a Spiritual Warfare Manual for Use in the Home*, 1996.
*Stop Them before They Stop You*, 2009.
*Taking the Battle to the Enemy's Gate*, 2011.
*The Chain Breaker*, 2010.
*The Dining Table of Darkness*, 2005.
*The Enemy has Done This*, 2003.
*The Evil Cry of Your Family Idol*, 2003.
*The Hidden Viper*, 2011.
*The Internal Stumbling Block*, 2005.
*The Lost Secrets of the Church*, 2012.
*The Militant Christian*, 2012.
*The Mystery of First Fruit Offering*, 2007.
*The Mystery of Mobile Curses*, 2005.
*The Mystery of Sleep*, 2012.
*The Power of Biblical Giving*, n.d.
*The Problems of Incomplete Deliverance*, 2005.
*The Pursuit of Success*, 1999.
*The School of Tribulation*, 2011.
*The Serpentine Enemies*, 2001.
*The Skeleton in Your Grandfather's Cupboard*, 2005.
*The Star Hunters*, 2002.
*The Star in Your Sky*, 2005.
*The Terrible Agenda*, 2009.
*The Wealth Transfer Agenda*, 2005.
*Victory over Satanic Dreams*, 1996.
*Victory over the Storms of Life*, 2012.
*Violent Prayers to Disgrace Stubborn Problems*, 1999.
*War at the Edge of Breakthroughs*, 2004.
*Wasted at the Market Square of Life*, 2010.
*Ways to Provoke Divine Vengeance*, 2012.
*When the Deliverer needs Deliverance*, 2007.
*When the Enemy Hides*, 2011.
*When the Wicked is on Rampage*, 2012.
*When You are Under Attack*, 2012.
*When Your Labour Needs Deliverance*, 2012.
*Whilst Men Slept*, 2009.

# BIBLIOGRAPHY

*Why Problems Come Back*, 2009.
*Your Foundation and Your Destiny*, 2001.
*Your Turnaround Breakthrough*, 2012.
*Your Uzziah Must Die*, 2012.


(2) Books by David O. Oyedepo used here (all published by Dominion Publishing House, Lagos)

*All You Need to Have All Your Needs Met*, 2004.
*Anointing for Breakthrough*, 1992.
*Anointing for Exploits*, 2005.
*Born to Win*, 1986.
*Breaking Financial Hardship*, 1995.
*Breaking the Curses of Life*, 1997.
*Commanding the Supernatural*, 2006.
*Conquering Controlling Powers*, 1997.
*Covenant Wealth*, 1992.
*Exploits of Faith*, 2005.
*Exploring the Riches of Redemption*, 2004.
*Exploring the Secrets of Success*, 1998.
*Financial Prosperity: Testimonies of Financial and Business Breakthrough*, 2003.
*Force of Freedom*, 1995.
*Fulfilling Your Days: Scriptural Principles for a Long Life*, 1998.
*Keys to Answered Prayer*, 1986.
*Keys to Divine Health*, 1986.
*Making Maximum Impact*, 2000.
*Manifestations of the Spirit: Unveiling the Seven Spirits of God*, 1997.
*Maximise Destiny*, 2006.
*Operating in the Supernatural*, 2004.
*Overcoming the Forces of Wickedness*, 1994.
*Possessing Your Possession*, 2006.
*Releasing the Supernatural: an Adventure into the Spirit World*, 1993.
*Riding on Prophetic Wings*, 2000.
*Ruling Your World*, 2005.
*Satan, Get Lost! Outstanding Breakthroughs in Spite of the Devil*, 1995.
*Showers of Blessings: Rains of the Spirit*, 1997.
*Signs and Wonders Today: a Catalogue of the Amazing Acts of God among Men*, 2006.
*Success Buttons*, 2005.
*Success Strategies: Putting in Your Hand the Scriptural Password to Unending Success*, 2003.
*Success Systems*, 2006.
*The Blood Triumph*, 1995.
*The Hidden Covenants of Blessings*, 1995.

*The Law of Faith*, 1985.
*The Mandate: Operational Manual*, 2012.
*The Miracle Meal*, 2002.
*The Miracle Seed*, 1985.
*The Release of Power*, 1996.
*The Unlimited Power of Faith*, 2011.
*The Winning Wisdom*, 1996.
*The Wisdom that Works*, 2006.
*Understanding Financial Prosperity*, 2005.
*Understanding the Anointing*, 1998.
*Understanding Your Covenant Rights*, 2003.
*Walking in Dominion*, 2006.
*Walking in the Miraculous*, 1998.
*Walking in the Newness of Life*, 2005.
*Winning Faith*, 2004.
*Winning Invisible Battles*, 2006.
*Winning the War against Poverty*, 2006.
*You shall not be Barren*, 1998.


(3) *Other works*

[Omino, John], *Satanism: How the Devil is Trapping God's People*, Nairobi: Pawak Computer Services, 2000.
Africa Progress Report, *Equity in Extractives*, launched 10 May 2013 at WEF on Africa, Cape Town.
Akala, Winston Jumba, 'The Challenge of Curriculum in Kenya's Primary and Secondary Education: the Response of the Catholic Church', in Grace *et al.*, *International Handbook*, 619–35.
Allen, John L., *The Future Church: How Ten Trends are Revolutionizing the Catholic Church*, New York: Doubleday, 2009.
Ashforth, Adam, *Madumo: a Man Bewitched*, University of Chicago Press, 2000.
Atkin, Nicholas, and Frank Tallet, *Priests, Prelates and People*, New York: Oxford University Press, 2003.
Baitu, Juvenalis, 'The Moral Crisis in Contemporary Africa', *AFER*, 45, 3 (2003), 248–62.
Bakker, Janel Kragt, *Sister Churches: American Congregations and their Partners Abroad*, New York: Oxford University Press, 2014.
Barrett, David, George Kurian and Todd Johnson, *World Christian Encyclopedia: 2ⁿᵈ Edition*, New York: Oxford University Press, 2001.
Barrett, David, and Todd Johnson, *World Christian Trends AD 30—AD 2200: Interpreting the Annual Christian Megacensus*, Pasadena, CA: William Carey Library, 2001.
Behrend, Heike, '"Satan gekreuzigt": Interner Terror und Katharsis in Tororo, Westuganda', *Historische Anthropologie*, 12, 2 (2004), 211–27.

—————— 'The Rise of Occult Powers, AIDS and the Roman Catholic Church in Western Uganda', *Journal of Religion in Africa*, 37 (2007), 41–58.

—————— *Resurrecting Cannibals: the Catholic Church, Witch-Hunts and the Production of Pagans in Western Uganda*, Woodbridge, Suffolk: James Currey, 2011.

Benedict XVI, *Africa's Commitment*, Nairobi: Paulines, 2011.

Berger, Peter L., *The Sacred Canopy: Elements of a Sociological Theory of Religion*, New York: Anchor, 1967.

—————— 'Max Weber is Alive and Well, and Living in Guatemala: The Protestant Ethic Today', *The Review of Faith and International Affairs*, 8, 4 (2010), 3–9.

—————— *Adventures of an Accidental Sociologist: How to Explain the World without Becoming a Bore*, Amherst: Prometheus, 2011.

Berger, Peter L., Brigitte Berger and Hansfried Kellner, *The Homeless Mind: Modernization and Consciousness*, London: Penguin, 1974.

Berger, Peter L., Grace Davie and Effie Fokas, *Religious America, Secular Europe? A Theme and Variations*, Aldershot: Ashgate, 2008.

Borer, Tristan Anne, *Challenging the State: Churches as Political Actors in South Africa 1980–1994*, Notre Dame, IN: University of Notre Dame Press, 1998.

Bowers, Paul, 'African Theology: its History, Dynamics, Scope and Future', *Africa Journal of Evangelical Theology*, 21, 2 (2002), 109–25.

Bruce, Steve, *Secularization*, Oxford University Press, 2011.

Bwangatto, Ambrose John (ed.), *Africa is not Destined to Die: Signs of Hope and Renewal*, Nairobi: Paulines, 2012.

Calderisi, Robert, *Earthly Mission: the Catholic Church and World Development*, London: Yale University Press, 2013.

Carmody, Brendan, 'Catholic Church and State Relations in Zambian Education: a Contemporary Analysis', in Grace *et al.*, *International Handbook*, 543–62.

Casanova, José, 'Global Catholicism and the Politics of Civil Society', *Sociological Inquiry*, 66, 3 (1996), 356–73.

Catholic Charismatic Renewal [Ghana], *Healing and Deliverance Training Manual*, Kumasi: CCR, 1996.

Catholic Health Care Association of Southern Africa, *In the Service of Healing: a History of Catholic Health Care in Southern Africa*, Johannesburg: Cathca, 2011.

Centre for Development and Enterprise, *Under the Radar: Pentecostalism in South Africa and its Potential Social and Economic Role*, Johannesburg: Centre for Development and Enterprise, CDE In Depth no. 7, 2008.

Chadwick, Owen, *A History of the Popes 1830–1914*, Oxford University Press, 1998.

Clapham, Christopher, 'Governmentality and Economic Policy in Sub-Saharan Africa', *Third World Quarterly*, 17 (1996).

Clapham, Christopher, review of Stephen Ellis, *Season of Rains: Africa in the World*, London: Hurst, 2011, in *International Affairs* 87, 6 (2011), 1548.

Collier, Paul, *The Bottom Billion: Why the Poorest Countries are Failing and what Can be Done about it*, Oxford University Press, 2007.

Comoro, Christopher and John Sivalon, 'Marian Faith Healing Ministry', in Thomas Bamat and F. Wiest (eds), *Popular Catholicism in a World Church: Seven Case Studies in Inculturation*, Maryknoll, NY: Orbis, 1998, 157–82.

Congregation for Divine Worship, *Instruction on Prayer for Healing*, dated 14 Sept. 2000, Vatican.

Czerny, Michael, 'The Second African Synod and AIDS in Africa', in Orobator, *Reconciliation*, 193–202.

D'Antonio, William V., James D. Davidson, Dean R. Hoge and Mary L. Gautier, 'American Catholics and Church Authority', in Lacey *et al.*, *Crisis*, 273–92.

Douglas, Mary, 'Sorcery Accusations Unleashed: the Lele Revisited 1987', *Africa*, 69 (1999), 177–93.

——— 'The Devil Vanishes', *Tablet*, 28 April 1990, 513–14, reprinted in Fardon (ed.), *Mary Douglas*, 95–9.

Dover, Kenneth, *Marginal Comment: a Memoir*, London: Duckworth, 1994.

Ellis, Stephen, *The Mask of Anarchy: the Destruction of Liberia and the Religious Dimension of an African Civil War*, London: Hurst, 2001.

Enwerem, Iheanyi M., *Crossing the Rubicon: a Socio-Political Analysis of Political Catholicism in Nigeria*, Ibadan: BookBuilders, 2010.

Fardon, Richard (ed.), *Mary Douglas: a Very Personal Method: Anthropological Writings Drawn from Life*, London: Sage, 2013.

Fukuyama, Francis, *The Origins of Political Order: from Prehuman Times to the French Revolution*, New York: Farrar, Straus and Giroux, 2011.

Gellner, Ernest, *Postmodernism, Reason and Religion*, London: Routledge, 1992.

——— *Conditions of Liberty: Civil Society and its Rivals*, London: Hamish Hamilton, 1994.

——— 'Anything Goes', *Times Literary Supplement*, 16 June 1995, 8.

——— 'The Importance of Being Modular', in John A. Hall (ed.), *Civil Society: Theory, History, Comparison*, Cambridge: Polity Press, 1995, 32–55.

Getui, Mary N. and Peter Kanyandago (eds), *From Violence to Peace: a Challenge for African Christianity*, Nairobi: Acton, 2003.

Gifford, Paul, *Christianity and Politics in Doe's Liberia*, Cambridge University Press, 1993.

——— *African Christianity: its Public Role*, London: Hurst, 1998.

——— *Ghana's New Christianity: Pentecostalism in a Globalising African Economy*, London: Hurst, 2004.

——— *Christianity, Politics and Public Life in Kenya*, London: Hurst, 2009.

Gleason, Philip, *Contending with Modernity: Catholic Higher Education in the Twentieth Century*, New York: Oxford University Press, 1995.

Government of Kenya, *Report of the Presidential Commission of Inquiry into the Cult of Devil Worship in Kenya*, n.d.

Grace, Gerald R. and Joseph O'Keefe (eds), *International Handbook of Catholic Education: Challenges for School Systems in the 21st Century*, Dordrecht: Springer, 2007.

Greenpeace, *The Plunder of a Nation's Birthright; a Drama in Five Acts*, launched 10 Oct. 2012.

Hastings, Adrian, *In Filial Disobedience*, Great Wakering: Mayhew-McCrimmon, 1978.

—— *The Church in Africa, 1450–1950*, Oxford University Press, 1994.

Hebga, Meinrad, 'Christianisme et négritude', in A. Abble et al, *Des Prêtres noirs s'interrogent*, Paris: Editions de Clef, 2nd ed, 1957, 202–23.

Holland, Heidi, *Dinner With Mugabe: the Untold Story of a Freedom Fighter who became a Tyrant*, London: Penguin, 2008.

Hope, Anne, and Sally Timmel, *Training for Transformation; a Handbook for Community Workers*, Gweru: Mambo Press, 1984.

Hornsby-Smith, Michael P., *Roman Catholic Beliefs in England: Customary Catholicism and Transformations of Religious Authority*, Cambridge University Press, 1991.

Hornsby-Smith, Michael P., *Roman Catholics in England: Studies in Social Structure since the Second World War*, Cambridge University Press, 1987.

Horton, R., 'African Conversion', *Africa*, 41, 2 (1971), 85–108.

Ilo, Stan Chu, *The Church and Development in Africa: Aid and Development from the Perspective of Catholic Social Ethics*, Nairobi: Paulines, 2013.

John Paul II, Apostolic Constitution *Ex Corde Ecclesiae*, 1990.

Johnson, Mary and Patricia Wittberg, 'Reality Check', *America*, 13 Aug. 2012.

Jordan, J.P., 'Catholic Educators and Catholicism in Nigeria', *AFER* 2 (1960).

Ka Mana, *Christians and Churches of Africa; Salvation in Christ and Building a New African Society*, Maryknoll, NY: Orbis, 2004.

Kairos Theologians, *Challenge to the Church: a Theological Comment on the Political Crisis in South Africa*, Braamfontein: the Kairos Theologians, 1985.

Kalilombe, Patrick, 'Praxis and Methods of Inculturation in Africa', in Ryan (ed.), *Theology of Inculturation*, 38–48.

Kanyandago, Peter, 'Rich but Rendered Poor: a Christian Response to the Paradox of Poverty in Africa', in Peter Kanyandago (ed.), *The Cries of the Poor in Africa: Questions and Responses for African Christianity*, Kisubi: Marianum Publishing, 2002.

—— 'Violence in Africa: a Search for Causes and Remedies', in Getui *et al.*, *From Violence to Peace*, 2003, 7–40.

——'"Let us First Feed the Children" (Mark 7, 27): the Church's Response to the Inequitable Extraction of Resources and Related Violence', in Orobator, *Reconciliation*, 2011, 171–80.

Katongole, Emmanuel, *The Sacrifice of Africa: a Political Theology for Africa*, Grand Rapids: Eerdmans, 2011.

Lacey, Michael J. and Francis Oakley, *The Crisis of Authority in Catholic Modernity*, New York: Oxford University Press, 2011.

Lado, Ludovic, *Catholic Pentecostalism and the Paradoxes of Africanization: Processes of Localization in a Catholic Charismatic Movement in Cameroon*, Leiden: Brill, 2009.

Landes, David S., *The Unbound Prometheus*, Cambridge University Press, 1969.

Linden, Ian, *Global Catholicism: Diversity and Change since Vatican II*, London: Hurst, 2009.

Magesa, Laurenti, 'African Renaissance: the Jubilee and Africa's Position in the International Context', in Peter Kanyandago (ed.), *Marginalised Africa: an International Perspective*, Nairobi: Paulines, 2002, 13–27.

———— 'On Speaking Terms: African Religion and Christianity in Dialogue', in Orobator, *Reconciliation*, 2011, 25–36.

———— *Anatomy of Inculturation: Transforming the Church in Africa*, Maryknoll, NY: Orbis, 2004.

Martin, David, 'Pentecostalism: a Major Narrative of Modernity', in David Martin, *On Secularisation: towards a Revised General Theory*, London: Ashgate, 2005, 141–54.

———— *Pentecostalism: the World their Parish*, Oxford: Blackwell, 2002.

Massa, Mark S., *The American Catholic Revolution: How the '60s Changed the Church Forever*, New York: Oxford University Press, 2010.

Milingo, Emmanuel, *Face to Face with the Devil*, Broadford, Victoria: Scripture Keyes Ministries, 1991.

Mombe, Paterne-Auxence, 'Moving beyond the Condom Debate', in Orobator, *Reconciliation*, 2011, 203–13.

Moore, Henrietta L. and Todd Sanders (eds), *Magical Interpretations, Material Realities: Modernity, Witchcraft and the Occult in Postcolonial Africa*, Abingdon: Routledge, 2001.

Morey, Melanie M. and John J. Piderit, *Catholic Higher Education: a Culture in Crisis*, New York: Oxford University Press, 2010.

Mutahazi, Emmanuel, 'Process and Method in the Theology of Inculturation', in Ryan, *Theology of Inculturation*, 2004.

Ngona, Dieudonné, 'Theology of Inculturation in Africa Today', in Ryan, *Theology of Inculturation*, 2004, 15–37.

Niehaus, Isak, *Witchcraft and a Life in the New South Africa*, Cambridge University Press for International African Institute, 2013.

Njoku, Stephen Uche, *Curses: Effects and Release*, Enugu: Christian Living Publications, 1993.

Noll, Mark, *The New Shape of World Christianity*, Downers Grove: InterVarsity Press, 2009.

Norris, Pippa and Ronald Inglehart, *Sacred and Secular: Religion and Politics Worldwide*, second edition, Cambridge University Press, 2011.

O'Malley, John W., *What Happened at Vatican II*, Cambridge, MA: Harvard University Press, 2008.

Oliver, Roland, *The Missionary Factor in East Africa*, London: Longmans, 1952.

Omolade, Richard, 'Challenges for Catholic Schools in Nigeria', *International Studies in Catholic Education*, 1, 1 (2009), 30–41.

Orobator, Agbonkhianmeghe E., 'The Synod as Ecclesial Conversation', in Orobator, *Reconciliation*, 2011, 1–10.

——— (ed.), *Reconciliation, Justice and Peace: the Second African Synod*, Nairobi: Acton, 2011.

——— (ed.), *Practising Reconciliation, Doing Justice, Building Peace: Conversations on Catholic Theological Ethics in Africa*, Nairobi: Paulines, 2013.

Peel, J.D.Y., *Religious Encounter and the Making of the Yoruba*, Bloomington and Indianapolis: Indiana University Press, 2000.

Piot, Peter, *No Time to Lose: a Life in Pursuit of Deadly Viruses*, New York: W.W. Norton and Company, 2012.

Pobee, John S., and Gabriel Ositelu II, *African Initiatives in Christianity: the Growth, Gifts and Diversities of Indigenous African Churches: a Challenge to the Ecumenical Movement*, Geneva: WCC Publications, 1998.

Pype, Katrien, *The Making of the Pentecostal Medodrama: Religion, Media and Gender in Kinshasa*, New York: Berghahn Books, 2012.

Ryan, Patrick (ed.), *Theology of Inculturation in Africa Today: Methods, Praxis and Mission*, Nairobi: CUEA, 2004.

Schoffeleers, Matthew, 'Ritual Healing and Political Acquiescence: the Case of the Zionist Churches in Southern Africa', *Africa*, 61 (1991), 1–25.

Schuth, Katarina, 'Assessing the Education of Priests and Lay Ministers', in Lacey *et al.*, *Crisis*, 317–47.

Simpson, Anthony, *'Half-London' in Zambia: Contested Identities in a Catholic Mission School*, Edinburgh University Press for International African Institute, 2003.

Soede, Nathanael Yaovi, 'The Enduring Scourge of Poverty and Evangelization in Africa', in Orobator, *Reconciliation*, 2004, 181–90.

Sow, Ibrahima, *Le maraboutage au Sénégal*, Dakar: IFAN Cheikh Anta Diop, 2013.

Tarimo, Aquiline, *Applied Ethics and Africa's Social Reconstruction*, Nairobi: Acton, 2005.

Tentler, Leslie Woodcock, 'Souls and Bodies: the Birth Control Controversy and the Collapse of Confession', in Lacey *et al.*, *Crisis*, 2011, 293–316.

Theuri, Matthew M., 'Religion and Culture as Factors in the Development of Africa', in Mary N. Getui and Matthew M. Theuri (eds), *Quests for Abundant Life in Africa*, Nairobi: Acton, 2002.

Thomas, Keith, *Religion and the Decline of Magic*, London: Penguin, 1973.

——— 'Diary', *London Review of Books*, 10 June 2010.

Thompson, E.P., *The Making of the English Working Class*, London: Gollancz, 1963.

Trevor-Roper, Hugh, *The European Witch Craze of the Sixteenth and Seventeenth Centuries*, London: Penguin, 1969.

UNICEF, *Children Accused of Witchcraft: an Anthropological Study of Contemporary Practices in Africa*, Dakar: UNICEF/WCARO, 2010.

Watson, Rupert (ed.), *Pills, Planes and Politics: the Wisdom of Imre Loefler*, Nairobi: Salmia Trust, 2008.

Wijsen, Frans, *Seeds of Conflict in a Haven of Peace: from Religious Studies to Interreligious Studies in Africa*, Amsterdam: Rodopi, 2007.

Williamson, Sidney George, *Akan Religion and the Christian Faith: a Comparative Study of the Impact of Two Religions*, Accra: Ghana Universities Press, 1965.

Wuthnow, Robert, *Boundless Faith: the Global Outreach of American Churches*, Berkeley: University of California Press, 2009.

# INDEX